KJL-578-918

ABOUT THE AUTHOR

Michael Bibring was educated at the London School of Economics where he graduated with an LLB (Hons). He qualified as a solicitor in 1979. He has lectured extensively including at the University of Westminster, Middlesex University and to various groups of surveyors. He contributes to the Commercial Property Law Programme produced by Television Education Network and has written for the *Estates Gazette, Estates Times* and *Taxation* magazine. Until recently he was the head of the Property Department of Finers where he was responsible for landlord and tenant negotiations, rent reviews and development work. He has now given up private practice to take up a main board position at Marylebone Warwick Balfour Group PLC and this new dimension to his career has allowed him to write from the perspective of client as well as adviser. He is married to Linda and has two children, Lee and Nikki. When not working he is a keen sportsman.

*This book is dedicated to
Linda, Lee and Nikki, my
biggest critics ... and fans!
And to my father, Harry –
my immeasurable inspiration.*

CONTENTS

INTRODUCTION
AND
GUIDE TO USE OF THIS BOOK

You are not a solicitor and this is not a legal textbook. This may be a statement of the obvious but it is important that this book is used as it is intended: it is a way for surveyors to clearly identify some of the important legal issues that affect their working lives and impact on the way they do business in England and Wales. Please remember that Scottish and Irish law is different.

In the commercial sector there are many areas where it would be difficult for a surveyor to do the best for his client without having a good working knowledge of legal issues. In some cases it would be simply impossible to do the job. Imagine trying to negotiate for a retail tenant whose lease is coming to an end without having any idea of the ramifications of the Landlord and Tenant Act 1954. This book is intended to address some of these issues and give you a working knowledge of many areas of law with which you will be concerned on a daily basis. I have assumed that as general practice commercial surveyors you have some familiarity with the subject matter of this book and the areas dealt with in it.

Commercial property transactions are often very complicated. It is naive to expect surveyors to be able to negotiate complex transactions without having some knowledge of the legal consequences of their negotiations. The modern commercial surveyor must be aware of legal niceties in order that he can gain the upper hand and improve the position of his clients. He must avoid falling, or allowing his clients to fall, into traps.

I am a great believer in lawyers and surveyors working together as a team in order that they can best protect and advance the position of their clients. Consultants in both professions must have some idea of what the other is trying to achieve in a deal. It is absolutely no use for a solicitor to be ignorant of the property ramifications of his negotiations; nor is it sensible for surveyors to have no legal knowledge. The purpose of this book is to ensure that surveyors can have a ready guide to the legal implications of certain areas of their work but without intending that they become experts in the law.

This book, which is designed more as a manual than as a textbook, is addressing general legal principles and areas to watch out for. It does not pretend to be a tome of legal references, cases, statutes, etc. There are many law books that fulfil this function in relation to the issues discussed in this book and you will see that I refer to some of them. For example, many of the chapters refer to various cases relating to the issues mentioned. These cases tend to reflect the most recent or interesting developments in the area in question and I have not sought to refer to all the cases on the relevant subject. None of the various stand-alone chapters are intended to be a treatise on the subject matter referred to in them. They are intended to stimulate thought and pro-voke good and pro-active advice and perhaps just give the reader the edge when he is negotiating with another surveyor. I am also hoping that some of my ideas, thoughts and opinions will be of use in the negotiation process.

Nor is the book a substitute for legal advice. There are many areas where surveyors must obtain legal advice and must refer their clients to lawyers. Again take an example of a renewal under the Landlord and Tenant Act 1954. I think it would be very poor practice indeed for sur-veyors to serve the legal notices that are so important in the renewal process, and even more so if they were to do so without consultation. This is particularly important given the speed and frequency with which the law changes.

In case you should think that these comments are part of a conspi-racy requiring you to use solicitors rather than your own profession for part of your work, you should know that I am a firm believer in recip-rocity. I think that it would be equally dangerous for a solicitor to serve a Section 25 notice without any reference to the landlord's surveyor. The surveyor will have a practical understanding of exactly who is in occupation, what the property looks like, etc. All this may have a sig-nificant bearing on the service of a legal notice.

I say all this to emphasize the need for our professions to work in tandem. Practitioners in both fields cannot possibly do their job with-out an understanding of each other's profession. Just because I would not undertake a development transaction without seeing the site does not mean that I am doing so to the exclusion of the surveyor whose views, advice and knowledge will obviously be vital.

I would therefore suggest that where you are involved in commer-cial property transactions which involve any of the areas considered in this book, you refer to the relevant chapter (all of which have been written so that they stand alone but also cross-refer to other relevant points in other chapters) and hopefully that will give you a feel for some of the legal issues that may be involved. You can then either refer to one of the more detailed legal textbooks relating to the subject in question, consult with the solicitors acting for you or your client, or if you feel confident that there is no need for further legal advice, move forward in the knowledge that you are aware of the legal consequences of the matter in hand.

Most of this book is concerned with leasing transactions, although there are one or two issues in the last chapter that are of interest in sales and purchases too. In dealing with leases you should be aware of the Code of Practice published in December 1995. This does not have the force of law but sets out a code of conduct in carrying out commercial lease transactions in England and Wales. Since it has been endorsed by a number of powerful representative groups, I suspect that despite its voluntary status one ignores it at one's peril. There is a Standing Committee that has been set up to monitor how it operates in practice and I thoroughly recommend you to read it. The longest chapter in the book, Chapter 1, is devoted to privity of contract. This is purely because the regime is relatively new and still a current 'hot topic'. I thought surveyors would want more time devoted to this important new change. If further reading on privity is required, I thoroughly recommend the College of Law pamphlet entitled *Privity of Contract: A Practitioner's Guide*. (See Recommended reading.)

So far as the remaining chapters are concerned, it would be remiss not to mention issues that arise in relation to massive subjects like rent reviews, alienation and 1954 Act renewals. These subjects are therefore given their own chapter but it is important to recognize that these three chapters are not comprehensive works on their subject matter; Bernstein and Reynolds' *Rent Review Handbook*, *Woodfall on Landlord and Tenant* and *Hill and Redman's Law of Landlord and Tenant* are but three examples of legal works that discuss these issues in the depth they deserve. The chapter on break clauses and the short chapter dealing with obligations to trade each deal with specific issues that often confront commercial property surveyors involved in lease negotiations and where perhaps a little more legal knowledge might just help you gain the upper hand in negotiating.

As for the last chapter, the pot-pourri, this contains some thoughts on specific topical issues which interest me and which I hope you will also find stimulating. All of the chapters have numbered paragraphs for ease of reference and where I have felt it may assist, I have included diagrams to help illustrate a point.

None of the chapters pretends to deal comprehensively with all the issues that affect the relevant subject; but I hope I have concentrated on some of the more important and interesting aspects and, in some cases, some current issues. I have tried to identify some issues where having a little legal knowledge may help tip the balance in your favour in negotiations; this is very much the style of the annual 'Forty Tips and Traps' lectures which I have given to surveyors over the last few years and which largely have inspired this book.

I have used a number of legal terms and expressions and I have included a glossary at the back. I have also set out a list of the statutes, as they have been referred to in the book, in the Recommended reading section.

It seems clear to me from various dialogues that I have had with surveyors in conferences and informally that there is a need for a book of this nature and I hope that in using it you will find that you are able to add a further dimension to the advice that you give your clients.

The law is correct as at February 1997 but I must stress that some of the issues in this book relate to points where the courts are constantly deliberating and changes may well arise. By way of a small example, in the course of writing the chapter on the 1954 Act the law on service of Section 27 notices changed! For this reason it is very important indeed that you keep up to date; the *Estates Gazette*, *Property Week* and *Property Law Bulletin* are three excellent publications that will help you to do this.

I should like to thank my long suffering secretary, Angie, who has not only undertaken the vast majority of the typing of this book (including deciphering my completely illegible handwriting) but whose calm efficiency has helped give me the time to write. I should also like to thank the Property Managers' Association for allowing me to refer to some statistics returned from their surveys.

Finally, I should also like to thank my wife, Linda, and children, Lee and Nikki, for their patience and understanding, as I have disappeared to write for large chunks of many weekends.

MICHAEL A. BIBRING 1997

CHAPTER 1

PRIVITY OF CONTRACT

1. PRE-ACT POSITION

1.1 Privity of contract

1.1.1 Until 1 January 1996 all leases were subject to the doctrine of privity of contract. This provided that where a landlord granted a lease to a tenant, then the tenant was liable throughout the term of that tenancy; his obligations to pay rent and observe covenants applied notwithstanding an assignment of the lease and irrespective of whether the tenant remained in occupation of the premises. The liability related to the rent as increased on review and of course original tenants are rarely party to, or consulted in connection with, any rent review where they have already assigned the lease.

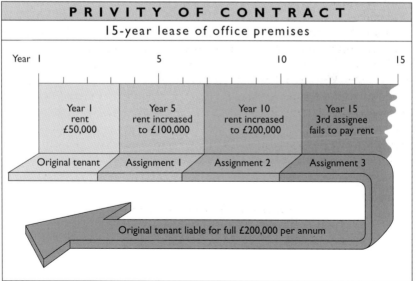

PRIVITY OF CONTRACT
15-year lease of office premises

Year 1 — 5 — 10 — 15

| Year 1 rent £50,000 | Year 5 rent increased to £100,000 | Year 10 rent increased to £200,000 | Year 15 3rd assignee fails to pay rent |

Original tenant / Assignment 1 / Assignment 2 / Assignment 3

Original tenant liable for full £200,000 per annum

LIVERPOOL
JOHN MOORES UNIVERSITY
AVRIL ROBARTS LRC
TEL. 0151 231 4022

1.1.2   It is not uncommon for an original tenant to find that he has to meet a liability of one of his successors long after he has assigned his lease.

1.2   Privity of estate

1.2.1   The doctrine of privity of contract did not apply to a tenant who was not the original tenant. This might seem curious, but not so if you remember that such a tenant was not a party to the original contract. Liability for subsequent tenants arose under the doctrine of privity of estate which stated that a tenant's obligations under a lease subsisted during that time that he had an estate in the lease. After an assignment the doctrine of privity of estate did not impose any obligation upon any tenant other than the original tenant for breaches of covenant that were to occur after assignment.

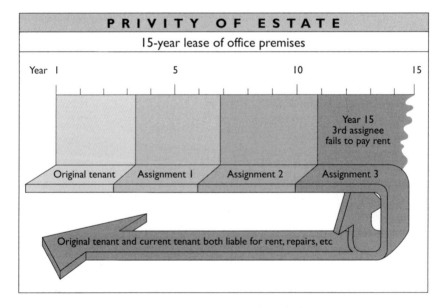

PRIVITY OF ESTATE

15-year lease of office premises

Year 1   5   10   15

Year 15
3rd assignee
fails to pay rent

Original tenant / Assignment 1 / Assignment 2 / Assignment 3

Original tenant and current tenant both liable for rent, repairs, etc

1.3   In practice the doctrine of privity of estate rarely operated, since modern leases nearly always imposed an obligation on assignees to directly covenant with the landlord throughout the duration of the term of the lease and not just for such time as they were in possession of the premises.

1.4   Accordingly, one way or another, most commercial tenants found themselves liable to pay the rent, repair the property and otherwise perform the covenants contained in leases, long after they ceased to have any interest in the property.

1.5   Tenants had been seeking change to these doctrines for many years. The boom market of the late 1980s effectively meant that the lobby fell on deaf ears, but as the recession began to bite the tenants' lobby increased and in March 1993 the Government announced that there would be change in the Law. The Landlord and Tenant (Covenants) Act 1995 (1995 Act) was passed in 1995 and came into force on 1 January 1996.

1.6   The 1995 Act conveniently splits into two parts. Some of the 1995 Act applies only to new tenancies and some applies to both new and old tenancies. It is absolutely essential that surveyors fully understand the difference between a new and old tenancy and this is dealt with in paragraph 3 below.

2.   SUMMARY OF THE NEW LAW

2.1   As it affects new leases only

2.1.1   Tenants are automatically released on an assignment.

2.1.2   Landlords can require a tenant to guarantee his chosen assignee. This concept is called an authorised guarantee agreement and you will have no doubt have heard this referred to by the ghastly abbreviation AGA. For the sake of brevity only, I use that expression in this book.

2.1.3   The parties to a commercial lease (but not residential leases) are allowed to set out criteria for withholding licence to assign.

2.1.4   Landlords are able to seek a release from liability but only on request; this procedure is not automatic.

2.2   As it affects all leases, both old and new

2.2.1   Landlords are required to notify arrears of rent, certain service charges and other liquidated sums due from the tenant – called fixed charges in the 1995 Act – within six months of the current tenant's default or they are not able to recover these from the former tenant.

2.2.2   Former tenants (or guarantors) who are required to pay a fixed charge following default by the current tenant can, if they do make full payment of that fixed charge, call for an overriding lease (see paragraph 9 below).

2.2.3   Former tenants and guarantors whose liabilities arise as a result of certain lease variations which occur after their assignment are not liable for any increased liability which is referable to those variations (see paragraph 10 below).

2.3   The 1995 Act applies to commercial and residential tenancies although the amendments to the Landlord and Tenant Act 1927, that allow the parties to set out the criteria for granting licences to assign, only apply to commercial tenancies.

2.4   The 1995 Act prohibits contracting out.

3.   NEW OR OLD?

3.1   Since the 1995 Act has different consequences for new tenancies and old tenancies it is absolutely essential that before any action is taken relating to any lease, everyone knows whether it is a new lease or an old lease.

3.2   The cut-off date is 31 December 1995 and leases granted after that date are new tenancies subject to the overriding exception that they will still be old leases if the commitment to grant or take that lease was made before 1 January 1996.

3.3   Accordingly, if the date on the lease is 1996 or later it will be a new tenancy unless there was an agreement for lease, or an option to grant that lease, or a court order providing for the grant of that lease, which was made in 1995 or earlier.

3.4   Note that the relevant date is the date upon which the lease is granted and not the term commencement date. This prevents anti-avoidance.

3.5   Obviously there is nothing wrong in granting a lease in 1996 with a term commencing in 1995 and if by doing that one could have made the lease an old tenancy to which privity of contract would have applied it would have been easy to avoid the new regime.

3.6   A lease granted in 1996 or afterwards with a term commencing before 1996 will be a new tenancy unless the commitment to take that lease by way of agreement, court order or option was made earlier than 1 January 1996. You should also know that back dating a lease (or indeed any other legal document) is simply not legal.

3.7   So, in determining whether a lease is a new tenancy the relevant date is the date upon which it is granted (subject to considering if there was an earlier commitment). If one is to avoid unnecessary detective work all leases that are granted should contain a simple statement as to whether or not they are a new tenancy and if not, why not.

3.8   Assuming that a lease does not say whether or not it is a new tenancy, you may need to enquire whether there was an old agreement for lease, option or indeed a court order. Mere correspondence or negotiations regarding a potential lease pre-1996 will not be sufficient unless it was a formal agreement for lease or an option. This may need careful investigation where one is proposing to purchase an investment subject to a lease where the initial covenant is of prime importance and the purchaser is relying on privity of contract liability applying to the tenant who was the original covenant to underpin any subsequent assignments.

3.9   Options

3.9.1   Prior to the 1995 Act coming into force, options were sometimes used by organizations who thought that they might one day carry out a sale and leaseback and where they might wish to offer an investment with their covenant underpinning the lease for its full term. Any lease granted pursuant to that option would not qualify as a new tenancy and therefore privity would apply. Accordingly when a sale and leaseback is contemplated, assuming that this is during the life of the option, the organization would then be able to sell subject to a lease to itself which, since it is created pursuant to the option entered into before the 1995 Act, is not a new tenancy. There may be good commercial reasons why a company or individual planning a sale and leaseback would choose to do this. The freeholder would need to weigh up the difference in the value of the investment with its covenant subject to a new tenancy as opposed to an old tenancy, against the risks that the company would have as original tenant taking an old tenancy as opposed to a new tenancy. If there were no substantial advantages in capital terms, then the vendor would then have the choice whether to exercise the option and take an old lease or structure the lease outside the option arrangements so that the lease simply becomes a lease granted after 1996 and thus a new tenancy under the 1995 Act. The arrangement would have the advantage of giving choice to the landowner without any value restriction. It is of course too late now to create any such option.

3.9.2   Also, contractual options to renew set out in leases granted before the 1995 Act came into operation would have the effect of providing that a lease granted pursuant to that contractual option would be an old tenancy and not a new tenancy. I have seen leases granted in this manner, particularly in circumstances where the parties want to grant a lease for, say, seventy years but for stamp duty reasons structure the arrangement by granting a thirty-five-year lease with an option for a further lease.

3.9.3   I mention these points in order to emphasize the continuing need to ascertain whether a lease which on the face of it appears to be a new tenancy, is in fact a new tenancy, or whether a pre-commitment to it or option for it renders it an old tenancy. The mere passage of time will not be sufficient and practitioners will need to be on their guard. Obviously to the extent that a two-tier market develops, this may become very important.

3.9.4   You will see from the above that a contractual option to renew will render the renewal lease an old tenancy with all its privity ramifications. This is not the case in respect of statutory renewals under the Landlord and Tenant Act 1954.

3.10   1954 Act renewals

3.10.1   If an old tenancy is renewed under the 1954 Act, then if that
renewal is completed after 1 January 1996 it will be a new tenancy. Paragraphs 3 and 4 of Schedule 1 to the 1995 Act deal
with this, providing that the court may take into account the
operation of the 1995 Act in both looking at the rent and the
other terms of the new tenancy.

3.10.2   In commercial lease renewals that fall into this category, the
landlord may well want to amend the alienation provisions of
the lease to give him more control over assignments, given that
once he consents to an assignment he is losing the covenant of
the original tenant that he would otherwise have had under
privity. This needs to be looked at very carefully, particularly for
example, in circumstances where the tenancy is being renewed
to, say, a company which is not of great covenant strength albeit
supported by a strong parent company guarantor. The package
of tenant and guarantor may well have been acceptable to the
landlord when he originally granted the lease now being
renewed, but in the context of a weak tenant being released on
assignment the landlord may well want to look carefully at the
circumstances under which the premises can be assigned, or the
rent that is to be paid, particularly since an AGA can only be
required of a tenant and not the guarantor. (See paragraph 5
below.)

3.11   Five other points are worthy of mention before we leave the
question of whether or not a lease is a new tenancy:

3.11.1   Variation or surrender and re-grant?
Variations to leases often operate as a surrender and re-grant.
For example, if a landlord and tenant were to change the
demise, such an extensive variation would almost certainly
operate as a surrender of the old lease and re-grant of a new
lease. In those circumstances, if it is a pre-1996 lease that is
being varied, the re-grant would become a new tenancy and one
will have created, perhaps unintentionally, a new tenancy from
an old one. Similar circumstances might arise where parties
entered into an agreement for lease before 1 January 1996 and
when they come to complete the lease they change important

terms. If the lease granted after 1 January is not granted 'in pursuance of ... an agreement entered into before that date' then the post-1995 lease will in fact be a new tenancy. The variations in the agreement for lease, or the lease to be granted, may well provide ammunition to a tenant seeking to obtain a release on assignment but of course the alienation provisions may not have been amended to take account of the fact that the lease is a new tenancy; after all, the parties entering into the original agreement for lease would not have anticipated that it might be a new tenancy.

3.11.2 Rent review

(i) Rent reviews are agreed or determined by reference to the rent that a notional tenant would pay for a hypothetical lease. Leases normally assume that on the relevant review date a lease is to be granted by a willing landlord to a willing tenant. Since future review dates will inevitably be post 1 January 1996 such a notional lease can only be a new tenancy and therefore free of privity of contract. Does this mean that the hypothetical tenant is taking a lease notionally without privity of contract liability? He might pay more for such a product than he would for a lease subject to the doctrine of privity of contract. If however the lease is an old lease, the tenant owns, and is reviewing, a lease with full privity liability. The position is of course worsened by the fact that the hypothetical lease will normally incorporate the terms of the lease being reviewed and thus include an alienation clause in the same form as that contained in the actual lease. It will not contain a clause that gives the landlord more control and in particular one which allows him to set out the criteria for assignments. (See paragraph 6 below.)

(ii) Before the 1995 Act took effect some lawyers and surveyors were busily drafting assumptions that the hypothetical lease be construed as an old lease. Whether this is in fact necessary will depend on whether the courts adopt a commercial approach rather than a literal approach. There are a number of cases regarding rent reviews where the courts have attempted to apply what they have called 'a presumption of reality' and looked for a commercial approach which does not leave a windfall profit in the hands of the landlord.

This was particularly so during the appeals relating to headline rents (see paragraph 7, chapter 2). Only time will tell whether the point is taken in the courts and how they will deal with it. You will have to be alive to this argument. My own view is that the courts would not be terribly sympathetic to a landlord trying to foist a higher rent on the tenant by dint of such reasoning. Clearly there is nothing that can be done now by tenants to protect themselves against this position and we shall have to wait and see whether this comes before the courts.

3.11.3 Overriding leases

Overriding leases granted after a former tenant pays up following a demand for a fixed charge will, of course, be granted after the 1995 Act came into force but that fact will not make them new tenancies. Where the lease out of which an overriding lease is created was a new tenancy, the overriding lease will be a new tenancy but in all other respects it will not. You cannot create new from old.

3.11.4 Disclaimer

Where a contractual guarantor undertakes to guarantee the obligations of a tenant, that guarantee nearly always provides that if there is a disclaimer of the lease by a liquidator or trustee in bankruptcy of the original tenant, the guarantor can be called upon to enter into a new lease following that disclaimer.

The question arises whether any such tenancy entered into after the 1995 Act came into force would be a new tenancy or an old tenancy for the purposes of the 1995 Act. Obviously on the face of it, it should be a new tenancy since the lease will be granted post 1996. However, although the 1995 Act is silent on the point I think that a better interpretation would be for that lease to still comprise an old tenancy. The lease would not have been granted other than as a result of the obligation contained in the contractual guarantee and I think that one could make a good argument to state that the lease is granted in pursuance of an agreement entered into before 1996, i.e. the agreement contained in the contractual guarantee in the original lease. Although the 1995 Act does not deal with the issue, there are similarities with overriding leases where you cannot create new from old. In the same way as the overriding lease owes its existence to the pre-1996 old lease, so would such a lease being taken by the guarantor of the tenant whose liquidator has disclaimed an old tenancy.

3.11.5 Forfeiture

Where a lease is forfeited and there is an application for relief from forfeiture which is not made by the current tenant, if the person successfully applies for relief after the 1995 Act is in operation the resulting lease will be a new lease. This will apply whatever the status of the forfeited lease. In those circumstances one will have been able to create new from old and this may be a very good reason why landlords might in the future choose to oppose applications for relief or agree to them on terms whereby the alienation covenant is changed.

4.   RELEASE ON ASSIGNMENT

4.1   Tenant release

4.1.1   Arguably the most publicised and well-known part of the 1995 Act is Section 5 which provides that a tenant is released from the tenant's covenants of a tenancy as from the date of assignment. The principle recommendation of the Law Commission in its 1988 report was to remedy the wrongs of privity of contract.

4.1.2   Section 5 is clear. Tenants are released on assignment of leases which are new tenancies. The release procedure is automatic. Once a tenant has been released, he ceases to be entitled to the benefit of the landlord's covenants from the date of assignment. Effectively a line is drawn and so far as the outgoing tenant is concerned his interest in the premises will cease.

4.1.3   These changes in the law only apply for new tenancies: for leases that do not fall within the definition of new tenancies (as to which see paragraph 3 above) there is no change to the existing rules relating to privity.

4.1.4   The basic rule releasing tenants is subject to one or two notable and important exceptions:

(i) As you will see from paragraph 5, an outgoing tenant can be required to stay in the firing-line after the assignment, and guarantee performance by the assignee. It was thought to be perfectly reasonable that although an outgoing tenant is released, a landlord is entitled to look to him to guarantee the performance of the tenant that the tenant himself has chosen. The main problems with the old privity regime tended to emanate from assignees a long way down the line and over whom an original tenant had no control. The requirement for an AGA addresses this concern. Tenants can be asked to guarantee the assignee they choose and impose upon the landlord, but no one else.

(ii) It would also not be fair if tenants could take advantage of the release mechanism by unlawfully assigning. For that reason, unlawful assignments and assignments by operation of law are excluded by Section 11 of the 1995 Act: these do not have the effect of releasing a tenant from liability. The tenant will only be released on the next assignment which is not an excluded assignment. Excluded assignments are effectively transparent for the purpose of the release provisions of the 1995 Act.

4.2   Landlord release

4.2.1   The 1995 Act provides for release provisions to apply to landlords as well as tenants. Outgoing landlords, again only of new leases, may seek release from liability. However, in the case of an outgoing landlord, the release provisions are not automatic. The landlord must apply for a release. The rationale for this is that, by and large, tenants need the consent of their landlords before they can assign and therefore landlords have the opportunity of consenting, or not, to the proposed assignment. They can see who is taking the tenant's place and evaluate the change in covenant. They have the right (albeit not necessarily absolute) to say no. Very rarely, however, do landlords need to apply for a tenant's consent to assignment of the reversionary interest. If, therefore, landlords were automatically released on assignment of the reversionary interest, where a tenant were to have no input whatsoever, landlords would be able to avoid liability without the tenant having any control.

4.2.2   The procedure that the 1995 Act has introduced requires the landlord to apply to the tenant for a release. The application must be made within a four-week period either side of the assignment of the reversion and the tenant either consents to the release, in which case the landlord will be released from liability (and will no longer have the benefit of tenant covenants in each case from the date of assignment), or the tenant will object. If the tenant objects the matter will ultimately be decided by the County court. The court will need to ascertain whether the tenant is reasonable in withholding consent to the release.

4.2.3   If the tenant fails to do anything within four weeks following receipt of the landlord's notice, then the release will take effect from the date of the assignment.

4.2.4   In multi-let buildings it is necessary for all tenants to consent and one of the clear difficulties that sometimes faces a landlord is the situation where he applies for a release of his liability but does not obtain it from all of the tenants. This is worrying since it is often in that type of situation where a landlord will have obligations to provide services, management, etc. and tenants will want to be satisfied that any new landlord is of sufficient covenant strength to perform the obligations to the same standard. It is quite likely that where tenants are faced with applications for release they will get together to take action collectively, especially if they are anxious to ensure that the landlord remains on the hook.

4.2.5   Where a landlord has not been granted a release on assignment of his reversion he will have the opportunity to request a release on subsequent disposals of the reversionary interest.

4.2.6   Landlords will have to try and ensure that, to the extent that they are not released, they have the opportunity of applying for release on future assignments. The four-week window either side of the assignment of a reversionary interest will still apply and therefore it is essential that in these circumstances landlords are aware of subsequent dealings with the reversion. The sale documentation should provide for this, otherwise a landlord who is not released may simply not know of the next opportunity for a release. None the less, this is likely to cause all sorts of problems in practice.

4.3 Personal covenants

4.3.1 Probably the most dangerous aspect of the new release procedure, in so far as it relates to landlords, is that landlords may inherit liability for onerous covenants given by original landlords, say in the development of property. Developers often undertake substantial construction obligations in agreements for lease and purchasers of the reversion will need to ensure that they do not inherit these. The practice is certainly emerging whereby obligations such as these are made personal and do not pass on to successor landlords, thus removing the requirement for release.

4.4 Old law position

4.4.1 Under the law prior to the 1995 Act, original landlords were liable in privity of contract but successor landlords were only ever liable pursuant to the doctrine of privity of estate. The position of course is the same for both landlords and tenant save, as mentioned in paragraph 1.3 above, privity of estate was very much a theoretical doctrine for tenants since they nearly always had direct contractual liability anyway, by virtue of direct covenants imposed in licences to assign. This is not something that in practice affected landlords and therefore the new requirement to apply for release is more onerous for landlords (other than original landlords) than was the pre-1995 Act position.

4.5 Sublettings

4.5.1 The 1995 Act does not deal with sublettings but it is clear that on sublettings, even where granted out of an old lease, a landlord cannot require a direct covenant for the full term from his subtenant. It would be quite wrong if the subtenant could be required to give a direct covenant to the superior landlord for the entire duration of the term through the licence to underlet. The intermediate landlord granting the sublease would not be able to obtain such a covenant and therefore why should the subtenant be in a position whereby he has to give such a covenant to his superior landlord? This position is the same whether subleases are granted out of old or new tenancies. The sublease will be a new tenancy. Landlords must make absolutely sure that their licences to underlet allow them to require direct covenants from the subtenant and then each of its assignees. It may also be possible for the landlord to require that the subtenant and each assignee of the sublease enters into an AGA with the superior landlord.

4.6   Summary

4.6.1   To summarize, the 1995 Act's main principle relating to privity is to release both tenants and landlords on assignment after which they are not liable under their covenants. Equally, where one party is released it no longer has the benefit of the other's covenants. Although the 1995 Act goes about this in slightly different ways for landlords and tenants the principle is the same.

5.   AUTHORISED GUARANTEE AGREEMENTS

5.1   As we have seen, where a tenant lawfully assigns a lease, and where that assignment is not an excluded assignment, he will be released from liability on completion of the assignment. He no longer underwrites the liabilities and obligations of his successors. The old privity regime would have made that tenant liable throughout the duration of the tenancy and although he might have held rights against assignees under indemnity covenants, he would have remained principally liable under privity of contract.

5.2   In new tenancies the only way the tenant lawfully assigning can be left on the hook is if the landlord requires him to give an AGA by virtue of which he guarantees compliance with the tenant covenants by the assignee but no one further down the line.

5.3   An AGA must be entered into pursuant to a condition, lawfully imposed, requiring it. Since for commercial leases the 1995 Act has changed the provisions of the Landlord and Tenant Act 1927 and now entitles the parties to set out criteria for granting (or withholding) licence to assign, it is quite normal to see leases setting out conditions in the alienation clause requiring a tenant to enter into an AGA on any assignment. Sometimes this is qualified to apply only where it is reasonable to do so but many leases have an absolute obligation on tenants to enter into an AGA and it is doubtful that such a liability would have a particularly adverse impact on rent review. Assuming it does not, it is certainly a precise way for a landlord to protect his position. The requirement is clear and the tenant knows exactly where it stands. On any assignment, although the tenant will be released it will have to guarantee the assignee that it foists upon the landlord. Since we have been working under the new regime there has been some resistance from tenants negotiating new leases to the acceptance of alienation clauses that require them to enter into an AGA. Well-advised tenants, notably multiple retailers, and some commentators argue that such a requirement should only apply 'if it is reasonable in all the circumstances'. If a tenant is able to negotiate this, then fine, but I do believe it is reasonable for the AGA requirement to be an absolute and automatic one; after all, this clearly follows the logic of requiring the tenant to back up the assignee that it is asking the landlord to accept.

5.4 It is no good trying to draft an AGA in such a way that the outgoing tenant is responsible to guarantee assignees further down the line than the next assignee. To the extent that this is done the document will not comply with Section 16 and will not qualify as an AGA. Note that if one has been over-zealous in the drafting it is likely that the whole document will not be tainted since the Section says that the agreement does not qualify as an AGA 'to the extent that it purports' to include these outlawed requirements. By implication, it is all right to the extent that it does not. To make the position absolutely safe one can insert a severance clause which will then have the effect of severing from the document any part of it that would otherwise render the document invalid.

5.5 The 1995 Act does not seek to set out the form that an AGA should take but many leases do have a form attached to the lease.

LIVERPOOL JOHN MOORES UNIVERSITY
LEARNING SERVICES

5.6   This follows the practice that grew up before the 1995 Act, and which still exists, for landlords to set out the form of guarantee that would be required from contractual guarantors of assignees. The form is very often set out in a schedule to the lease.

5.7   It is important that one bears in mind the risk that if a form of AGA is attached to the lease then that form must stand the test of time for the entire duration of the term. If the law of guarantees were to change during the life of the lease, the landlord may regret having attached a form of AGA to a lease. By and large, however, this practice does commend itself in that it is clear to all parties what will be required on assignment.

5.8   The 1995 Act does not set out what can go into an AGA save that it is clear that the guarantor can be made liable as primary obligor. The 1995 Act also makes it clear that the guarantor's obligations cannot go beyond that of the assignee he is guaranteeing. There is specific reference in Section 16(5) to what happens on a disclaimer and the 1995 Act allows an AGA to require the guarantor to enter into a new tenancy if there is a disclaimer. Remember that the law of guarantees and disclaimer was recently considered in the House of Lords in *Hindcastle Limited* v *Barbara Attenborough Associates Limited and Others* **1996 EGCS 28**. It is clear that a disclaimer releases the tenant but not his guarantor. The 1995 Act does not alter this in any way.

5.9   Subject to the above the general law of guarantees applies to AGAs.

5.10   One point that is worth mentioning at this stage is that Section 16 of the 1995 Act makes it clear that AGAs can only be required to be entered into by tenants. There is nothing in the 1995 Act that permits the landlord to require a contractual guarantor to enter into an AGA when the tenant who he is guaranteeing seeks to assign.

5.11   Landlords must be wary of the traditional structure where a lease is granted to a tenant of little substance supported by a more substantial entity as guarantor, perhaps a parent company. Problems may well arise for the landlord when he is asked to consent to an assignment by the insubstantial tenant even to an assignee of greater covenant strength. The insubstantial outgoing tenant was of course being supported by a substantial guarantor. Section 16 does not say that the landlord can require the original contractual guarantor to enter into an AGA.

5.12 This raises one very important difficulty, primarily as a result of the provisions of Section 25 of the 1995 Act which states that any agreement relating to a tenancy is void to the extent that it would exclude, modify or otherwise frustrate the operation of any provisions of the 1995 Act. Since one of these provisions is that which draws a line after an assignment, it is arguable that a contractual obligation upon a contractual guarantor to guarantee the tenant not only whilst he is a tenant, but also whilst he is liable under an AGA, may be void.

5.13 If it is not permissible to require a contractual guarantee to last beyond the time when the tenant is liable to the landlord under the tenant covenants then clearly the landlord would be in a difficult position, being unable to insist on a contractual guarantor entering into an AGA.

5.14 There has been much written about this in the property press but I still believe that a technical reading of Section 24 of the 1995 Act saves the day for landlords. This section states that where a tenant is released from a tenant covenant then any guarantor who has guaranteed compliance with those tenant covenants is also released to the same extent that the tenant is released *from the tenant covenants*. This would seem to imply that where a contractual guarantor remains liable to guarantee the tenant's liability, not under the tenant covenants but pursuant to obligations set out in an AGA, the contractual guarantor's liability can remain. Landlords normally provide for a contractual guarantee to last not just whilst the lease is vested in the tenant (and thus release the contractual guarantor on assignment) but whilst the tenant is liable to the landlord under the lease covenants and/or pursuant to an AGA.

5.15 In addition to this, it is absolutely essential that the AGA does not merely provide for a liability whilst 'the lease is vested in the assignee'. If this were the case then the tenant would be off the hook if the assignee were to unlawfully assign. As we have seen from paragraph 4.1.4 (ii) above, an excluded assignment would not otherwise release a tenant and it would be wrong if the tenant were released from any obligations under an AGA in such a manner. (There have been articles on this subject in the *Estates Gazette*, i.e. 11 May 1996, page 118 – see Recommended reading.)

5.16 None the less, landlords have to be very careful where they are granting a lease to a tenant on the strength, not of the covenant status of the tenant, but because it is being supported by a strong contractual guarantee. Certainly when considering assignment from the insubstantial tenant, landlords need to weigh up the strength of covenant package that they are losing against the strength of covenant package they are gaining. It is not merely a question of looking at the tenant in a vacuum. Apples must be compared with apples. It may be that a practice will develop whereby in circumstances where in the past a landlord may have granted a lease to an insubstantial tenant supported by a substantial guarantor, the landlord would, instead, grant the lease to both entities as direct tenants. Both would then be tenants for the purpose of Section 16 and both could therefore be required to enter into an AGA.

5.17 AGAs are normally going to be entered into by the assigning tenant but there are circumstances where an AGA will be entered into by earlier tenants. As you will have seen from paragraph 4.1.4 (ii) above, where there is an excluded assignment it is transparent for the purpose of the 1995 Act. Accordingly, when the assignor under that excluded assignment comes to enter into a lawful assignment which is not an excluded assignment, it is perfectly reasonable for the landlord to require him to enter into an AGA with the new assignee. This will be the time when the tenant who assigned pursuant to the excluded assignment is released and at that stage he can be required to enter into an AGA. The rationale is easy to follow if you work on the premise that AGAs can be required from tenants who are released and tenants are not released on excluded assignments.

5.18 AGAs are no more than guarantee agreements and therefore the general law relating to guarantees will apply to them. It is important that landlords and tenants do not vary leases without making the outgoing tenant who has entered into an AGA party to that variation. In certain cases guarantors are released from all liability where there is a variation of the contract that they are guaranteeing compliance with, and where they are not party to that variation. The variation may be such as to release the tenant entering into an AGA from all liability under the lease. I have certainly seen AGAs drafted in such manner as to require the guarantor to enter into deeds of variation. This must be very carefully considered, especially in view of the provisions of Section 18 of the 1995 Act considered in paragraph 10 below.

6.   AGREEING CRITERIA

6.1   Until the 1995 Act a landlord has not been able to dictate expressly in the lease what is and what is not reasonable. If the tenant is prohibited from assigning or underletting without the landlord's consent then either by implication, or expressly, the landlord cannot unreasonably withhold consent. Landlords have not, however, been able to go on to say what is and what is not reasonable. The courts have regarded this as a matter for *them* to decide.

6.2   Section 22 of the 1995 Act changes all this but only for what is described in the 1995 Act as a 'qualifying lease'. This is a new tenancy but not a residential lease, i.e. a lease by which a building is let wholly or mainly as a single private residence. All commercial leases are included and it would seem that the definition of 'qualifying lease' also covers and includes leases granted for the commercial purpose of allowing the tenant to run a business of granting residential tenancies. After all, such a lease would not have let the building 'wholly or mainly as a single private residence'.

6.3   The 1995 Act allows the landlord and tenant to set out the conditions for granting consent to assignment of a qualifying lease. The provisions can appear in the lease or they may be agreed between the parties at a later date provided it is prior to application for licence to assign. If a new lease is granted and the parties have not specified criteria in that lease, there is nothing to stop them from doing so in the future, so long as they do so before a tenant makes application for licence to assign.

6.4   Broadly speaking, where the parties specify circumstances for withholding consent to an assignment, or conditions subject to which a consent will be granted, then the landlord is not regarded as unreasonably withholding consent to an assignment if the withholding is on the grounds that the circumstances exist. Similarly if consent is given subject to those conditions, the consent will not be deemed to have been given subject to unreasonable conditions. The circumstances and conditions may be factual and capable of objective analysis, in which case they are absolute. Where they are framed by reference to a matter being determined by the landlord or someone else, the landlord's or third party's power to determine must be exercised reasonably or there must be an unrestricted right given to the tenant to have the determination reviewed by someone else, whose determination will be conclusive.

6.5   Where the criteria are factual and do not need further determination (e.g. ' any assignee must be a public company quoted on the London Stock Exchange') it is an objective test capable of simple verification and therefore absolute. If a tenant were to agree to a clause including this as a prerequisite for assignment, then the landlord would have the absolute right to refuse consent to assignment to a private company, however strong the prospective assignee's covenant might be. The landlord would not be unreasonably withholding consent since the circumstances for withholding consent (the assignee being a public company) would not have been met.

6.6   If, however, the circumstances were not factual but clarifying them needed determination (e.g. 'no assignment other than to a company of covenant strength equal to the assignor') the determination by the landlord would still have to be exercised reasonably or there would have to be reference to a third party determination and the third party's determination would be binding.

6.7   Factual or discretionary tests

6.7.1   So, where there are circumstances or conditions set out in the alienation clause in a qualifying lease the first task is to determine whether they are factual or discretionary.

Obviously very careful thought needs to be given before factual tests are set out, since if these are to last the lifetime of a lease, both parties must be satisfied that they will give the necessary protection throughout the term. The problem is perhaps more for the tenant than for the landlord because of the way Section 22 of the 1995 Act is worded. The section states that where a circumstance or condition is specified the landlord is not regarded as unreasonably withholding licence if the circumstance exists or licence is given subject to the condition.

6.7.2   If there were a factual test that the assignee must be a public company, the landlord would not be unreasonable in withholding consent if a private company was put forward. Equally, if a public company is put forward the 1995 Act is drafted in such a way that the landlord would still be able to withhold consent if it is reasonable to do so on the facts. The test is likely to provide that it is a prerequisite that the assignee is publicly quoted and the tenant needs to show this before he can even get off the starting-block. Once a public company assignee is put forward, the landlord must still be satisfied, acting reasonably, that it is of reasonable covenant strength. It is, of course, possible to draft the condition so that any public company assignee will be sufficient to satisfy the landlord. This is unlikely to commend itself to landlords and it is certainly not the normal way to deal with this.

6.8   Building leases

6.8.1   There is one exceptional type of case – building leases. Section 19 1(B) of the Landlord and Tenant Act 1927 used to provide for a different treatment of building leases. This will still continue for old tenancies but no longer for new qualifying leases, now that building leases have been brought into line with all other qualifying leases. So far as old tenancies are concerned, building leases with provisions requiring consent prior to assignment are deemed not to require consent where the landlord is notified of the deal within six months, save during the last seven years of the term, where Section 19 of the 1927 Act applies in the usual way. As I say, this is no longer the case for new tenancies as a result of Section 22 of the 1995 Act which introduces a new Section 1(D) into the old Section 19.

6.9 Landlord's dilemma

6.9.1 Since June 1995 when the 1995 Act was originally passed, people have been giving thought to the type of conditions that need to be inserted in commercial leases after 1 January 1996. The obvious dilemma for commercial landlords is a simple one:

(i) The 1995 Act no longer gives them the protection, comfort and security of privity of contract;

(ii) On assignment they will lose the covenant of the original tenant (subject to it entering into an AGA);

(iii) They have the right to strictly control assignment, either by absolutely prohibiting it or by setting out stringent criteria at the outset; and

(iv) If they persuade the tenants to agree to an absolute prohibition on assignment or, more likely, stringent criteria, will they be able to let the premises and, assuming they can, what effect will this have on rent review? As you will know, rent reviews are agreed or determined by reference to the rent a notional tenant would pay for a hypothetical lease on the same terms; clearly the more stringent the alienation clause becomes, the less attractive it will be to notional tenants and the more likely it will be that the actual tenant will seek a discount at review to reflect the fact that notional tenants would not pay so much for a lease with oppressive alienation provisions.

6.10 Use of disregards on review

6.10.1 A clear balance must be obtained which reflects the desire that landlords have to protect the covenant status of the original tenant against the impact that provisions designed to do this may have on rent review. Clearly if the parties agree to do so, it would be possible for a landlord to set out strict criteria for assignment and then provide for a review clause with false assumptions directing the valuer to ignore these on rent review. For a landlord to persuade a tenant to agree to this, he would no doubt have to be in a strong bargaining position. However there is nothing wrong with this approach if the parties set out to achieve it, although clearly the courts are likely to strive for the 'presumption of reality' that came to the fore during the headline rent cases (see paragraph 7 of Chapter 2 below) and certainly where it is not absolutely clear that the false assumptions have this effect.

6.11 So what type of covenants can one expect to see and is one seeing? As lawyers and surveyors began to put their thinking caps on once it became clear that the 1995 Act was going to get on the statute books, a number of innovative clauses began to emerge. Alienation clauses have become extremely long and relatively complicated and an extraordinary amount of time and effort is spent negotiating them. Perhaps now that the 1995 Act has been with us for a little while, one has begun to see this settle down and in many sectors landlords have begun to return to the position prior to the 1995 Act where the alienation clauses merely required them to act reasonably in considering whether or not to consent, perhaps bolstered by an invariable right to call for an AGA. None the less, alienation clauses do exist where there are specific tests and it is worth looking at some of these in more detail.

In measuring any financial tests the whole covenant package of assignees needs to be considered and, as mentioned above in paragraph 5.11, landlords must be careful where the proposed assignee is a worthless company backed by a substantial parent guarantor. There will probably then be problems when that assignee seeks to assign, in that only it and not its parent, can be required to give an AGA. Similarly, if the original lease is granted to a combination of insubstantial tenant backed by a parent guarantor, or indeed any other form of security, it is essential that the landlord looks at the assignee's status by reference to the covenant package that it has and is giving up. This package of original tenant and original contractual guarantor must be considered and the assignee must be looked at in the light of that, not just the covenant strength of the original tenant.

6.12   Financial tests

6.12.1   Formulae relating to net asset value and net profits of proposed assignees were thought to be one way of specifying criteria. It is not unusual to see a net profit test whereby a proposed assignee must be able to show that they have achieved net trading profits pre-tax equal to or better than three times the rent passing for a period, normally three years, before the application for licence to assign. This is a tried-and-tested method for evaluating covenant strength in forward funding agreements and certainly one has seen this type of provision find its way into alienation clauses. It sometimes works for headquarter office buildings, but there are inherent dangers with the letting of shops, restaurants, etc. Assume, for example, a lease granted to one of the national high street retail chains with this as the major test in the alienation clause. If that original operator has two or three hundred units, its covenant strength measured by reference to profits is likely to be far greater than three times the rent passing under those premises. So any assignee passing such a test may still not be anything like as good as the original tenant. If that is the only test for an assignee, it is clear that the landlord is likely to run the serious risk of down-grading the strength of covenant on assignment. Landlords can take comfort, of course, from the fact that Section 22 of the 1995 Act is drafted in such a way as to still allow the landlord to withhold consent if it is reasonable to do so. The requirement to meet the net profit test is a prerequisite to moving forward and testing the rest of the assignee's covenant. However, landlords must be very careful if they are relying on this in circumstances where the type of test that they have agreed is not sufficient to weed out patently unacceptable assignees. They will be relying on the court saying that a refusal is reasonable against the background of a specific test of acceptability. Perhaps one of the best advantages given to landlords by these net profit tests is the fact that the assignee must normally have shown net profits for perhaps three years prior to the licence to assign. This at least shows that the assignee has been around for some time and has been consistently making profits that should be sufficient to pay the rent. It will stop the landlord from having to deal with start-up businesses which can often be a big concern, particularly in the retail and leisure sectors. If one uses profit tests, very careful drafting is needed in order to ensure that one knows what is being measured. For example, the fact that huge profits have been made may be irrelevant if they are extraordinary items and not normal trading profits.

6.12.2 Net asset value, capital adequacy and gearing tests are also sometimes helpful to landlords in giving a good idea as to the strength of the covenant, including its borrowings.

6.12.3 However, there are significant problems with financial tests and a report prepared by a working party of representatives of various funds, together with some surveyors, lawyers and accountants, under the aegis of the Association of British Insurers (ABI) was dismissive about such tests being imposed in institutional leases. Their concern was that no test, or even any combination of tests, could be applied consistently in such a way as to provide a reliable result. It is perhaps somewhat surprising that the report was so dismissive, since there are clearly situations where financial tests of one sort or another may well assist a landlord. However, given that this report was commissioned with a view to looking at standard type clauses to insert in leases in order to exercise control over assignments, the insertion of such financial tests, which were openly condemned by the report, may well involve running the risk that such tests might affect the institutional acceptability of the lease.

The working party is reviewing the impact of the 1995 Act generally and is considering revising ABI policy in 1997.

6.13 Comparative covenant strength and equivalence tests

6.13.1 Tests that provide for assignees to be of equivalent or better covenant strength can be dangerous in that if the original tenant is a very strong covenant, this may effectively preclude assignment. If a landlord is granting an original lease to, say, one of the top-one-hundred PLCs and requires any assignee to be of equal covenant strength, then even though this may need third party determination, or the landlord to act reasonably, since it is not a factual/objective test, the net effect of it may be to make assignment very difficult indeed. Original tenants agreeing to this type of test must be very careful. The irony, of course, is that the stronger the original tenant the more the landlord wants to protect its original tenant covenant strength and the more careful the original tenant has to be. Equally, in those circumstances, if the landlord is trying to protect that covenant strength with equivalent covenant status alienation provisions, the very insertion of such a clause may be something which would be used against the landlord on review and thus attack the yield that the landlord would otherwise be able to obtain and the growth that would be obtained from the premises. These are the very things the landlord is trying to protect.

6.13.2 Where there is a covenant comparison test, the parties will need to decide exactly what date is taken for the comparison. Should the assignee be of equivalent covenant strength with that of the original tenant at the date the original lease is granted or when the licence to assign is applied for? Arguably it should be the former since, firstly, that is the time when the landlord agreed to accept the covenant and, secondly, it may well be that the original tenant is seeking to assign the lease in order to keep a lid on its financial commitments in circumstances where its covenant strength is deteriorating. Conversely if the date for comparison is the earlier date this may be historic and the original tenant may be a much stronger covenant at the date application for licence is made. It is at that date that an assignment will have the effect of taking that covenant away from the landlord. Perhaps take the higher of the two: this will certainly protect the landlord, although for obvious reasons it is not likely to find favour with tenants.

6.13.3 I think there are very difficult points arising from equivalent covenant status clauses. Not only can they cause great difficulties for original tenants who are strong, but they are also difficult to evaluate unless there are factors which are to be taken into account when making the appropriate comparison. Covenant comparison tests can also be phrased so as to allow refusal of consent if the value of the landlord's interest in the premises is to be diminished. There is no doubt that imposing a condition such as this will give the landlord a significant amount of control but, once again, perhaps at the expense of growth by way of increased rent at review. Tests like this are often fiercely resisted by occupiers, particularly in the retail and leisure sector. In its report the ABI working party acknowledged this and perhaps tests like this are more sensible only in secondary locations. They have certainly not commended themselves to well-advised tenants in primary locations and I doubt they will.

6.14 Performance of covenants

6.14.1 Leases sometimes provide that it is a condition of licence to assign that the tenant pays his rent and observes his covenants. I think there are many dangers indeed in such a test, even if it is watered down by words such as 'material' and 'substantial'. There have been many problems arising from these sort of clauses in break clauses (see Chapter 4) and I would very strongly recommend that tenants do not agree to provisions such as this. If a landlord is concerned to ensure that the assignee is likely to be able to comply with lease covenants a condition along those lines can be easily inserted. This rightly looks forward to the proposed assignee's likely performance, it does not look backwards. Breach of existing covenants should not be a reason for withholding consent. It was not a reason prior to the 1995 Act, even in the case of disrepair of premises unless the disrepair was extremely substantial and I do not advocate this as a test for the future.

6.14.2 Perhaps it is fair to both parties to provide for a pre-condition that the rent is paid up to date, but tenants can get into difficulties if such a condition relates not only to the rack rent, but also other moneys reserved as rent such as service charges. It may not be at all fair to require service charges to be paid before an assignment in circumstances where, say, there is a bona fide dispute. This may indeed operate as a sword of Damocles. I think that as a general principle it is important that this type of clause looks forward to evaluate future performance; it is not right for it to look back as a way of punishing an assignor who has been in breach or as a way of making him comply with his obligations at a time when he needs the landlord's help.

6.15 Diplomatic immunity and residence restrictions

6.15.1 Landlords may be keen to impose conditions prohibiting a transfer to assignees who enjoy diplomatic immunity or where

they are resident outside the UK. If there is a residence requirement it may be that one would choose not to impose a restriction on the assignee being resident in the UK but to provide for
the residence to be either in the EU or just in a jurisdiction
where there are arrangements for enforcement of judgments
reciprocal with the United Kingdom.

6.15.2 Certainly, restricting assignees to UK residents has a certain
merit, in that it might just be speedier to enforce judgments and
indeed there might be more likelihood that assets are in the UK
to support any judgment that is obtained. Until quite recently it
had been thought that there may be a general ability to withhold consent without any form of condition simply on the basis
of unreasonableness where the assignee is resident outside the
UK. Doubt was cast upon this in the case of *Kened Limited and
Another* v *Connie Investments Limited* **1995 NPC 84** (also
referred to in Chapter 3, paragraph 3.18) where the court held
that it was unreasonable to take issue with a guarantor resident
in Luxembourg on the basis that enforcement of judgement
debts in Luxembourg was not a terribly difficult task.

6.16   Obtaining of consents as a prerequisite

6.16.1 Certainly there is no reason why conditions cannot be imposed
requiring that the appropriate superior landlords' or mortgagees' consents are obtained but tenants need to ensure that if
a condition such as this is imposed, it relates to leases or mort-
gages that are in place at the date the lease is granted; they can
then see the basis upon which consent can be withheld by the
appropriate landlord or mortgagee.

6.17   Standing of assignee

6.17.1 It is certainly not unusual to provide that it is reasonable to
withhold consent if the proposed assignee is not of sufficient
financial standing to enable it to comply with the tenant
covenants in the lease. Of course this is not the same as an
equivalent covenant test nor is it the same as a historic look at
performance. It is merely a requirement for the assignee to
prove that it can comply with the tenant covenants and,
arguably, insertion of a specific condition along these lines is no

more than a statement of the position that assignees were in before the new changes where they sought landlord's licence to assign against the background merely that the landlord could not act unreasonably.

6.18 Inter group

6.18.1 Landlords need to be very careful to exercise an element of control over assignments inter group. The ABI report suggested that assignments to associated companies be prohibited completely and this is certainly one way of protecting the position, although it may not find favour with many tenants. Perhaps it is not necessary in order to give the landlords the measure of control that they need. It is important that if there is an assignment inter group the landlord is not in any worse position than before the assignment. The assignment is likely to have been effected to accommodate the tenant's needs in relation to some form of reconstruction of its corporate affairs and if that is the case, clearly it would not be reasonable for a landlord to suffer as a consequence.

6.18.2 Perhaps this is one situation where an equivalence test would be reasonable and sensible. If a tenant is assigning inter group as part of some form of reconstruction, it is not an easy proposition for the tenant to argue that the assignee that it has provided to the landlord should be of less covenant strength than was the tenant. If one goes this route then again one will need to decide the date upon which the comparison is taken and there may be a good reason to provide for the test of equivalence to be at the date of licence to assign or the date of the original grant, whichever produces the better result for the landlord.

6.18.3 There is one further problem with inter group assignment and that is where originally there was a contractual guarantee to support the tenant. If one accepts that the inter group assignment should put the landlord in no worse position than it was before, then I think it is perfectly reasonable for the landlord to insist that on any such assignment, if there was an original contractual guarantor, then he is required to provide a contractual guarantee for the assignee as well. The principle is straightforward. If a landlord is to permit an inter group assignment then it should do so only on terms whereby it is not prejudiced.

6.19 Other tests including requirement for a costs undertaking

6.19.1 Other tests that I have seen and which can be negotiated include reference to the number of trading outlets of an assignee, its position with credit rating agencies, surrender back clauses, provision of rent deposits, etc. I have also seen leases include a condition requiring that the assignee's solicitors undertake to pay the assignor's legal and surveyor's fees in relation to the application for licence to assign, whether or not licence is granted.

6.19.2 There have been difficulties in the past where tenants have sought undertakings such as this. The courts have not been inclined to provide that it is reasonable to insist on receiving such an undertaking to be given before the landlord begins considering the application. Obviously if an undertaking cannot be obtained, then if the licence does not proceed to completion the landlord's professionals are likely to be involved in undertaking work for which they will not be paid by the assignee. In the first instance decision of *Dong Bang Minerva (UK) Limited* v *Davina Limited* **1995 1 EGLR 41** the court said that undertaking work pursuant to an application for landlord's consent was part of the overhead of being a landlord. In practice landlords do not tend to accept this as part of their overheads. They would not normally expect to pay their professionals for considering abortive applications for licence to assign and thus the professionals themselves often have to bear these costs. The court of appeal in the *Dong Bang Minerva* case appears to have ducked the issue, since both parties to the appeal agreed there was no issue before them, if the undertaking was for reasonable costs. In the case in question, the undertaking sought to make the indemnifier 'fully' responsible for 'all costs'. The court felt that the landlords had acted unreasonably in relation to this specific undertaking and for that reason the appeal was dismissed; the court did not give a ruling on whether it was generally reasonable for a landlord to require an undertaking. Costs can often be quite substantial and clearly inserting an obligation for the assignee's solicitors to give an undertaking to be responsible for costs is one way round this! I think that following the Court of Appeal decision, it is important that any such undertaking only seeks to make the assignee's solicitors responsible for *reasonable* costs. If a landlord does this he should be all right.

6.20 I hope that I have given you a flavour of the type of tests and conditions that can be inserted in relation to new commercial leases. The insertion of specific circumstances for withholding licence or conditions subject to which licence is granted must be considered on 'a deal-by-deal basis' since what is right for some properties and tenants will clearly not be right for others. Furthermore, the experience in certain sectors is very different from that in others. For example, at present in the leisure sector where twenty-five and thirty-five-year leases with no breaks abound, one is seeing complicated alienation clauses and extensive tests; in the office market this is not so common and it is not all that rare to see a shorter-term lease with a more straightforward alienation clause relying on perhaps just reasonableness and the requirement for an AGA. Protecting rental growth, covenant status and institutional acceptability are at the heart of the debate. This is a complicated area which surveyors and lawyers alike are just beginning to get to grips with and probably there is no better example of property negotiation where lawyers and surveyors must act in tandem.

7. LANDLORD RELEASE AND ARREARS

7.1 Landlord's liabilities were also controlled by the doctrine of privity of contract until the 1995 Act. Before then, other than the original landlord who would be liable to the tenant in privity of contract, a landlord would only be responsible during the time of his ownership of the reversion: he would be liable in privity of estate. This concept must be read against the background that, of course, commercially an original landlord was keen to obtain an indemnity from someone to whom he sold the reversion and normally a chain of indemnity covenants was created. Under the 1995 Act the position has changed.

7.2 For new tenancies, on an assignment of the reversion, landlords are now only released from their liabilities if they make an application to the tenant requesting a release. That request must be made before or within four weeks after the landlord's assignment. The tenant receiving the application then has four weeks to respond to the notice. The tenant can accept or passively do nothing, in which case the landlord will be released. Alternatively, the tenant may object, in which case the matter is referred to the County court for it to decide whether the application for release is reasonable.

7.3 A release from liabilities sounds as if it should be the ideal scenario for a landlord, but it may not always be so. Landlords must note that where they are released from liabilities then from the date of that release they will cease to be entitled to the benefit of tenant covenants.

7.4 In multi-let buildings it may be very difficult for landlords to be effectively released because they will need the consent of all the tenants to whom leases have been granted. Bearing in mind that landlords will lose the ability to enforce tenant covenants after they are released, landlords will want to assiduously avoid the possibility of being released by some tenants and not others.

7.5 Section 26 of the 1995 Act states that nothing in the 1995 Act is to be read as preventing a party to a tenancy from releasing a landlord from its covenants. Arguably, therefore, one can insert a provision in new leases providing for release as an automatic process.

I do not believe that it is possible to do this without contravening the general anti avoidance provisions of Section 25 unless perhaps the clause itself states that the landlord would be automatically released upon obtaining similar personal covenants from the successor. Tenants are likely to accept this in some cases, although where the landlord is providing substantial services the tenant may well want to ensure that it has the opportunity of considering the quality of the covenant providing those services in the future and of course an automatic replacement of one landlord by another would defeat that. For those reasons Section 25's anti avoidance provisions may come to the aid of a tenant. One is seeing covenants that are specified to be personal and which do not run with the land. This is particularly important, and quite prevalent in development agreements, agreements for lease and the like where there may be construction obligations which, for example, a purchasing fund would not wish to inherit. It has become more and more normal to see covenants of this nature expressed as personal covenants.

7.6 Another way of practically and effectively controlling liabilities is to create single-purpose vehicles to take on the liabilities in the first place. This will enable the company itself perhaps to be disposed of, leaving all the liabilities in one vehicle. There would then be no need for an assignment of the reversion; the new owners would simply acquire the landlord company. Buying companies creates its own problems, and there may be difficulties and additional expense for the purchaser doing its due diligence, negotiating warranties and indemnities, etc. This may prevent dealing with disposals in this way, but it is an avenue that may be appropriate in certain circumstances.

7.7 When a landlord is seeking to dispose of his reversion, assuming that he wishes to seek a release, then as mentioned above he must make his application to the tenant. If he is unfortunate, in that the tenant refuses the release and either the landlord does not challenge that refusal or it is upheld in the court, then all is not lost. The landlord will have a second bite at the cherry. Former landlords can be released from liabilities so long as they make application again before or within the four-week window of any future assignment of the reversion. The motto is clearly 'if at first you do not succeed try try try again!'

7.8 One major catch behind this is that a landlord may well not know that his purchaser is planning to dispose of the reversion. This may be some years after the first disposal. I think that this potential pitfall can be avoided. It should be possible for contractual documentation to contain an obligation by a purchaser to notify his vendor if he, the purchaser, is planning to dispose of the reversion at some time in the future after completion of his acquisition from the vendor. This contractual obligation could be protected at the land registry and this should enable a purchaser to have the opportunity to forward plan on any potential disposal by a purchaser. Whether this is in practice something that owners of property wish to concern themselves with is quite another matter, but there are clearly situations where it may be appropriate.

7.9   This new regime for providing landlords with the opportunity to be released has thrown up a need for tenants to take on board yet another management function. In order that tenants can monitor an application for landlord release they must have a system able to deal with it. Without this it would be quite possible for a landlord to serve notice upon his tenant that he is proposing to dispose of his reversion, seek a release from the tenant and for the tenant to totally ignore that request, allow the four-week period to elapse and then find that the landlord will have been released by default. Certainly many multiple retailers and users of more than one set of premises do have systems that are designed to deal with this and, hopefully, prevent release from occurring merely by default or mismanagement. Active management by tenants is required and this is no different to the sort of procedures that tenants have long been used to in responding to 1954 Act Section 25 notices, rent review trigger notices and the like. I suspect, however, that there may be situations where tenants' advisers may come under pressure and no doubt even negligence suits may result from failure to properly deal with notices of this nature (much as they have in relation to Section 25 notices, trigger notices and other time of the essence machinery where an aggrieved tenant may have litigated against either his landlord or perhaps – more worryingly for the readers of this book – the tenant's advisers!).

7.10   Where a landlord is not released from his obligations in relation to a new tenancy, the outgoing landlord will remain jointly and severally liable with the incoming landlord but also both of them will have the benefit of the tenant covenants.

7.11   Section 23 of the 1995 Act alters the position in relation to arrears of rent.

    For new tenancies the vendor will retain the right to sue for old arrears unless he assigns that right. If he assigns the right, the purchaser of the reversion will obtain the right to sue in place of the vendor. This is exactly the opposite for old tenancies.

    The new landlord, however, can forfeit for old arrears or breaches unless the right of re-entry has been lost by waiver or release.

Accordingly, where is there an assignment of the reversion of an old lease then if there has been no assignment of rent arrears only the vendor can sue for them, although the purchaser can forfeit! It is becoming quite normal for arrears to be assigned to purchasers and I believe this is much more practical because the right to sue is then held by the person who has the new contractual relationship and indeed, the rights of forfeiture.

7.12   Where one is dealing with an acquisition of a reversion containing a mixture of old and new tenancies it is important for rights to be assigned. Without a formal assignment in relation to arrears arising under the new tenancy(ies), the vendor will have the right to sue, whereas in relation to those arising under the old tenancy(ies) the purchaser will have the right to sue. This can cause enormous management headaches. I would urge very careful enquiry on the acquisition of any investment where there is a mixture of old and new tenancies and there is something to be said for an assignment under the 1995 Act in relation to arrears arising under new tenancies so that at least there is a consistent approach to arrears. As I have said, I think this has much to commend it in that the owner of the reversion will be making the call as to when to sue and how to negotiate. Equally, a vendor allowing for such an assignment will need to be compensated himself in that, by definition, the arrears that he is allowing his purchaser to control will have arisen during the time that he was the landlord. It is quite usual for the contract to deal with this and provide for the purchaser to inherit the right to sue on the basis that he is accountable in whole or in part for the arrears so that he becomes something of a collecting agent for the vendor. Obviously if there is an assignment of the right to sue, the question of how much of the arrears are to be recovered for the benefit of the vendor is something to be negotiated at the time of the disposal of the reversion and matters to be taken into account will of course include the likelihood of recovery, discounts for net present day value and so forth. It is also quite normal for the purchaser inheriting such rights to sue, only to be obliged to account for arrears collected, net of all collection costs. If he is collecting arrears for the benefit of the vendor then his costs should at least be paid by the potential beneficiary and it is arguable that the purchaser should be paid a fee for the collection of the arrears – perhaps a percentage of moneys recovered.

8.   PROMPT RECOVERY

8.1   In paragraph 2 of this chapter we looked at a summary of the new law and divided that into two sections: firstly as it affects new leases only and secondly as it affects all leases, both old and new.

Paragraphs 4 to 7 inclusive concerned themselves only with new tenancies and we now move forward to look at the three parts of the 1995 Act that affect both old and new tenancies. This paragraph, 8, deals with prompt recovery and the following two paragraphs deal with overriding leases and the variation of leases respectively.

8.2   One of the major reasons behind the lobby for reform leading to the 1995 Act concerned the fact that tenants who had long since forgotten about leases that they had assigned, were called upon to meet liabilities that had arisen, in some cases, many years later and after perhaps several rent reviews. This seemed intrinsically wrong and the 1993 announcement that there would be legislation in the field of privity of contract made it clear that measures would be introduced to encourage prompt recovery of arrears.

8.3   The principal provisions are outlined in Section 17 of the 1995 Act. Where a landlord wishes to claim rent or service charges from a former tenant or a former guarantor who remains liable under privity of contract (or in the case of a new tenancy pursuant to an AGA) or if there is a desire to claim any other liquidated sum payable under such a lease from a former tenant, the landlord must serve a Section 17 notice on that former tenant within a six-month period starting from the date the amount became due. Without such a notice being served the rights to recover from the former tenant will be lost.

8.4   It is important to remember that Section 17 applies only to former tenants as defined and not to an existing tenant or to an existing contractual guarantor. Unless there is some contractual obligation requiring a claim within a certain period the statute of limitations is all that will control the speed of the landlord. This is not, of course, the mischief to which the 1995 Act was directed. The legislators' concern was to ensure that people who no longer had a direct relationship with the landlord were given notice of arrears within a specified, and relatively short, period. Contractual guarantors must make their own arrangements. Section 17(3) does not give them the right to receive a Section 17 notice and, when giving the contractual guarantee, if they want to receive notice of any arrears that have been accumulated by the tenant whose liabilities they are guaranteeing, they must provide for the landlord to be contractually obliged to give them notice of arrears. Section 17 does not provide for a notice to be given to them.

8.5   Two interim measures were introduced:

8.5.1   Arrears that were due before 1 January 1996 had to be claimed before 1 July 1996. Obviously that period is now up and former tenants will no longer have to worry about pre-1996 arrears unless they received a Section 17 notice before 1 July 1996, or unless proceedings were issued against them before the 1995 Act came into force; and

8.5.2   The prompt recovery provisions of Section 17 do not apply to any claim where proceedings were instituted against a former tenant on or prior to 31 December 1995.

8.6   Section 17 notices do not apply to all arrears. The Act uses the expression 'fixed charges' and Section 17 notices only apply to rent, service charges and liquidated sums. Service charges are given the meaning attributed to them in Section 18, Landlord and Tenant Act 1985 and it is, therefore, possible that certain service charges recoverable in commercial leases will not be caught by the Section 17 notice procedure. If, for example, promotion costs are included in a service charge (although this is discouraged in the recently published guide to service charge practice – see Chapter 7, Part A, paragraph 1) and there is no procedure for recovery of them separately as a liquidated sum, then these would be outside the scope of service charges as defined under the 1995 Act. Technically, if there was a liability to pay those service charges going back many years a landlord would not necessarily be excluded from suing for them. Liquidated sums are fixed amounts due for failure to comply with a covenant in the lease. Occasionally, continuous trading clauses provide that a tenant is liable for a fixed amount for every day that it closes its shop. I have seen provisions such as this in leases, for example at Thurrock Shopping Centre, and although it might be somewhat incongruous for tenants to insert provisions stating that a breach of covenant would give rise to a sum being payable by way of liquidated charges, inserting such a clause would have the effect of allowing the tenant to receive a default notice in respect of those damages, since breach of the continuous trading clause would give rise to a liquidated sum being due.

So, where one wishes to sue for a fixed charge a Section 17 notice must be served within six months of the arrears becoming due. It is important that one appreciates the obligation is for notice to be given within six months and not within two quarters since of course the two are not the same. Arrears that become due on 25 March will be out of time if a notice under Section 17 is served on the September quarter-day; this is of course 29 September, more than six months after 25 March. The same will apply to Section 17 notices served on the December quarter-day in respect of arrears arising from moneys that became due on the June quarter-day. Practitioners will have to watch this very carefully since I suspect the courts will be unforgiving in considering notices served late, and perhaps rightly so, bearing in mind that the 1995 Act is crystal clear. Notices must also be served on a prescribed form and it is no use merely dropping the tenant a line saying that it is less than six months since arrears became due and they are claimed under Section 17 of the 1995 Act. This will not be sufficient and again the courts will not come to the aid of a practitioner who seeks to recover arrears in this way.

8.7 It may be possible, however, for this piece of legislative drafting to be used for the benefit of landlords. As you will see in paragraph 9, below, any person who receives a Section 17 notice and meets the claim in full is entitled to claim an overriding lease under Section 19 of the 1995 Act. This is something landlords may wish to avoid. Accordingly, it may be that they would want to serve notice on a former tenant that arrears are due but ensure that the recipient does not have the right to call for an overriding lease. If a landlord was to informally seek payment of arrears, but not serve a Section 17 notice, then if the tenant were to pay the arrears in full without taking proper advice and then subsequently seek the advice of a lawyer or surveyor as to its rights to claim an overriding lease, that former tenant may well find that it will have paid in circumstances where it does not have a right to call for an overriding lease. If a landlord adopts this approach, he will have to ensure that, in order not to lose the right to sue, a formal Section 17 notice is served within the statutory time periods should the former tenant not pay up on receipt of the informal notice. The advantage, therefore, of serving an informal request and hoping the tenant pays is merely one which bases its premise on the fact that the tenant will not seek advice until after payment. This is not likely to be something that would arise very often, but the possibility does of course exist.

8.8 Landlords must take seriously the fact that a tenant is entitled to an overriding lease if it meets a Section 17 claim in full. This is quite deliberate. The legislators were endeavouring to provide a regime whereby someone paying has the right to go back into a leasehold relationship with his landlord.

8.9 Accordingly, if a landlord has a range of tenants against whom proceedings may be issued, the 1995 Act provides a practical way of ensuring the landlord considers whether or not to make life miserable for the weak tenant. If he does so and that weak tenant finds the money to pay, then the weak tenant would be able to seek an overriding lease putting it in a position of controlling other former tenants, or indeed the current tenant, and perhaps even forfeiting the lease. This is a great comfort for weak tenants since they know landlords will not necessarily seek them out if there are more substantial former tenants (and don't forget this expression includes old guarantors) against whom a claim can be made.

8.10 Landlords should also check carefully what their mortgagees or superior landlord may have to say about them risking the creation of overriding leases by dint of serving a Section 17 notice and finding that the recipient pays up in full. Although the 1995 Act makes it clear that mortgagees cannot object to an overriding lease (the 1995 Act is silent about superior landlords) it is likely that superior landlords and, more so, mortgagees may want to insert obligations in their documentation requiring consent before a Section 17 notice is served so that they can ensure that they do not find that their investment/security is fettered by perhaps a greedy intermediate tenant/borrower serving a Section 17 demand without properly thinking through the consequences of his actions. This is certainly the practice being adopted in post-1995 Act investment loan documentation.

8.11 As long as a Section 17 notice is served, no more money can be claimed in relation to the arrears that are the subject of the notice unless the notice itself anticipates that there may be a greater sum due. In those circumstances which of course would arise where a rent review or final service charge figure is still to be determined, the notice must make reference to the fact that there is to be a further claim. Any such further claim would then need to be made within three months of the final determination, perhaps by an arbitrator in a rent review.

8.12 One will need to consider carefully whether the mere service of a Section 17 notice might constitute waiving a breach of covenant. There is an obligation to serve such a notice within six months and the notice on the prescribed form states that the landlord 'intends to recover from you [the arrears]'. This is a clear statement of an intent by the landlord to seek moneys from a tenant and arguably waive a non-continuing breach of covenant. I would have thought, however, that a court may well be sympathetic to a landlord in these circumstances. It is difficult to see how the court could punish a landlord for serving a notice in circumstances where Section 17 makes it clear that the notice must be served within the time-scale if it is to be a valid Section 17 notice.

9. OVERRIDING LEASES

9.1 So as we have seen, Section 19 of the 1995 Act gives former tenants who pay in full following receipt of a Section 17 notice the right to claim an overriding lease. The effect of this is to interpose the former tenant between the landlord and the current lessee. The rationale behind this is that the former tenant previously had lease obligations which it has now been required to discharge and the previous obligations were incurred at a time when it was a tenant and had rights over the property, therefore since the landlord has sought fit to seek payment by the former tenant as a result of those liabilities, it is fair for the former tenant to be able to again have a leasehold interest in the property.

9.2   If a former tenant makes a request within twelve months of the fixed charge being paid in full then the landlord is obliged to grant the overriding lease to that former tenant. The lease will be for a term equal to the remainder of the term of the relevant tenancy plus three days. That three-day nominal reversion may in itself be cut down if the lease in question is a sublease and the effect of that would be to displace the landlord's reversionary interest. This is necessary because if one grants a lease for the same length of time as a superior lease then, unless there is a nominal reversion even of a matter of days or hours, then that sublease will in fact take effect as an assignment and not a sublease. Of course Section 19 has been drafted with that in mind.

9.3   One needs to look at the terms of the overriding lease. Broadly speaking it will contain the same covenants as are in the relevant tenancy but personal covenants will not be reproduced. Nor will any spent covenants. Accordingly if the relevant tenancy was granted in, say, 1985 for a term of twenty years with a break in 1995 then an overriding lease granted in 1997 (or indeed any time after 1995) would not have a break clause included in it. If the relevant tenancy did not express the date for the break but merely said that one party had the right to determine 'at the expiry of the fifth year of the term', that wording should not be repeated in the overriding lease. The reason for this is that although Section 19(4) provides for covenants that operate by reference to the commencement of the term to be inserted by reference to the commencement of the overriding tenancy, this does not apply to the extent that the covenant is spent (Section 19(4)(b)).

9.4   As I have mentioned, personal covenants will not be reproduced. I think there is one potential difficulty here. Quite often tenants, particularly of multiple retail premises, negotiate personal concessions. These can vary from relatively straight-forward and minor concessions, such as an exclusion of the obligations to maintain plate-glass insurance, to more funda-mental personal covenants such as the exclusion of the need to obtain landlord's consent for alterations or even perhaps a waiver of subletting restrictions, etc.

9.4.1   Since the 1995 Act was passed, when acting for tenants I have been seeking to negotiate that personal concessions such as these are given not only whilst the lease is vested in my client but also whilst any overriding lease might be vested in it. I do not think that there is any good reason why a landlord should not accept such a provision since the logic that one particular named party should have the benefit of the covenant applies just as much if that party is tenant under an overriding lease, as it does if it is tenant under the lease being negotiated at the time. You should however be aware of the decision of *Max Factor Limited* v *Wesleyan Assurance Society* **1996 NPC 70** (see Chapter 3, paragraph 2) where a personal break was held to be lost on assignment and not capable of resurrection on assign-ment back to the party having the benefit of it. Perhaps this casts some doubt on such tactics. The principle being that the personal concession is lost when the original tenant comes back in another capacity, i.e. tenant under an overriding tenancy. Never the less, the situations are not identical and little can be lost by specifically providing for concessions to be repeated in an overriding lease. The Max Factor break did not say that it would apply if Max Factor were tenant whether as original tenant or following assignment back to it; had it done so the result may have been different.

9.4.2   It is also arguable, of course, that since the provisions of Section 19(3) of the 1995 Act specifically exclude personal covenants, when it comes to granting an overriding lease a landlord might seek to object to such covenants being repeated in the over-riding lease (even if a specific amendment allowing for this had been negotiated in the original lease) on the grounds that the original amendment frustrates the operation of the 1995 Act in seeking to find a way around Section 19(3) and thus infringes Section 25 (the Section that prohibits contracting out). I do not think a court would necessarily have a great deal of sympathy with this but it must remain a possibility and I am not aware of any litigation on this yet.

9.5   When negotiating an overriding lease, the tenant's covenants must be very carefully thought through. Section 19(2)(b) provides that unless the parties agree to modifications (subject to the exclusion of personal and spent covenants as referred to above) the overriding lease should contain the same covenants as in the relevant tenancy 'as they have effect immediately before the grant of the lease'.

9.6   Section 19 does not provide for variations, even if reasonable, and it may be the case that simply repeating the covenants does not give them the same effect as they had in the relevant tenancy. To that extent perhaps the court would be sympathetic to an application by an aggrieved party for a variation to the terms of the overriding tenancy on the ground that to repeat the wording of the relevant tenancy verbatim would not give them the same effect as they had immediately before the grant of the lease.

For example, if a landlord were to grant a lease to a tenant and the provisions of the rent review clause made it clear that tenant's improvements were to be disregarded but did not go on to say that improvements carried out by undertenants would be disregarded then, technically speaking, if that tenant were to:

9.6.1   Carry out substantial improvements which had a rental value and which should be excluded; then

9.6.2   Assign its lease; then

9.6.3   Default in the payment of rent leading to the original tenant being

      (i) Served with a Section 17 notice;
      (ii) Paying up; and
      (iii) Calling for an overriding lease;

the original tenant would be interposed as the overriding lessee. It would become tenant of an overriding lease with the same landlord with whom it had done the original deal. If there were to be no alteration in the wording of the rent review clause, and the review clause that had been negotiated in the original lease were simply to be transposed into the overriding lease, then the landlord would be entitled to take into account the same improvements that this tenant had carried out whilst tenant, on the basis that they are improvements carried out by someone who is now an undertenant and only immediate tenant's improvements are to be disregarded! This needs to be watched very carefully when negotiating an overriding lease. Similarly, one needs to be wary of provisions dealing with the time that the tenant's improvements are carried out. Many disregards exclude tenant's improvements carried out 'after the date of this lease', if that wording is simply copied over unaltered into the overriding lease then the improvements would not be disregarded since they will have been carried out by the original tenant prior to 'the date of this lease' (i.e. the overriding lease).

9.7   An overriding lease is not necessarily a new tenancy even though by definition, of course, it will be granted after the 1995 Act came into force. Effectively its status follows the lease in respect of which it is being granted. If the lease which was vested in the former tenant was a new tenancy, the overriding lease will be a new tenancy. If not, the overriding lease will not be a new tenancy. It is worth stressing, however, that the ability to obtain an overriding lease applies to both old and new tenancies.

9.8   The 1995 Act contains a provision relating to costs of the overriding lease and the tenant must pay the landlord's reasonable costs (and not just its legal costs) for the grant of the overriding lease. This, of course, is a fundamental change from the Costs of Leases Act 1958 or, indeed, current practice. The rationale is that the landlord has not caused the breach which has led to the Section 17 notice which has led to the call for an overriding lease and therefore should not have to pay the costs. The former tenant obtaining the overriding lease will have to pay stamp duty on it.

9.9   The 1995 Act deals with the position of competing claims. Claims are dealt with on a first-come-first-served basis but if claims are made at the same time, earlier covenants have priority save that former tenants who are lessees come before former tenants who are guarantors.

9.10 The 1995 Act recognises the fact that mortgagees' consent may be needed and it is expressly stated that mortgagees' consent is deemed given. It is silent on the position about head landlords. Mortgagees should ensure that loan documentation and security documents in relation to investment loans allow the mortgagee to put itself in a position where it can control the service of Section 17 default notices so that the mortgagee does not find that its borrower inadvertently, or through bad management, serves a Section 17 notice on a weak tenant who then pays. In those circumstances, if the weak tenant calls for an overriding tenancy the effect of the service of that notice and any resultant payment may well be to weaken the investment and thus effect the mortgagee's security. The implications must be considered before arrears are demanded and this is a matter of equal importance to both mortgagees and the landlord borrower.

9.11 Where an overriding lease is granted to a former tenant who has paid up pursuant to a Section 17 demand, the former tenant's motive behind paying may be to ensure that when it gets its hands on the overriding lease it can forfeit for non-payment of the arrears that have fallen due under the relevant tenancy and then re-occupy the premises. Caution may be the order of the day here. If there is a payment due under a lease of, say, one quarter's rent and that payment is sought by the landlord and paid by a former tenant giving rise to the right to claim an overriding lease, the payment that would otherwise give rise to the ability to forfeit the relevant tenancy will have been made. It is difficult to see in those circumstances how the former tenant who becomes the landlord of the previously defaulting tenant can forfeit for non-payment of rent. By definition, the rent has been paid. Accordingly, if the intention of the former tenant is merely to forfeit and gain possession it should note that it is likely to be able to do this only on arrears that may arise on the next rent payment day or when there is some other breach but not the one that has given rise to the claim for an overriding tenancy.

9.12 Since the right to claim an overriding lease is linked to the service of a Section 17 notice, there is a problem on existing leases for tenants who do not receive a Section 17 notice but have a liability to indemnify a former tenant who does receive one. For example, if there is a strong original tenant who has assigned his lease to a weaker assignee, and the landlord acting sensibly and commercially only serves his Section 17 notice on the strong original tenant, that strong original tenant is the only person who can insist upon obtaining an overriding lease. He will still have a right of action under the indemnity covenants against his assignee, who may well find himself in a position of having to discharge that liability without the corresponding right to obtain an overriding tenancy.

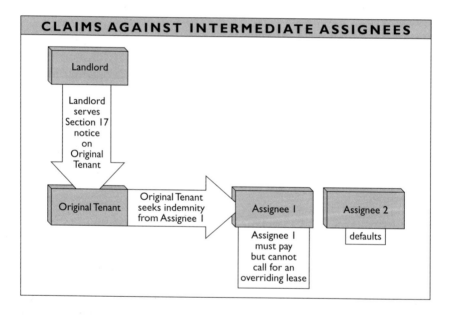

9.13   In his Blundell Memorial Lecture (extracted in the August 10 1996 edition of the *Estates Gazette*) Steven Fogel argues the possibility of the assignor seeking payment under this indemnity by serving a Section 17 demand and thus allowing its assignee to become its tenant. This would arise in circumstances where the assignor gives a default notice to protect its right to make its assignee honour an indemnity owed to it. Although Section 17 provides for notice to be served by a 'landlord', Section 17(6) defines 'landlord' as including anyone who has the right to enforce payment of the fixed charge. So, if rent is due and demanded from an assignor and the assignor demands it from its assignee (who is also a former tenant) and does so by serving a Section 17 notice, arguably he can be described as a landlord under Section 17(6). If the court allowed for this interpretation the assignee would be entitled to its overriding lease after all.

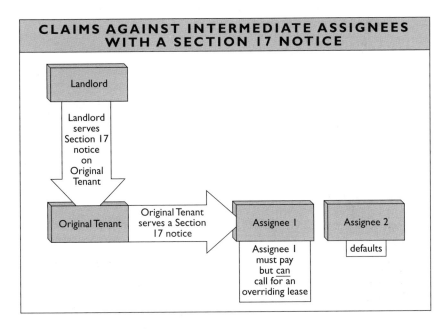

CLAIMS AGAINST INTERMEDIATE ASSIGNEES WITH A SECTION 17 NOTICE

9.14 Why would an assignor serve a Section 17 notice? Obviously it would not if it could recover under the indemnity without doing so. However, Steven Fogel's point is that in order to protect its right to sue on the indemnity the assignor might have to serve a Section 17 demand because the demand arises 'in respect of' rent and because therefore the assignor is arguably within the definition of 'landlord' under Section 17(6). Whilst this would give the assignee the right to call for an overriding lease and thus rescue him from the position outlined in paragraph 9.12 above, it is a strained reading of Section 17(6). That Section clearly says landlords include anyone who has a right to enforce payment of the fixed charge. Arguably the assignor does not have that right since his right is not to enforce payment of the rent (the fixed charge) but to claim on an indemnity. I suppose much will depend on the way the indemnity is worded and clearly the assignor must consider whether to serve a Section 17 demand on its assignee and take advice before it is too late. If it does not and a Section 17 demand is subsequently held to be necessary in order to recover the money, then that demand must be served within six months of when the charge becomes due. If it is not, the assignor will have lost its rights to recover from the assignee.

I am not sure that it was the intention of the draftsman of Section 17 to allow for assignees to be able to obtain an overriding lease from assignors in the circumstances. Equally, however, it does appear to be a theme of the 1995 Act that payment by a former tenant is to be geared to receipt of a Section 17 notice which, in turn, gives rise to the rights to claim an overriding tenancy. On this basis it is not stretching the imagination too far to allow for an assignee to be able to insist on the assignor serving a Section 17 notice to protect its indemnity and, perhaps, such a liberal approach ought to be encouraged in order to protect the assignee from ending up in the position that I outlined in paragraph 9.12. It might be ducking the issue a little to say that the position will need to be considered in the light of the specific indemnity covenant but this is unquestionably the case. If the indemnity makes it clear that the assignee must pay by way of indemnity all rent due and gives the assignor the right to claim by way of enforcing payment of that rent as if it were enforcing payment of rent by its tenant, then I suspect the point might be beyond question. In practice, however, I think there will probably be litigation on this particular issue. If an assignee receives a demand by its assignor to pay up under an indemnity there is little to be lost by the assignee refusing to pay until it receives a Section 17 notice. The assignor will then be forced to consider whether to serve a Section 17 notice, allowing for the possibility that the assignee would claim an overriding tenancy from the assignor. If it chooses not to do so and a period of six months elapses after the date the charge becomes due, then the assignee will no longer have to pay up under the indemnity. For Section 17 to arise the assignee will have to be a former tenant and therefore no longer entitled to the tenancy. If it is still the current tenant then it is not entitled to claim an overriding tenancy because it is not entitled to a Section 17 notice.

I am not quite sure what would happen in circumstances where the assignor were to claim under an indemnity and by simply serving a notice (not a Section 17 notice) and follow this up with proceedings, no doubt issued under Order 14, claiming summary judgment. Arguably the assignor can do this since the sum will be clearly shown to be payable and in those circumstances if judgment is issued and enforced, all of this may be done within a six-month period. This position exists, however, in any circumstances where a claim is made against a former tenant and, given the clear language of Section 17 stating that the former tenant is not liable unless it receives a Section 17 notice within six months, perhaps it is therefore arguable that any proceedings brought by a landlord, or in my example the assignor, would be stayed until the six-month period is allowed to elapse. If this is not done then clearly landlords or assignors would be able to circumvent the need to serve a Section 17 notice, and therefore disenfranchise the former tenant from being able to obtain its overriding lease.

10.   VARIATIONS

10.1   The last of the principle amendments of the 1995 Act concerns variations of tenancies and again this applies to both old and new tenancies. The 1995 Act restricts liabilities of former tenants where that tenancy is varied.

10.2   The former tenant is not liable to the extent that the amount payable refers to what is called a 'relevant variation' of the tenant covenants. Section 18(4) of the 1995 Act defines 'relevant variation' and the definition encapsulates alterations to the tenant covenants where the landlord has an absolute right to refuse to allow the alteration, or would have done if the alteration had been sought by a former tenant immediately before the assignment by him, but between that assignment and the variation the landlord and subsequent tenant have varied the lease to allow for the alteration. This is best shown by a diagram – see overleaf.

One needs to be very careful in deciding whether variations are those where the landlord has an absolute right to refuse. For example, Section 3 of the Landlord and Tenant Act 1927 allows a tenant to carry out certain improvements and if there is an

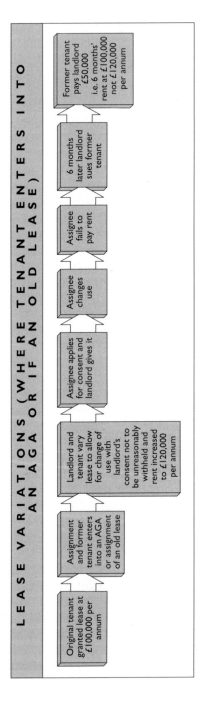

LEASE VARIATIONS (WHERE TENANT ENTERS INTO AN AGA OR IF AN OLD LEASE)

Original tenant granted lease at £100,000 per annum

Assignment and former tenant enters into an AGA or assignment of an old lease

Landlord and tenant vary lease to allow for change of use with landlord's consent not to be unreasonably withheld and rent increased to £120,000 per annum

Assignee applies for consent and landlord gives it

Assignee changes use

Assignee fails to pay rent

6 months later landlord sues former tenant

Former tenant pays landlord £50,000 i.e. 6 months' rent at £100,000 not £120,000 per annum absolute covenant prohibiting them, in these circumstances statute will have intervened and the alterations would not be 'relevant variations' for the purposes of Section 18.

10.3   The intent behind Section 18 is to prevent a tenant from becoming liable to pay a sum of money that is only due because of an alteration to the tenant covenants over which it has no control. Until the Court of Appeal decision in *Friends Provident Life Office* v *British Railways Board* **1995 48 EG 106**, many practitioners had felt that without there being a surrender and re-grant an original tenant would be liable for all these liabilities notwithstanding any variation of the terms of the lease. There was even a case, *GUS Property Management Limited* v *Texas Homecare Limited* **1993 27 EG 130**, cited in *Friends Provident* that indicated that original tenant liability was different to that of a guarantor's liability and would not be released in any way by a variation of the lease. It had been thought that original tenants were liable irrespective of any variations and that their position was different to that of a guarantor whose liabilities would be discharged by fundamental variations to the contract which was being guaranteed. *Friends Provident* said that this was wrong and the effect of *Friends Provident* is much the same as Section 18. Now the position is governed by Section 18 for both old and new leases and it is clear that where there is a relevant variation the former tenant cannot be made liable for an increase in the rent referable to it.

10.4   Parties to lease documentation must be very careful to ensure that when they are varying leases, they do not effect a surrender and re-grant. A variation in the demise or the lease term, both of which would go to the root of the legal estate would have that effect and if there is to be a surrender and re-grant then anyone who was liable under the previous lease would be off the hook since that lease would be surrendered. From the landlord's perspective this would obviously not be a good idea and furthermore the new lease granted would, by definition, be a new tenancy to which the old privity regime would not apply.

10.5   Landlords must be particularly careful about the position regarding guarantors. There are many cases where guarantors are released from their liabilities where there is a lease variation.

If it is intended that a lease is varied, it is ideal for all guarantors to be included in the deed of variation. Where this is not possible one does run the risk of the guarantor arguing that it has been released. However, perhaps the most likely position following both *Friends Provident* and now the enactment of Section 18 and also, of course, the fact that guarantors are released from tenant covenants as we have seen earlier, would be for the guarantor like the former tenant to be partially released to the extent that variations to the lease are relevant variations and an increase in rent for which they would otherwise be liable is referable to that relevant variation.

10.6 If an AGA is entered into it is doubtful that the document can bind a tenant to join in a deed of variation since this would no doubt fall foul of Section 25 in that it is not consistent with the approach of Section 18 and therefore could well be held to frustrate the provisions of the Act. Again, perhaps a landlord could insert such a clause but include a severance clause to save the day in case it has been over-zealous.

10.7 Although Section 18 applies to old and new tenancies it will not apply for variations effected before 1 January 1996 and in those cases the former tenant must rely upon *Friends Provident*. So far as new leases are concerned, Section 18 only has relevance in relation to former tenants who are liable as authorised guarantors. In all other cases, of course, they will have been released anyway by dint of the assignment.

10.8 It is my experience that very often variations to tenancies are not given the thought that they really deserve. Quite apart from the fact that they might inadvertently give rise to a surrender and re-grant, there are now questions of the extent to which they release former tenants from liabilities and there is also the overriding danger that guarantors might simply be released by not having been made a party to a variation. The moral of the story is quite simply that there must be very careful legal and surveying input where the parties are proposing any variation to contractual lease documentation.

10.9 Finally on the question of variations, do not forget that if one calls for an overriding lease, then any protection that one might have had previously as a former tenant not liable for rent increases referable to relevant variations, would disappear once one is tenant under an overriding tenancy.

11. CONCLUSION

11.1 As I have mentioned in the introduction to this book, privity and the 1995 Act has been afforded a disproportionate amount of treatment in the book. The new regime is something with which all practitioners are slowly coming to grips and obviously it has fundamentally changed the way one conducts business. It is absolutely essential that the surveying profession has a good working knowledge of the fundamental principles of the 1995 Act in order to advise its clients properly.

11.2 Readers may wish to read the Blundell Memorial Lecture on the 1995 Act and its implications, given in two parts by Steven Fogel and Trevor Moross, a slightly abridged version of which appears in the *Estates Gazette* of 10 August 1996 and 17 August 1996. There are regular articles on the 1995 Act in the property press and clearly practices and procedures are developing, as will case law, and perhaps there will even be early reform of this hastily drafted legislation.

11.3 There have been interesting surveys on the reaction of the property industry to the new privity rules. The British Property Federation, McKenna and Co and the *Estates Gazette* published an article in the edition of the *Estates Gazette* on 12 October 1996 looking at the reaction of the market to the first six months. Although the survey concluded that after some absurdly long and ill-conceived alienation clauses, things were now settling down, it was still felt that the market was confused. The final comment referred to in the article, is one to which lawyers and surveyors alike can relate:

> At present too much time is spent arguing about the 1995 Act.

It will be interesting to watch developments in this field of law.

CHAPTER 2

RENT REVIEWS

I. GENERAL PRINCIPLES

I.I The fundamental purpose of rent review clauses is to adjust the rent so that it keeps pace with inflation and variations in property values. Certainly since the 1960s and 1970s it has been commonplace for leases granting terms lasting beyond five years to contain rent review clauses and certainly a lease lasting for longer than five years would not be regarded as institutionally acceptable without a mechanism for adjusting the rent.

I.2 Until the downturn in the property market at the beginning of the 1990s it was almost unheard of for rent reviews to be anything other than upward-only. As long ago as 1978 the House of Lords recognized that an upward-only review clause was not only to the financial advantage of a landlord but also to tenants, since without such a clause landlords would not be happy to grant a long lease. Strained logic perhaps, but none the less upward-only clauses really are the order of the day. Accordingly, the cases and issues concerning rent review clauses tend to occur in relation to upward-only review clauses although as we will see in Chapter 6 there have been a number of cases where tenants seeking renewals under the 1954 Act have argued for an upward and downward review.

I.3 One variation to this theme is the 'threshold provisions review clause' where rent can go up or down but not below the rent originally agreed. See *Secretary of State for the Environment* v *Associated Newspaper Holdings Limited* **1995 EGCS 166** for a case where the court had to construe whether a clause was a threshold review clause or a traditional upward-only review clause. Normally this would be quite clear but in this case it was not: the Court of Appeal held the review clause was a ratchet clause, i.e. a traditional review clause.

1.4   Other methods are also sometimes used for reviewing rent, notably, reference to the retail price index or provision for compounding the initial rent. In the 1980s in certain sectors, notably retail sheds and restaurants, rents were often reviewed to a percentage of rentals in other sectors, in order to ensure that there could be a proper rent review in an immature market. For example, in the early days of freestanding restaurants on retail parks it was not unusual to take a percentage of retail rents within Class A1 of the Use Classes Order since there were simply not enough restaurants in the market being reviewed to give the appropriate comparable evidence.

1.5   In previous years of high inflation and rocketing property prices where rent review intervals were falling below five years, one occasionally saw landlords seeking to review the rent review clause itself. This would give the landlord the ability to review at shorter intervals if that was then market practice. This has now all but disappeared.

1.6   Turnover provisions provide another method of reviewing rent. Here rent is increased according to the level of turnover achieved in the unit. This is quite popular in relation to units in railway stations and airports, and some of the larger shopping centres in the United Kingdom have units where the rents are reviewed in this way. Perhaps one of the problems with turnover rent reviews in the United Kingdom is that they have tended to provide for the tenant to pay a base rent (often as high as 80% or 90% of the market rent of the property) or a percentage of turnover, whichever is the higher. Provisions such as this are often seen by tenants and their advisers as allowing the landlord to 'have his cake and eat it' and do not properly reflect a partnership between landlord and tenant which is the basis by which a landlord would normally seek to justify the requirement for a lease providing for rent to be reviewed by reference to turnover.

1.7   This chapter does not endeavour to deal with all the types of clauses or indeed all of the issues in relation to rent review. I have concentrated on some of the more important topics and issues that have arisen in the courts and in practice in recent times. There are many books devoted to rent reviews. In particular, I believe that any practitioner dealing with rent reviews on a regular basis will need a copy of the *Rent Review Handbook* by Bernstein and Reynolds on his desk at all times (see Recommended reading).

2.   TIME OF THE ESSENCE AND RENT REVIEW CLAUSES

2.1   The general principle is that time is not of the essence for rent review clauses. This was laid down in **United Scientific Holdings v Burnley Borough Council 1978 AC 904**. This House of Lords decision made it clear that unless there is an express time of the essence clause or an implication that time must be of the essence, time-limits in rent review clauses do not go to the root of the clause itself.

2.2   There have been many situations where the courts have had to decide whether time was of the essence in relation to specific rent review clauses. Clearly where there is an express provision making time of the essence there is no difficulty. The problem for the courts, and indeed advisers, arises where one has to decide whether the terms of a rent review clause, or indeed other provisions in a lease, show an intention to depart from the norm and to imply that time is of the essence.

2.3   It is reasonably clear that where a rent review clause contains a timetable with specific consequences flowing from a failure by one of the parties to comply with that time-scale, time-limits in relation to those obligations are of the essence. There have been a number of decisions along these lines, many of them concerning trigger notices where landlords serve notice triggering the review and in such notice provide for the rent to be at their suggested level unless it is disputed in accordance with the terms of the review clause. In **Mammoth Greeting Cards v Agra 1990 29 EG 45** the High Court had to consider whether time was of the essence where the parties had specified that were the tenants to fail to serve a counter-notice within two months, the rent would be conclusively fixed at the amount stated in the landlord's trigger notice. Here it was held that time was of the essence for the service of the counter-notice. The counter-notice that the tenant had served 'out of time' was of no effect and the rationale for this is that where the parties set out in clear language a timetable and specify what is to happen if the timetable is not met, it must be within their contemplation that non-compliance would lead to certain results. In order to achieve these results it is necessary to treat time as of the essence. In this particular case the expression used was 'conclusively fixed' and, therefore, the court felt that the parties must have intended time to be of the essence.

2.4 It is difficult to advise with any certainty since the courts are not always terribly consistent in this area. In *North Hertfordshire District Council v Hitchin Industrial Estate Limited* 1992 37 EG 133 the question arose again. The rent review clause stated that it was a 'condition precedent' that the landlord should serve at least one year's notice of their intention to vary the rent. The court said the condition precedent was just that: it was an essential requirement for the machinery to be put in action. However, it did not provide a contra-indication to the general rule that time was not of the essence. The expression was not interchangeable with time of the essence language. The decision does not sit well with many other cases, particularly *Chelsea Building Society v R and A Millet (Shops) Limited* 1993 EGCS 156 where again there was a condition precedent and again the condition precedent related to the service of a landlord's rent review notice. It was held here that time *was* of the essence and the judge refused to follow *North Hertfordshire*. There are certain differences between the two notices but when one carefully analyses them it is difficult to see that the distinction is so great as to justify a completely opposite result.

2.5 Although I should emphasize that this book is dealing with the law in England and Wales, the position is similar in Scotland. In *Visionhire Limited v Britel Fund Trustees Limited* 1992 10 EG 9595 the Scottish courts had to consider a case where a rent review clause gave a landlord a period in which he could initiate the rent review. If nothing was done within the relevant period the tenant had an opportunity to make a proposal as to the amount of the new rent and then the landlord had a three-month window to object, failing which the tenant's proposal became the new rent. Once again the courts were looking at a clause which set out a timetable and consequences for non-compliance and they found that this wording provided a sufficient contra-indication of the general principle that time is not of the essence. The time-periods outlined in the review clause were held to be of the essence.

2.6   It is obviously essential that lawyers and surveyors alike ensure compliance with time-limits where there is any danger that non-compliance might give rise to a loss or even just a post-ponement of rights. The books are littered with reports of cases where tenants have failed to properly deal with counter-notices. Where trigger notice procedures are provided for and time is deemed to be of the essence, the consequences of failure to comply with counter-notices can be very expensive. *Barrett Estate Services Limited v David Greig (Retail) Limited* 1991 36 EG 155 and *Patel and Another v Earlspring Properties Limited* 1991 46 EG 153 both illustrate the point that counter-notices must be clear and unambiguous. They must be correctly drafted.

2.6.1   If a lease calls for service of a counter-notice then, quite simply, the most expedient way of ensuring compliance is for surveyors and lawyers to work together in producing a formal counter-notice that repeats the wording of the lease verbatim. By doing so and stating that the notice is a formal counter-notice as provided for in the rent review machinery they will minimize the possibility of costly errors.

2.6.2   It is surprising how often such a simple procedure is not complied with. For example, in *Patel* the counter-notice (which was held to be valid) was a letter simply stating that the business had recently been purchased and the turnover was not sufficient to meet the rental the landlord was suggesting; the tenant went on to ask the landlord to reconsider the rental figure. Whilst the Court of Appeal bent over backwards to help the tenant and suggested that the court should approach issues of this nature 'with a sensible degree of common sense' it is not terribly difficult for a tenant to avoid this type of litigation by simply ensuring that the notice is carefully and properly drafted.

2.7   *Bickenhall Engineering Company Limited v Grand Metropolitan Restaurants* 1994 EGCS 146 was yet another case where a tenant's counter-notice was in question. In this case the lease stated that if the tenant did not serve his counter-notice specifying an alternative rent, the rental figure in the landlord's notice stood. The Court of Appeal found that time was not of the essence. The tenant's counter-notice did not contain a deeming provision here and there was no timetable within which the counter-notice needed to be served. The Court of Appeal did give their views on various conflicting appeal decisions and the case is worth looking at from that point of view.

2.8 Assuming that a rent review clause does require service of a counter-notice, not only must the notice be correctly drafted but also it must be served properly. It may be necessary to prove service and, of course, if a lease is sufficiently clear to make time of the essence it will no doubt have set out the basis upon which a counter-notice must be served. For a tenant to fail to deal with this properly is simply inexcusable. In circumstances where rent is reviewed in an upwardly direction an invalid counter-notice,

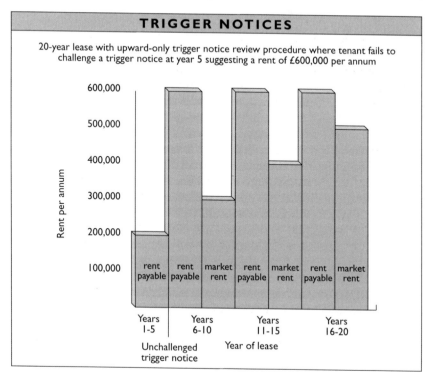

whether it is invalid because of the way in which it is drafted or the fact that it is not served properly, may well come back to haunt the tenant (or his advisers) time and again. The tenant may have to pay a very high rent (as specified in the landlord's trigger notice) and in an upward-only review clause this may be disastrous. Indeed the market rent might never again during the life of the lease reach the rental level fixed upon the tenant by an inequitable, but unchallenged, trigger notice.

The graph on the previous page illustrates the disastrous consequences for the tenant who has failed to protect his position. Here, even in a rising market the unchallenged trigger notice leaves the passing rent at a level higher than market rent for the entire duration of the term.

2.9 So it is clear that the parties to a lease may impliedly provide for time to be of the essence. There may be statutory provisions that would come to the aid of a party who would otherwise suffer as a result of this. In *Fordgate Bingley Limited* v *National Westminster Bank PLC* 1995 EGCS 97 the court had to consider a situation where the rent review machinery provided for the previous rent to be payable for the next review period and for the notice of increase to be of no effect if the new rent had not been agreed and there had been no application for arbitration by a certain date. In *Fordgate* the landlord failed to apply for the appointment of an arbitrator until nearly three months after the latest time prescribed by the lease and it was clear in these circumstances that there was an implication that time was of the essence since the lease had provided for what was to happen if the time-limit was missed. There was none the less an application under Section 27 of the Arbitration Act 1927 for an extension of time in which to refer the determination to arbitration and the court allowed the Section 27 application.

2.10 Other provisions in the lease may also indicate the necessary contra-indication to displace the general principle that time is not of the essence. For example, an association between the dates of service of rent review notices and the exercise of a break clause may well render the rent review timetable of the essence of the rent review clause. Much will depend on whether the court is satisfied that failure to comply with the timetable would prejudice the party exercising the break from deciding whether or not to do so. If that party needs to know what the new rent is likely to be in order to assist in deciding whether to opt to break, then it may well be that the mechanism for agreeing or determining that rent will be of the essence of contract. In fact, quite often break clauses are not drafted like this, even where the tenant may well have intended to negotiate a break that gives it the opportunity to consider the level of renewed rent before making up its mind about whether or not to determine the lease. I shall look at this in a little more detail in paragraph 5 of Chapter 4.

2.11 In *Central Estates Limited* v *The Secretary of State for the Environment* **1995 EGCS 110** the Court of Appeal analysed the various cases where there was a relationship between a break clause and the rent review clause such as to make time of the essence. In this particular case the rent was to be reviewed in an upward and downward direction and the break clause was mutual yet it was still held by the Court of Appeal that there was a sufficient relationship so as to make time of the essence. The court made it clear that there must be some period of time after the service of a rent review notice in which the tenant had to consider whether to serve a break clause notice. This obviously makes sense because if time is not of the essence then that period might well simply be eroded before the tenant can make up its mind whether to exercise its right to break.

2.12 So there are various cases where the courts have had to consider whether time is of the essence impliedly. It is obviously helpful for the courts to give guidance to practitioners in deciding whether time is impliedly of the essence and certainly practitioners need this guidance. However, where one is involved with the drafting of a new lease it seems to me that best practice requires a simple statement making it clear whether or not the parties intend time to be of the essence. There is no need to leave this to the judgement of the courts. If it is the intention of the parties to make time of the essence, then they should say so. *United Scientific* (see paragraph 2.1) allows the parties to expressly provide for time to be of the essence and they should either make a statement to that effect or state that time is not of the essence. There seems to be little good reason why a clause not expressly making time of the essence (and therefore not presumably intended to do so) does not contain a statement negativing this possibility and thus excluding the possibility that the court might say that some other provision in the lease impliedly makes time of the essence for the rent review machinery. Why leave such an important matter to chance, particularly given that many of the cases turn on the most fine details imaginable?

2.13 If one is facing a situation where a rent review is being activated in circumstances where perhaps the court might hold time to be of the essence then clearly there are very good reasons indeed why the parties and their advisers should ensure that all time-limits are strictly adhered to and complied with so that no chances are taken whatsoever.

3. COMPARABLE PREMISES, ASSUMPTIONS AND DISREGARDS

3.1 Where the rent is to be reviewed to the market rent it is obviously necessary for the parties to agree the rent that should be paid for the premises. If they cannot do this, then the matter will have to be determined for them by a third party. This procedure involves compiling evidence of comparable property and in order to do that and ensure that one is comparing apples with apples, it is necessary for all the terms and indeed the length of the term of the lease of all comparable premises to be similar to those of the subject premises.

3.2 The key word is 'comparable'. Imagine the situation where a prospective tenant is offered two sets of premises. Lease A is for a term of twenty-five years with no ability to assign or change the use and substantial repairing obligations and Lease B is for a similar term but with a tenant-only right to break early, rights for the tenant to change the use and assign and perhaps a more limited repairing obligation. The prospective tenant will unquestionably be more attracted to the terms of Lease B and will no doubt even be prepared to pay more for Lease B. He may even refuse to enter into Lease A.

Accordingly, if there is in existence a lease granted on the terms of Lease A, then when it comes to reviewing the rent payable for that set of premises, if the landlord were to offer as a comparable set of premises a lease granted on the terms of Lease B, the tenant would no doubt seek a hefty discount to compensate it for the fact that it does not enjoy the benefits that are enjoyed by the notional tenant of the 'comparable premises'.

3.3 Rent reviews where rents are to be reviewed to market rents nearly always turn on the evaluation of comparable evidence and since one is looking at the effect on review of all lease clauses it is important to bear this in mind when negotiating all such provisions. Do not confine your thoughts about review to the discussions concerning the review clause itself: it should be at the back of your mind in thinking about all other lease clauses.

3.4 Ideally the rent review clause will guide the parties, and any third party who is required to resolve a dispute between them, as to the terms of the notional lease to be valued on review. Where this is the case, disputes tend to revolve around the effect of the terms of the notional lease.

If a lease does not set out specifically what terms are to be included in the notional lease, then it may be for the court to fill in the gaps or interpret what they believe the parties may have intended.

Where all the terms are inserted, the question tends to be a matter of valuation and where the courts become involved, decisions of the courts tend to pretty much turn on the facts of individual cases; not so where the lease of the subject premises is simply silent as to the terms of the notional lease. Decisions of the courts in relation to matters of this nature tend to be of more relevance.

3.5 In giving the parties guidance, the rent review clause will direct the third party surveyor to assume certain matters and disregard others. Quite often the issues between landlords and tenants when negotiating rent review clauses concern such assumptions and disregards. The guiding principle should be that these assumptions and disregards should be drafted so as to allow the rent to be reviewed in a fair and equitable manner. In order to do this, certain matters need to be assumed and certain matters need to be disregarded. This is wholly different to the creation of 'false assumptions' or 'false disregards' designed to improve the position of the party inserting them.

3.6   For example, it is essential that in valuing premises one disregards improvements carried out by a tenant at his own cost where he was not under any obligation to the landlord to improve the premises. If one does not do that, the rent will be valued by reference to the premises as bettered (and made more valuable) by those improvements. The tenant will have therefore paid for the improvements themselves and then find he is liable to pay a higher rent because he occupies 'improved premises'. This is obviously not fair and the disregard of improvements is an example where one needs to move away from the position in reality: it is no use reviewing the premises in their improved state. This is one of those situations where the disregard is inserted to create fairness and not to unfairly improve the position of landlord or tenant. Indeed to exclude it would unfairly improve the landlord's position.

3.7   When one is looking at assumptions and disregards one needs to consider whether they are necessary to ensure a fair and equitable rent review or whether they are being inserted by a party seeking to improve his position. The disregard of improvements can conveniently be contrasted, for example, with a lease containing a very specific and restrictive user and a prohibition on any change of use but where the rent review clause directs the third party to assume an open user. This false assumption would clearly prejudice the tenant, since he would have all the onerous liabilities occasioned by a stringent restrictive user clause and the consequent constraints on assigning, but then find on review that he would not obtain any discount to reflect these prohibitive terms; he will have his rent valued by reference to much more valuable comparable property where there is a relatively relaxed user.

3.8   It is therefore essential that lawyers and surveyors carefully analyse proposed assumptions and disregards. They need to be carefully negotiated so that the review clause reflects something that is fair and reasonable and is not designed to enable the rent to be assessed on a basis which wholly prejudices one of the parties. There is a careful balance that needs to be drawn here and one which arises on virtually every rent review negotiation.

4. LENGTH OF TERM OF THE NOTIONAL LEASE

4.1 Where this is specified in the lease it is normal for the term to be defined either as the full length of the term of the lease which is being reviewed or the residue of the term of that lease that remains unexpired at the review date. A middle ground which one finds in many leases is for the notional term to be the residue of the actual term but with a minimum of, say, ten to fifteen years.

4.2 Much of the thinking behind this and the early drafting of provisions such as this in the 1970s and 1980s derived from the principle that landlords and investors wanted to see a twenty or twenty-five-year term on their leases and therefore wanted reviews to be on the basis of a term of that length. The debate tended to rage between landlords insisting on a notional term of the full twenty-five-year term and tenants requiring the rent to be valued by reference to a notional term equal to the unexpired residue on the basis that that was what they had in reality and therefore that was what should be reviewed.

4.3 The compromise referred to in paragraph 4.1 above found favour with both landlords and tenants since by reference to unexpired residue it met the tenant's need to review by reference to reality, whereas by having a fixed minimum, landlords were able to bring in as comparable evidence other relatively long institutional leases and also defeat a tenant's argument, which would grow in importance as the lease came nearer to its end and the residue became shorter, that a notional tenant would actually pay less for, say a five-year lease than it would for a twenty-five-year lease with five-yearly reviews, since it would not be able to write off its capital expenditure, fitting out costs, etc. over such a short period. Hence the residue/minimum compromise.

4.4 I think it is important to put this in context. In the market that has begun to develop in the 1990s, particularly for retail and office accommodation (but perhaps not so in the leisure sector where, if anything, leases are getting longer), tenants are very often keen to take short-term leases or leases with tenant's breaks. This gives them flexibility. If the notional term is twenty-five years then a tenant may well argue that this is much longer than he would require and in such circumstances he would not take the premises or would only take them at a discounted rental. Similarly, it may not always be the case that a landlord will want a very long notional lease for valuation purposes. If the tenant is taking a twenty-five-year lease of premises which contain expensive and perhaps old machinery, landlord's fixtures, air-conditioning plant, equipment, etc. and if the premises have a full tenant's repairing obligation, then one can see that if the landlord insists on a notional twenty-five-year term, this may prejudice him. In this situation, as at, say, the twentieth year of the term the tenant may well argue that he should be entitled to a significant rental discount to reflect the fact that the notional tenant is to be asked to take a twenty-five-year lease, on that date, of premises which contain this machinery, fixtures, etc. These will be costly to replace and undoubtedly worn out within twenty years or so of that date and therefore the tenant may well succeed in an argument for a rental discount to compensate for the liability to repair.

4.5   The moral of this story is to look at the kind of premises one is dealing with before agreeing the term of the notional lease to be inserted in the review clause. One is seeing more reference to unexpired residue with short minimums of ten to fifteen years at the most and it is becoming less and less normal for leases to be drafted requiring the notional term to be the full length of the original lease term. Of course there are still a significant number of relatively new leases that contain this wording, and where issues of valuation will no doubt arise on future leases; I would urge practitioners to look carefully at the subject matter of the premises in question in order to ascertain whether any point should be taken on any future review.

4.6   As I said earlier, cases in relation to reviews concern either interpretation of the wording included in the review clause or the interpretation of a review clause without wording that might otherwise have been included.

4.7   What happens where the lease does not deal specifically with the length of the term? In the case of *Lynnthorpe Enterprises*

Limited v *Sidney Smith (Chelsea) Limited* **1990 40 EG 130** the Court of Appeal had to consider a rent review clause where the rent was to be reviewed by reference to a notional term 'for a term of years equivalent to the said term'. The original term had been fifteen years and the question before the court was whether the notional lease was for a term of fifteen years from the review date or fifteen years from the original term commencement date (i.e. the unexpired residue). The court favoured the latter on the basis that the parties no doubt intended the notional letting to be on the same terms as those that existed in this particular lease. This case follows others in the same type of dispute (for example *The Ritz Hotel (London) Limited* v *Ritz Casino Limited* **1989 46 EG 95**). Both these cases reflected the court's desire to hold that the notional letting should reflect the terms of the subject lease as far as possible. As you will see in looking at many of the more modern cases on rent reviews, the courts strive for what they have called 'a presumption of reality' when they are interpreting rent review clauses.

4.8 If one takes residue as the length of the notional term, one needs to consider whether the lease should be valued on the basis that the tenant has the right to renew it under the 1954 Act. It was decided as long ago as 1979 in *Pivot Properties Limited* v *Secretary of State for the Environment* **1980 256 EG 1176** that the hope value of a renewal should not be excluded. The third party must assess the possibility of a renewal and it will then be a question of valuation evidence how this would affect rental bids.

4.9 So one can see there is an element of guidance. Unless the definition of term is quite clear as being equal to the term granted then the notional term will be a term starting from the relevant review date and the likelihood of renewal is not excluded. It is worth noting that in *Boots Chemist Limited* v *Pinkland Limited* **1992 28 EG 118**, a County court decision on landlord and tenant renewals which we look at in more detail in Chapter 6, paragraph 10, although the court said that it would order the notional term to be equal to the residue following the *Ritz* case, it criticized the *Ritz* wording as being ambiguous. One can only agree with this sentiment.

4.10 Before we leave the question of how long the lease should be, it is worth looking at the case of *Prudential Assurance Company Limited* v *Salisbury Handbags Limited* 1992 23 EG 117. This case concerned a lease for just under ninety-seven years granted in 1990 with seven-yearly reviews where the parties had omitted to state the length of the term of the hypothetical lease. The rent review clause required the parties to assume terms similar to those contained in the lease and the rent was to be reviewed to the best rent on such a letting, ignoring the rent review clause itself.

Because of the requirement to ignore the review clause the possibility existed of a horrendously high rent being foisted upon the tenant following the authority of *National Westminster Bank* v *Arthur Young* 1985 1 WLR 1123, a case where the court was faced with a rent review clause directing the valuer to exclude the clause itself which would have lead to a substantially higher rent being paid. It is easy to see that if a tenant is given a lease for a term of twenty-five years without review, he is likely to pay more for that than he would pay for a lease where he is having his rent reviewed upward-only at five-yearly intervals. Although it has now effectively been discredited and is therefore not likely to cause any future problems, the worry for the tenant in the *Prudential* case was that if the court was to hold that the notional term was the full ninety-seven years and since there was a specific direction to disregard the review clause, then, leaving aside for the moment the difficult valuation exercise (there would simply not exist many, if any, leases of nearly 100 years at market rent without review), the tenant would be facing the ridiculous situation of having to pay a rent on this basis. The judge in *Prudential* said that since the notional term was not specified, the term would be such as would be likely to be granted in the market as would produce the best rent to the landlord where there was no review. A five-year term was taken. This is the only result that could conceivably have been welcomed by the tenant. A term equal to the original term, ninety-seven years, or even the unexpired residue, would have been disastrous.

4.11 In *Millshaw Property Company Limited* v *Preston Borough Council* 1995 EGCS 186 the court was concerned with another long lease where the rent review provisions specified that the length of the notional term should not exceed the residue. At the review in the twenty-first year, some seventy-eight years were outstanding and the court held the length of term that should be taken was that which the landlord might reasonably expect to offer and the tenant might reasonably expect to accept to produce the best rent for an open market letting. This was the same principle as that in *Prudential* and clearly it would not have been reasonable in those circumstances to choose a length of term of seventy-eight years.

5. TERMS OF THE NOTIONAL LEASE

5.1 Having considered the length of the notional term it is necessary to look at the remaining terms of the notional lease that go to make up the comparables. Many of these will affect the review.

5.2 In order to consider the importance of ascertaining the terms of the notional lease, I think it is important to bear in mind that all of the terms of a lease are pivotal to the review clause. When negotiating any of the covenants, whether they be matters of obvious importance such as alterations, alienation, user or even

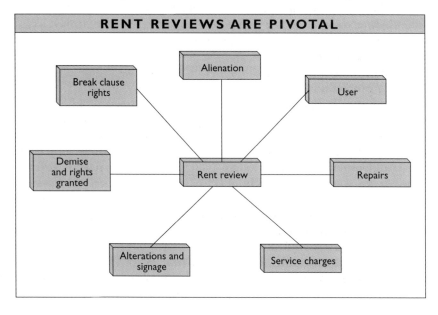

some of the more obtuse obligations in leases such as the right to erect signage, the parties should keep an eye on any rent review implications. It is obvious that a prospective tenant faced with a reasonably long lease and no rights to assign or change the use will pay less than a prospective tenant would for the same set of premises let on a lease of the same length of term, but with full and extensive rights to assign or change the use, etc.

5.3 I do not propose to go through the numerous cases dealing with discounts on review in respect of restrictions on use, alienation, alterations, etc. Many of these turn on their own facts and Bernstein and Reynolds' *Rent Review Handbook* deals with these more than adequately. I stress however, once again, the need for the parties and their advisers to negotiate these provisions with one eye firmly fixed on the rent review clause. Recent practice in relation to alienation has brought the point firmly home. Under the 1995 Act landlords and tenants of commercial premises are able, for the very first time, to specify the bases upon which a landlord will be reasonable to refuse to consent to assignment. Debate has raged on what is, and is not, likely to be acceptable to tenants and one of the big issues for landlords, of course, is that the tighter the alienation restrictions, the more likely a tenant will seek, and even obtain, a discount on review.

When negotiating the terms of a lease the parties should bear this in mind. The current approach of the judiciary is to interpret review clauses in a commercial way by reference to 'the presumption of reality' but clearly surveyors negotiating review clauses should not rely on this. They should ensure that leases reflect what they intend.

5.4 The question of the terms of a notional lease were recently considered in *Norwich Union Life Insurance Society* v *British Telecommunications PLC* **1995 EGCS 148**. This case concerned a rent review with a gearing formula. The lease did not provide for the notional lease to specifically exclude the gearing formula and indeed contained the words 'provided that the landlord and tenant undertook their respective obligations which they have undertaken in this lease'. The landlord was anxious to exclude the gearing provision and contended that these words were sufficient to do so. The court did not agree. It stated that to do this would be to re-write the parties' agreement. The court acknowledged that there was an element of illogicality in this, but none the less felt it was the right decision. This is obviously a case where the court came to the aid of the parties, but it is quite easy to ensure that where one is negotiating gearing provisions, they are excluded.

5.5 It is easy to see that if the reviewed rent of a restaurant is geared to say 125% of a retail property, then in looking at the market rent the tenant will seek a discount to reflect that in reality the lease in question requires him to pay 125% of that market rent. The gearing formula should therefore be disregarded. Normally the courts would seek to get to the same result and there are decisions to this effect, but not so in *Norwich Union*.

5.6 Similarly, if one is reviewing rent to the higher of market rent and the retail price index (RPI) increases, it is important that the reference to the RPI increase is disregarded from the notional term. Without that, the notional lease market rent would be less than the market rent obtainable for a notional lease without indexation provisions and, therefore, there is a need to exclude the indexation provisions in order to ensure that they do not create a self-cancelling absurdity. Whilst the court would be anxious to avoid this wherever possible, the parties should do their best to ensure that they draft provisions that do not need the court to come to their aid.

6.   LAST-DAY REVIEWS

6.1 Landlords are very often keen to have a rent review on the last day of the term or the penultimate day of the term. This avoids the need to go through the interim rent procedures set out in the 1954 Act.

6.2 Interim rents under the 1954 Act can go up or down. This is not often the case in a contractual review. Interim rents give discounts to the tenant which are simply not available in a standard open market rent review. Furthermore, a landlord would not obtain an interim rent if he failed to apply for one under Section 24(A) of the 1954 Act. This is another stumbling-block that simply does not exist if, instead of an interim rent, there is a contractual review.

One further advantage of the last-day review over the interim rent arises from the decision of the Court of Appeal in *Herbert Duncan Limited* v *Cluttons* **1993 2 WLR 710** (which I look at in paragraph 4 of Chapter 6). This case makes it clear that where privity of contract still applies, an interim rent award would not bind an original tenant who is no longer the tenant entitled to possession, whereas a rent review on the last day may well bind that tenant.

6.3   For these reasons landlords are often quite keen to ensure a new lease contains a last-day review.

6.4   If there is a last-day review, then for this to be of any meaningful advantage to the landlord in substantially increasing the rent that it might obtain from that which would be available under Section 24(A) of the 1995 Act by way of an interim rent award, the notional term to be valued on review must be longer than the merely unexpired residue. An unexpired residue of one day, even with the hope value of renewal, is not likely to yield a rent much greater than that which would be obtained under the interim rent procedure. It still might be of some help, however, if rents have fallen and the lease contains an upward-only rent review because under the 1954 Act the interim rent could be lower than the passing rent, although if that were the case, in practice it would be irrelevant since the landlord would not apply for the interim rent and the tenant cannot do so as the law currently stands, although there are proposals to change this (see Chapter 6). Assuming the landlord has got this right and has properly drafted an end of term review, landlords may gain from inserting one for the reasons set out above.

6.5   A landlord who wants to obtain a last-day review but who does not want to make a big issue out of this in the lease negotiations, perhaps hoping to 'slip it through' might simply state that rent is to be reviewed 'on each fifth anniversary of the date of commencement of the term'. If the definition of 'term' is drafted to include continuations under the 1954 Act the tenant must beware. The twenty-five-year lease will contain a rent review at the twenty-fifth year and for the reasons set out above this may prejudice the tenant.

6.6   Accordingly there may be a difference between a review clause:

6.6.1   That simply says 'subject to review on the [N] day of [N] in the years [a][b][c] and [d]; and

6.6.2   That provides for review on 'each fifth anniversary of the date of commencement of the term'.

6.7   There has been a recent case on the subject of reviews at the end of the contractual term. *Willison v Cheverell Estates Limited* **1996 26 EG 133** concerned a lease where a landlord had served a break notice and a notice under Section 25, 1954 Act. The tenant applied for a new tenancy and since Section 64 of the 1954 Act provides that the existing tenancy continues until the application is disposed of, the existing lease continued. The landlord was entitled to an interim rent running from the expiry of his contractual break. What he really wanted was to operate the contractual rent review provisions themselves, if he could do that. On the facts of *Willison* the court did not allow the landlord to do this but it seems reasonably clear in reading the Court of Appeal judgment that if the lease had been differently worded, the court might have come to a different result and might have allowed the landlord to operate a contractual rent review.

6.8   A tenant might want to argue that the very existence of a last-day review is, in itself, an onerous term entitling a tenant to obtain a discount on all rents agreed or determined on the rent reviews preceding the last-day review. If a landlord wants to avoid this argument it is possible that the review clause could disregard the existence of the last-day review on all of the reviews except that particular one!

6.9   I do not think we have seen the end of last-day reviews.

7.   HEADLINE RENTS

7.1   I want to spend a little time on headline rents, although they are much less of a problem nowadays. In the era of rent incentives that has been a part of the early 1990s, particularly in office lettings, the financial terms subject to which a tenant takes space

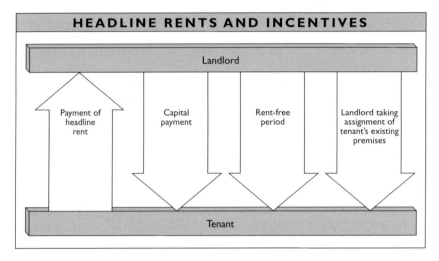

include far more than merely the amount of the rent that is being paid for the property. It is not uncommon for rents to be underpinned at a certain level and for the tenant to be compensated by being given substantial incentives. For example, premises that might be valued at £20 per square foot may perhaps be let at £40 per square foot, the tenant being given a very substantial rent-free period, a capital inducement or even a combination of the two. In these circumstances, the £40 per square foot figure is often called a headline rent.

7.2 On the basis that headline rents exist and many premises are let on headline rents, the question arises from time to time on review as to whether headline rents are good comparables or whether the headline element of other rent deals needs to be stripped out so that the parties trying to agree a rent review, or indeed the third party surveyor when they have failed to agree, should look at the net/real rent after taking away all of the incentives.

7.3 Headline rents are paid because the tenant receives an inducement. If the headline rent is to be used as the comparable for the rent payable on review every five years, the tenant will have a problem, since although his reviewed rent will be agreed or determined upon the basis that it is a headline rent with all the inducements that go with it, in fact, he will not have the benefit of those inducements and will have to pay the headline rent for the full five years. In reality no one would pay such a rent unless the rest of the package were to go with it but the High Court has had to consider five cases where landlords have sought to obtain headline rents on review. In three of the cases the landlord obtained a headline rent, in one the landlord would have obtained a headline rent if it were not for a 'double negative' in the assumptions/disregards of the review clause and only in one case did the court feel that the headline rent should be discounted. Accordingly, whilst the position has not been terribly clear, until recently landlords have been in the driving seat.

7.4 The Court of Appeal have now considered the whole area. In a consolidated appeal hearing which was heard in November 1994 the Court of Appeal have had considerable sympathy with the position of tenants.

7.5 The area in question is part and parcel of the ongoing discussion about when a rent review clause should reflect reality and when it should reflect an agreed set of assumptions and disregards that, when aggregated, lead to a situation that might be a long way off reality. It is not always easy to have a review that does not have false assumptions. If a review clause did not have any false assumptions, you would have all sorts of odd results such as the tenant paying a substantially increased rent because of goodwill attaching to the premises he might have been responsible for building up or, as I mentioned in paragraph 3.6 above, for improvements he has paid for himself, etc. Whilst the courts have said that where directions are not given, the review should be on the basis that would normally apply between an actual landlord and an actual tenant (i.e. *Basingstoke and Deane Borough Council* v *Host Group Limited* **1987 2 EGLR 147**), it is not at all unusual for there to be copious assumptions and disregards which adjust the real position so that it is fair and reasonable between the parties. There is a very good article considering this both from a legal and surveying perspective and which appears in the *Estates Gazettes* of 20 and 27 August 1994. The article is in two parts. The legal section is given by Jonathan Gaunt QC and the surveying section by Richard Main. It is an extract of the 1994 Blundel Memorial Lecture and I commend it.

7.6   The problem with headline rents is that the effect on a tenant can be quite devastating. Far from creating a false assumption that gives the tenant realism (as in the case of disregarding improvements – see *Ponsford* v *HMS Aerosols Limited* **1979 AC 63**), the headline rent debate very often gives the landlord a windfall profit.

7.7   Having looked at the basic concept of a headline rent we ought to look briefly at the decisions of the court regarding headline rents which were consolidated in a Court of Appeal case. Each of these turns on specific wording and in paragraphs 7.8 to 7.13 I have commented on the wording in the leases and the decision of the Court of Appeal, but if any reader is trying to ascertain either whether a headline rent exists in relation to an existing lease or is trying to either avoid such a construction or impose such a construction, I would strongly urge that detailed legal advice be taken on the exact wording. The consolidated appeal seems to make it clear that the decision of the court is likely to turn on very fine questions of interpretation. The cases that were considered in the Court of Appeal are as follows:
City Offices PLC v *Bryanston Insurance Company Limited* **1993 1 EGLR 126**;
Broadgate Square PLC v *Lehman Brothers Limited* **1994 04 EG 135**;
Co-operative Wholesale Society Limited v *National Westminster Bank PLC* **1994 11 EG 130**;
Scottish Amicable Life Assurance Society v *Middleton* **1994 10 EG 109**; and
Prudential Nominees v *Greenham Trading* **1994 EGCS 84**.

7.8   In the *City Offices* decision the clause stated that the rent that would be payable by the tenant would be the market rent 'after the expiry of any rent-free concession or fitting out period which might be given to the tenant'. In that decision there was also a disregard of any 'notional rent-free concession or fitting out period for which allowance would or might be given to the tenant'. The court held that the assumption would apply after any rent-free concession or fitting out period had expired. This would not be limited to fitting out periods alone but would include *any* concession. This disregard however had the effect of countering the assumption! The judge adjusted the headline rent downwards to that which would have existed if there had been no rent-free period. The other alternative of course – and this is no doubt what the landlord was seeking to achieve in drafting the disregard – would have been to disregard the whole effect of the rent-free period in the letting package. The rent could then have been taken at face value and a headline rent would have been awarded. The *City Offices* case really shows how one should not over-cook the position. Here, a badly drawn disregard was at odds with the assumption. If one looks at the other cases, it seems that without this disregard and the inconsistency it caused, a headline rent would have been awarded.

7.9 In the *Scottish Amicable* case, the rent review clause stated that the market rent was to be the rent 'at the rate payable following the expiry of any rent-free period or periods at concessionary rents which might be granted on a new letting of the demised premises or of comparable premises in the open market on the relevant review date'. Here the disregard included a disregard of 'any effect on rent of any initial rent-free period or periods at concessionary rents or other inducements which might be offered in the open market to prospective underlessees of the demised premises or any part thereof of comparable premises'. Here the judge said it was her job to look for the intention of the parties. Relying on *Basingstoke and Deane Borough Council v Host Group Limited* she felt that one should look at the review clause as a whole so as to give effect to the basic purpose of the clause and not to confer a windfall profit on the landlord. It seems as if the judge took the underlying commercial purpose and then pursued a close analysis of the assumption to support a decision to value the rent after fitting out discounts but before taking rental inducements into account.

7.10 In *Broadgate Square* the market rent definition provided for the rent payable after the expiry of any rent-free period of such length as would be negotiated in the market and again it was held that the expression 'any rent-free period' was not limited to fitting out periods and the arbitrator was wrong to discount down from the headline rent. There is a clear dichotomy between *Broadgate Square* and *Scottish Amicable*.

7.11 In *Co-operative Wholesale Society* again the assumption was that 'any rent-free period ... which may be offered in the case of a new letting in the open market shall have expired'. Here the arbitrator awarded the headline rent and the appeal to the High Court failed. Rich, J said that it must be assumed that any rent-free period has expired and the arbitrator was therefore right to order the headline rent.

7.12   In *Prudential Nominees* there was a headline rent awarded without discount and the assumption that there should be no reduction to be made on account of any rent-free period or concession was not restricted to fitting out periods.

7.13   The Court of Appeal's judgement in the consolidated appeal is effectively a victory for tenants. The court was extremely critical where false assumptions and disregards were created and it was clear that the court would lean against a construction which would require payment of rent upon the assumption that the tenant had received benefits that he had not in fact received. Accordingly the *Scottish Amicable* decision was upheld whilst the decisions in *Co-operative Wholesale* and *Prudential Nominees* were overturned on appeal. In the *Broadgate Square* case, however, the reference to the rent-free period being 'of such length as would be negotiated in the open market' made it impossible to confine the words to rent-free periods attributable to fitting out works and the appeal was dismissed.

7.14   The concept of headline rents is quite a difficult one. The Court of Appeal has made it clear that you can still have headline rents so long as the wording giving rise to the headline rent is unambiguous. Most commentators see the distinction that was made between the *Broadgate Square* case and the others as quite strained and the belief is that the courts will bend over backwards to ensure that a tenant does not have a headline rent foisted upon it. Probably if a draftsman wishes to achieve a headline rent on review, then he should simply take the *Broadgate Square* wording and repeat it verbatim. One would need to put this in context and it may well be that a court would still endeavour to lean against the construction that the *Broadgate Square* wording gives rise to a headline rent in relation to a different set of premises or circumstances. One must not lose sight of the fact that one of the reasons the headline rent cases originated was to try and avoid what became known as the 'Ninety-nine Bishopsgate Effect', i.e. the fact that property needed to be valued as vacant, having the consequential effect of giving the tenant negotiating a review the right to call for a discount to reflect the fact that since the notional premises are 'vacant', expenses would need to be incurred to get the premises up and running. Since the actual tenant would of course be running a business he would need a discount to compensate such a state of affairs.

A very good analysis of the headline rent cases appears in Bernstein and Reynolds (see Recommended reading) and indeed the book contains two precedents, one avoiding the Ninety-nine Bishopsgate Effect but not creating a headline rent and one defining open market rent as a headline rent. The latter follows the wording in *Broadgate Square*.

8.   VAT AND RENT REVIEWS

8.1   VAT needs to be considered in the context of rent reviews. Remember VAT is not payable on rent unless the landlord makes an election to charge VAT. Remember also that the 1996 Budget is to change the position regarding VAT on rent and it is now the case that where a landlord wants to elect to waive the exemption he can only do so if the tenant has an 80% recovery rate in relation to VAT (these proposals are extremely controversial and changes are inevitable before they are enacted; however, more on this later in paragraph 8.4 below). For that reason, some commercial premises have rents where the tenant pays VAT on top and some do not. Equally, some tenants have the ability to recover the VAT charged to them as input tax and some do not.

8.2   Before electing to waive the VAT exemption and charge VAT on rents, landlords must give some thought to whether this will deter tenants from their property or adversely affect the rental value. In the financial sector, for example, some tenants cannot recover VAT. Clearly if office accommodation is available to let in that sector, it is likely that some potential tenants will not be able to recover all of their VAT as input tax. Those tenants are likely to be less excited about taking premises where the rent has VAT on top, since the additional VAT will simply be an

LIVERPOOL JOHN MOORES UNIVERSITY
LEARNING SERVICES

added overhead cost. At present rates of tax this would add $17\frac{1}{2}\%$ to the cost of occupying the premises.

8.3   One way in which landlords can avoid problems on review is by a false assumption whereby on review it is assumed either that the landlord has irrevocably stated he will not charge VAT or that all notional tenants are able to recover all VAT in full. Properly drafted provisions of this nature should enable the landlord to avoid an argument by a tenant that it should have a discount on review to reflect the fact either that VAT is charged or that it may be charged in the future and that this potential cost might make the premises less attractive to tenants. The clear problem for tenants is that there is absolutely no reason why they should agree to a false assumption of this nature which gives the landlord the benefit of perhaps a higher rent in circumstances where the tenant may have to pay VAT and face the fact that his market for disposal is adversely affected or even reduced since it may include tenants who do not have full VAT recovery.

8.4   The position is more complicated now with the new proposals contained in the 1996 Budget, since the question of whether VAT can properly be charged and of whether an election to waive the exemption be allowed to stand, will depend on the tenant's recovery rate and, to the extent that this changes from time to time, the landlord's ability to charge VAT may change. Whilst I am not really an advocate of false assumptions, I think that there is much to be said for a landlord inserting an assumption along the lines of that set out in paragraph 8.3 above where the original letting is to a tenant who has the ability to recover VAT. It seems to me intrinsically unfair that the landlord should run the risk that the tenant may change its VAT status perhaps even more than once, and affect the landlord's position on rent review. This is all very new, of course, since at the time of writing this book the legislation giving effect to the budgetary proposals has not yet been drafted but clearly surveyors and lawyers need to be alive to this at an early stage. It seems from early commentaries on the likely legislation, that the position will need to be considered afresh on every rent payment date. I deal with this prospective legislation in a little more detail in Chapter 7, paragraph H.

9. IMPLEMENTATION OF THE REVIEW PROCESS

9.1 Normally rent reviews can be implemented by either the land-lord or the tenant. This tends to be the same for both upward-only reviews and reviews that are capable of decreasing the rent payable. At first sight it is difficult to see why a tenant would ever want to implement a review which was upward-only, but there may be situations where this would be in his interest. For example, he may be wishing to dispose of property and in order to have a degree of certainty he will want to know what the rent is likely to be. Furthermore, in an upward-only review it is normally the case that the existing rent continues to be payable until a new rent is agreed or determined and occasionally landlords persuade tenants to pay the excess (if any) with interest at a high rate. In these circumstances, even in an upward-only review, a tenant might be anxious to bring the review process to a head.

9.2 For far more obvious reasons a tenant might be quite anxious to implement a review where the rent could be reduced. *Harben Style Limited* v *The Rhodes Trust* **1995 17 EG 125** and *Royal Bank of Scotland* v *Jennings* **1995 35 EG 140** are two recent and conflicting cases concerning upward/downward reviews where the lease provided that the reference to a third party could only be made at the landlord's request.

9.3 In *Harben* the court refused to require the landlord to make an application to a third party. It would only do so if the rent review machinery had broken down and since the rent review clause made it clear that if there were no reference to the third party the rent were to stay the same, this was not the case. The *Royal Bank of Scotland* case conflicted with this and was decided after *Harben* and the *Harben* decision was referred to in the judgment. Again there was reference to a third party determination and again only the landlord could make the application and they did not do so. The High Court held that on a proper construction of the review clause the rent was not upwards-only and therefore either there was an enforceable requirement for the landlord to apply to the president of the RICS or an implied obligation to do so in order to make the clause work. The *Royal Bank of Scotland* case followed the

1983 decision of *Sudbrook Trading Estate Limited* v *Eggleton* **1983 1 AC 444** where the House of Lords required valuation machinery to be put in place in order to determine the level at which a freehold reversion could be purchased, the tenant having exercised the option to purchase the reversion. In the *Royal Bank of Scotland* decision the court made it clear that where it was not an upwards-only review it was necessary for the tenant to be able to move the matter forward to a third party reference and therefore, if necessary, a clause allowing the tenant to do so would be inserted.

As I say, the judge in the *Royal Bank of Scotland* case had seen the *Harben* decision although not the full report of it. If one looks at the two leases in detail the *Harben* lease did specifically provide for the eventuality that a review might not take place. The court felt this was sufficient to distinguish the case from *Sudbrook*. This did not arise in the *Royal Bank of Scotland* case. Practitioners felt that it was more logical to follow *Royal Bank of Scotland* and now that the matter has been decided by the Court of Appeal (**1996 EGCS 168**) and the Court of Appeal has upheld *Royal Bank of Scotland* this is unquestionably the better approach when analysing clauses of this nature. However, if one is negotiating the terms of a new lease, once again the message is 'use clear language'. Practitioners, particularly those advising tenants, should make it absolutely clear that where there is to be a potential downward review the tenants have the right to implement that review. The court may not always come to the aid of a tenant who does not provide for that and another 1995 High Court decision, *Fraser Pipestock Limited* v *Gloucester City Council* **1995 36 EG 141**, is a classic example of a situation where the court would not intervene to remedy a situation where machinery had broken down since they could not ascertain clearly what the parties intended.

9.4   Late in 1996 the High Court had to look at yet another case where the landlord was seeking to frustrate the implementation of an upward/downward rent review by failing to serve notices. The case in question was *Addin Investments Limited* v *Secretary of State for the Environment* **1996 EGCS 195** which was heard in the High Court in November 1996. The rent review provisions of the lease stated that rent would be higher than the original rent fixed for the first seven years, which was

£148,500, or such sum 'as shall be assessed as the current open market rent'. Accordingly, this was not an upward-only review but a threshold provision. The rent would not fall below the original rent but, subject to that, was upward/downward. The mechanism for review was set out clearly. There was provision for an assessment of the open market rent specified by the landlord in its notice, agreed by the parties or fixed by a third party. The rent review provisions stated that if there was a late assessment there was provision for back dating the tenant's obligation to pay the increase but no corresponding provision in favour of the tenant for a downwards adjustment. Initially rents rose and by July 1988 the rent had gone up to £440,000 per annum but by July 1995 both landlord and tenant realized that a fresh assessment would yield a lower figure. Remember the rent could go down but not below £148,500.

9.5 The landlords took a decision not to serve notice. Could the court order an independent assessment even though the landlord had not done what it needed to do to bring the rent review machinery into play?

9.6 The High Court made it clear that the landlords could not frustrate the purpose of the rent review clause, namely that the market rent should be payable throughout the lease. The provisions of the rent review clause were held to provide machinery for giving effect to the paramount purpose of establishing market rent and the tenant got its downward review. Interestingly, one other point was considered by the court. As I mentioned earlier, there was a provision for back dating the tenant's obligation to pay an increase but no corresponding provision in favour of the tenant. The court said that, if called upon, it would imply a corresponding refund provision in the case of a downwards assessment. This is only a High Court decision and, at the time of writing this, I have only seen the case summaries in the *Estates Gazette* and not a full transcript of the case, but this is an interesting concept.

9.7 It is also interesting to contrast these upward/downward decisions with the interim rent procedures of the 1954 Act. As I have said, these can also cause rent to go down but there is no provision in the 1954 Act which allows a tenant to apply for an interim rent in these circumstances. Could **Royal Bank of Scotland** and **Addin** be cited as authority for allowing a tenant to apply for an interim rent? I do not think so. I believe statute will have to intervene to provide for this but as you will see in the chapter on the 1954 Act, there are proposals for change of the 1954 Act and the proposals incorporate permitting a tenant to apply for an interim rent.

10. ASSUMPTIONS THAT THE PREMISES ARE FITTED OUT

10.1 One frequently sees rent review clauses containing an assumption that the premises are fully fitted out for trading.

10.2 The purpose behind such an assumption is to prevent the tenant from being able to allege that it should have a rental reduction to reflect the fact that in the market place any notional tenant would seek a rent reduction to compensate it for the time required to fit out its premises.

10.3 However, one of the problems with clauses of this nature is that they give rise to the potential interpretation that the tenant's fitting out works would be taken into account for review purposes. Clearly this is at odds with the general proposition that improvements carried out by and at the cost of tenants should be excluded and specifically disregarded from rent review clauses. In the case of **London and Leeds Estates Limited v Paribas Limited 1993 2 EGLR 149** the Court of Appeal effectively disposed of the argument that, in general, fitting out assumptions allow for tenant's fitting out works to be rentalized. The Court of Appeal made it clear that the purpose of such an assumption is to preclude the actual tenant from arguing that the hypothetical tenant is entitled to its discount, either on account of the actual state of repair, or because it requires different fitting out works to be carried out, the cost of which would necessarily have to be borne by the hypothetical tenant. The Court of Appeal in **London and Leeds** allowed for the possibility that the parties can specifically and expressly provide for tenant's fitting out works to be rentalized, but if they do not make express provision for this, then a fitting out assumption will not generally allow for such interpretation.

I think the matter has now been put beyond doubt by the High Court in *Ocean Accident and Guarantee Corporation* v *Next PLC* and *Commercial Union Assurance Company PLC* v *Next PLC* **1996 33 EG 91**. The High Court summarized the general approach to the construction of rent review clauses which was not in dispute before the court, namely that in the absence of an express provision to the contrary the premises are to be valued at review as they are, taking into account improvements irrespective of who effected them. The presumption of reality enunciated in *Co-operative Wholesale Society Limited* v *National Westminster Bank PLC* **1995 1 EGLR 97** should always be borne in mind. The court stated that fairness to the tenant makes it understandable that the parties would not expect the reviewed rent to be increased by reference to improvements effected by the tenant at its own expense. The High Court contrasted this with improvements made by the tenant pursuant to an obligation contained in the lease (which one would have expected to have been reflected in the original rent and other terms of the lease). Equally the presumption of reality favours a reviewed rent being fixed on the assumption that the hypothetical tenant would not have to move in and fit out: the actual tenant will already have done so. Again this was referred to in the *Co-operative Wholesale* case. Whilst the court made it clear that these principles were subject to the express terms of the lease in question, it did not feel that these assumptions, particularly the fitting out assumption, should allow for tenant's fitting out works to be rentalized. I think that the position is now beyond doubt and that unless a fitting out assumption clearly states that the tenant's fitting out works are to be rentalized, they will not be. However, this is something that must be given serious thought when the parties are negotiating a rent review clause, particularly if there is to be extensive fitting out work.

11.   CONCLUSION

11.1   Once again I should like to stress that this chapter is not intended to deal with all aspects of rent review clauses but merely some of the more interesting and current topical issues. There are an enormous number of issues that do need to be thought through when one is dealing with a rent review clause and since this book is not intended to be a comprehensive dia-tribe on rent reviews I make no apology for leaving a number of these out.

When negotiating rent review clauses landlords and tenants and their respective advisers must be clear in what they intend. When they are negotiating other clauses in leases it must be borne in mind throughout that there may be rent review implications. If this is done, the draftsman is accurate and one has a working knowledge of the rent review issues, then it is less likely that someone will be tripped up by some unforeseen rent review consequence of the negotiations in relation to another part of the lease. If a surveyor is negotiating a review then a good working knowledge of these issues and many more is needed in order to give the surveyor an edge over his opponent.

CHAPTER 3

ALIENATION AND USE

1. GENERAL PRINCIPLES

1.1 Most leases of commercial premises allow the tenant to assign the whole of the property with consent. Whether or not the lease expressly provides that the landlord must act reasonably in considering the tenant's application for consent, Section 19(1) of the Landlord and Tenant Act 1927 (1927 Act) contains a statutory implication that requires the landlord to act reasonably in considering an application for consent to assignment by a tenant. Exactly the same applies for underletting and again many leases provide that tenants can underlet the whole or, in some cases, even part of the demised premises with consent. The position regarding change of use is slightly different. It is governed by Section 19(3) of the 1927 Act, subsection 3 which contains no requirement for the landlord to act reasonably where a lease simply prohibits change of use without consent. The position regarding user can conveniently be divided up into three types of user clause:

1.1.1 An absolute user clause. This is where a lease absolutely prohibits any change of use;

1.1.2 A qualified absolute clause. This is where a change of use is permitted with landlord's consent and there is no express provision for such consent not to be unreasonably withheld. As mentioned above, there would be no statutory implication of this and, in these circumstances, Section 19(3) of the 1927 Act provides that the landlord can act unreasonably but may not demand a premium as a consideration for the grant of consent unless the change of use also involves carrying out structural alterations. If it does, there is no deemed provision stopping the landlord from demanding a premium. The 1927 Act does allow the landlord to require its costs to be paid; and

1.1.3   A qualified user clause. This is where the right to change is qualified by an obligation to seek landlord's consent and in circumstances where it is stated that the landlord cannot act unreasonably.

1.2   Section 19 allows a landlord to recover its legal costs and surveyors fees, so long as they are reasonable and incurred in connection with the application for consent. It is the Law of Property Act 1925, Section 144 that prevents the landlord demanding a premium for consenting to assignment or underletting. This section can, however, be excluded by agreement. It rarely is, but if it is the landlord can obtain a premium as consideration for granting consent.

1.3   For these reasons it is important to know when it is reasonable to approve an application for consent to assign and when it is reasonable to refuse.

Obviously this question is one that very often turns on individual facts since the question of reasonableness will depend on many factors relevant only to the circumstances of the case in question.

1.4   There have been many cases of reasonableness since the 1927 Act but there are two important new ingredients:

1.4.1   Before the Landlord and Tenant Act 1988 (the 1988 Act), if a tenant felt that his landlord was unreasonably withholding consent then there were only two courses of action open to him. Either he could seek a declaration from the court that consent was being unreasonably withheld, or take the law into his own hands by simply assuming that the refusal was unreasonable and, provided his assignee was prepared to do so, complete the transaction without obtaining landlord's consent. There was no statutory procedure before the 1988 Act for the dilatory landlord to be sued by his tenant for damages for unreasonably withholding consent. The 1988 Act fills this gap by providing a statutory duty by landlords to tenants in respect of licences to assign and licences to underlet and even consents for mortgaging or otherwise parting with possession of the premises. If a landlord acts unreasonably and breaches the statutory duties created by the 1988 Act then the landlord may well face an action for damages for breach of statutory duty. Also, the 1988 Act changes the burden of proof. This now falls squarely upon the shoulders of the landlord (i.e. the person who owes the duty): it is for the landlord to show whether consent is given within a reasonable time and/or whether any conditions imposed are reasonable. It is for the landlord to show whether it is reasonable for consent to be withheld. This reverses the traditional burden of proof. The 1988 Act does not deal with changes of use applications or indeed any other clause where a tenant is prohibited from doing something without his landlord's consent other than mortgaging or parting with possession.

1.4.2　The 1995 Act also impacts on the position regarding alienation. Firstly, as we saw in Chapter 1, the parties to a qualifying lease (effectively a new commercial lease) can set out agreed criteria for withholding consent. If the landlord and tenant both state it is reasonable to withhold consent in a given set of factual circumstances, then if those given set of circumstances apply, consent may be withheld and no court will intervene to say that the landlord is unreasonable in withholding consent. The documentation between the parties sets out the position and the court will not state that anything in the documentation which is specified as a valid reason for withholding consent is in fact unreasonable and invalid. Secondly, the background of decision making is now very different. Before the 1995 Act, when a landlord was considering an application for consent to an assignment he could do so in the knowledge that even if he was not absolutely and entirely satisfied with the covenant of the assignee he would retain the covenant of the original tenant (and probably all intervening tenants who will have contracted directly through licences to assign). Again, as we saw in Chapter 1, the 1995 Act changes all that for new leases and, subject to the possibility of obtaining an AGA from the outgoing tenant, the landlord will lose the covenants given by the outgoing tenant on assignment. At the very best the landlord will retain these until the next assignment at which stage he will lose the covenant of the assignor. It is very important for the landlord to bear this in mind in considering the application by the assignor for consent.

1.5　One further point that should be factored into the equation which has not yet been the subject of judicial intervention also arises from the 1995 Act. This Act allows the parties to specify criteria for withholding consent but, subject to that, the landlord's consent still cannot be unreasonably withheld. If specific criteria are not inserted, to what extent will their absence be held against the landlord in situations where the landlord is seeking to object?

Certainly if an assignor of a new lease seeks to assign that lease and the objection is grounded, say, merely on the fact that the proposed assignee is a private limited company, I suspect the court may well state that that is not a valid reason for withholding consent on its own. Had the landlord wanted to impose a condition prohibiting assignment to a private company, he could have done. That does not mean that any private limited company would automatically be a valid assignee. There may be very good reasons why the landlord would be reasonable in withholding consent to a specific proposed assignee but the landlord would have to prove this.

1.6   Time will tell how the courts look at cases where a landlord is accused of acting unreasonably in withholding consent in the new regime imposed by the 1995 Act.

1.7   For the 1988 Act to bite, a tenant must make a formal application in writing to the landlord for consent. This need not be in any particular form but if the tenant has merely telephoned his landlord asking for consent or perhaps even dealt with an agent (perhaps the landlord's surveyor or solicitor) where it is not clear that the agent is acting strictly as agent/attorney for the landlord, then the court may well feel that an application 'to the landlord' has not yet been made. In such an event the landlord's time for considering the request will not have started running. Although there is no specific time for giving consent, the 1988 Act requires the landlord to act reasonably (and this means with reasonable speed too) and a tenant and his advisers must make sure that they have done everything necessary under the 1988 Act in order to get time running. Similarly, once time is running a landlord must protect his position by responding quickly and in writing.

1.8   The 1988 Act is not the end of all problems for tenants but it does concentrate the landlord's mind. The days of landlords simply ignoring a tenant's request for consent have gone. It may even now be unreasonable for a landlord to refuse to deal with an application for licence to assign before his solicitors are in receipt of 'a solicitor's undertaking' to pay all costs whether or not the transaction proceeds to completion. Landlords do not want to face the consequences of paying their solicitors' costs, or even those of managing agents, if a licence to assign does not proceed. After all, it is the tenant who has instigated the procedure since it is he who wishes to assign his lease and it is only because of this that the landlord's professionals have had to undertake work. Why should the landlord have to pick up the costs of his lawyers and surveyors in these circumstances? In *Dong Bang Minerva (UK)* v *Davina Limited* (referred to in Chapter 1) the first instance judge said that one of the overheads of being a landlord may well be the obligation to deal with matters like this without cover for costs.

1.9 The Court of Appeal did not have to consider whether it was reasonable to ask for an undertaking at the outset because both parties before the Court of Appeal assumed that it *would* be reasonable so long as the undertaking sought for all 'reasonable' costs. Accordingly there is no judicial authority, but probably a landlord would be reasonably safe if he asks for an undertaking to pay reasonable costs before carrying out work. The downside is that, if this is wrong, the landlord might be in breach of the 1988 Act and face a damages claim. Caution must be the order of the day.

1.10 The 1988 Act does not deal with what is, and what is not, reasonable. The law prior to 1988 is still relevant. You should note however that Section 3 of the 1988 Act specifically provides that in certain cases it is reasonable to withhold approval. Section 3 deals with the obligations upon a superior landlord where the head lease prohibits the intermediate tenant from consenting to alienation by a subtenant without superior landlord's consent. The section imposes a duty on the superior landlord owed to the subtenant to act reasonably. Section 3(4) says that it is reasonable for the landlord not to give approval only in a case where, if he withheld approval and the tenant gave his consent the tenant would be in breach of covenant. Again, I should stress that although the pre-1988 cases are relevant there is a different background now that the 1995 Act has removed privity of contract for new leases.

1.11 Various principles were laid down in *International Drilling Fluids Limited* v *Louisville Investments (Uxbridge) Limited* **1986 1 AER 321**. The Court of Appeal set out seven principles to guide us in what is reasonable. Only six are now relevant; the seventh was that the onus in proving that consent had been unreasonably withheld was on the tenant. The 1988 Act now specifically provides that this onus is for the landlord to discharge. The six remaining principles of *International Drilling Fluids* can be summarized as follows:

1.11.1 The purpose of a covenant is to prevent the property being used in an undesirable way or by an undesirable tenant;

1.11.2 The relationship between the landlord and tenant is key and the landlord cannot refuse consent on grounds which have nothing to do with that;

1.11.3 The onus will be to show that the conclusions that led the landlord to justify its position were justified in the eyes of the reasonable man;

1.11.4 The landlord may disapprove of an assignee on grounds that he does not approve the purpose to which the assignee wishes to put the premises, even in cases where that purpose is not expressly forbidden by the lease;

1.11.5 The landlord normally needs to consider his own interests but there may be cases where the disproportion of benefit to the landlord and detriment to the tenant might make an otherwise reasonable withholding of consent unreasonable; and

1.11.6 In every case the facts and the circumstances of the case will prevail.

1.12 How long can the application take? We have all seen situations where applications for consent drag on for far too long. *Midland Bank PLC* v *Chart Enterprises Inc.* **1990 44 EG 68** found the court saying that a delay of just under three months in replying to an application for licence was unreasonable. However, probably the greatest lesson to learn from *Midland Bank* was not the delay in dealing with the application for landlord's licence, but the delay in bringing the matter to court. The original application for consent in that case was made on 15 February 1989. The case was heard on 28 February 1990! In most markets assignees will not wait around for the decision. By the time the matter comes to court they will have long gone and found other premises. It is partly for these reasons that the 1988 Act, with its introduction of liability in damages, was enacted.

1.13   In *Dong Bang Minerva* a much shorter delay led to an unreasonable withholding of consent claim being successful.

1.14   *Air India* v *Balabel* **1993 30 EG 90** and *CIN Properties* v *Gill* **1993 38 EG 152** make it clear that the basic test of reasonableness has not changed since the 1988 Act. The landlord must simply show that his conclusion was one to which a reasonable landlord might have come in the same circumstances. The landlord refused consent because the assignee was previously a director of a company which had failed to perform properly in another transaction. The court was satisfied that it was a basis for withholding consent and confirmed that the 1988 Act had not changed the basis upon which these matters were to be considered.

1.15   You will remember from Chapter 1, paragraph 6 that the provisions of Section 22 of the 1995 Act allow the parties to a new lease to set out the criteria which would be reasonable for withholding consent at any time prior to an application for consent. It might be important for the parties to bear this in mind since if they want to add these criteria after a lease is granted but before an application for licence is made they would have to sit down and agree them before the tenant were to make its application. Presumably this is not likely to be a big issue in practice since any such criteria would need to be agreed in any event on the basis that no party would have the contractual right to insist on inserting them. No doubt if the parties agreed to do so they could waive the requirement for the criteria to be agreed before the application by simply providing for a deed of variation to be completed after the application itself (although

Section 25 of the 1995 Act – the anti avoidance section – may prevent that). What is crystal clear however, is that the landlord cannot hold up the application for consent to assign a new lease on the basis that it wishes to agree such a set of criteria.

1.16 Just a further word about building leases. If they are new leases under the 1995 Act then they are subject to the same controls as any other qualifying lease. If they are old leases then if there is a qualified covenant against assignment or underletting, the provisions of Section 19(1)(b), 1927 Act only apply to dealings effected more than seven years before the term ends, although if there is provision for notice of the dealing to be given within six months, no consent will be required. A building lease is a lease of more than forty years made in consideration of erection, substantial improvement, addition or alteration of buildings. Section 19(1)(b) does not apply to leases granted by the government and local authorities and, of course, many building leases are granted by such entities.

2. CONSENT TO ASSIGNMENT AND PERSONAL COVENANTS

2.1 The Court of Appeal has made it clear that when determining the question of whether a refusal is reasonable, the particular covenant should be considered on its merits and the refusal should not necessarily be decided by construction of the lease as a whole.

2.2 In *Oil Property Investments Limited* v *Olympia and York (Canary Wharf) Limited* 1994 29 EG 121 the Court of Appeal had to consider an appeal by a tenant from a High Court decision upholding as reasonable a landlord's refusal to consent to an assignment.

2.3 Originally the lease had been granted to ICI Petroleum Limited. They were now called Enterprise Petroleum Limited (EPL). Back in 1987 the lease had been assigned to Olympia and York (Canary Wharf) Limited (O and Y) and following the administration of O and Y the administrator sought to assign the lease back to EPL.

Pausing there one would not have imagined any concern whatsoever. However, there were two factors here that made this case somewhat unusual:

2.3.1   The original annual rent was £360,000 and this had now risen to over £1 million. The lease had upward-only reviews and therefore the rent would never be less than that; and

2.3.2   The original lease gave the original tenant (and only the original tenant) a right to determine the lease at the tenth year of the term.

2.4   Accordingly, the court was asked to consider whether it was reasonable for the landlords to refuse consent for the assignment to EPL by the administrator of O and Y. EPL were of course the original tenant and the landlords were frightened that they would have the right to break whereas no other tenant would have such a right. This would therefore leave the landlords in the position of having a rental void of perhaps over a year and, no doubt, only the prospect of a much smaller rental once the property was let. There was evidence that EPL would, in fact, have wanted to exercise the option to determine.

2.5   The court dismissed the appeal, holding that the landlords would be severely damaged by the assignment, notwithstanding the fact that there was no objection to the covenant of EPL *per se*. An injunction against the assignment to EPL was continued until after the break date.

2.6   The case of **Max Factor Limited v Wesleyan Assurance Society 1995 41 EG 146** was a further High Court decision concerning personal covenants and alienation.

2.7   In this case Max Factor Limited were granted a lease with a mutual break and the break clause referred to the lessee as 'Max Factor Limited only'.
    The original tenant had assigned the lease and indeed the landlord's reversion had been assigned to the defendant Society. In 1993 Wesleyan Assurance Society consented to the assignment of the lease back to Max Factor Limited and in June of 1994 Max Factor sought to exercise the break.

Max Factor were contending that the break notice was valid and the Society responded that the break was no longer available since they had assigned, even though they had taken back the property as assignee.

2.8 Max Factor's application was dismissed and it was held that the right to determine was only vested in Max Factor whilst they had the lease vested in them as original tenant.

2.9 In the *Olympia and York* decision the court did not have to decide this question because it was agreed between all parties that the effect of the reassignment to the original tenant would have been to allow it to exercise the personal break: exactly what Max Factor were contending in this case. It has to be said, however, that the leading judgment in *Olympia and York* did question whether this agreed set of facts was correct and this questioning was quoted in the *Max Factor* judgment.

2.10 If *Max Factor* was decided correctly then there is an argument that *Olympia and York* was decided wrongly. *Olympia and York* is founded on the basis that it is reasonable to withhold consent in situations where the effect of the assignment would be to give the assignee a right that it does not have until the assignment is completed, whereas *Max Factor* says that where there is a personal right to break, that is lost upon assignment and would not be resurrected by the assignment itself. I think there are difficulties with the *Max Factor* judgment. If a break is given to Max Factor only, why should that break not be operable by Max Factor when they are again the tenant.

Perhaps some support for the *Max Factor* rationale can be taken from the 1995 Act to the extent that it deals with overriding leases. As we saw in Chapter 1, overriding leases will not include personal covenants. By analogy, therefore, if an original tenant had a right to break similar to that in the *Max Factor* case (i.e. personal to the original tenant) that break clause would not be repeated in an overriding lease. This is clearly the position under the 1995 Act and, therefore, perhaps this gives some credence to the decision in *Max Factor*.

I did say in Chapter 1, paragraph 9 that there may be nothing wrong with inserting a provision in a lease making it clear that, where a personal concession is negotiated, that would be repeated if the beneficiary of the personal concession were to take an overriding lease. Obviously there is no law on this either way but that is my view. It is of course possible that the *Max Factor* decision casts doubt on this on the basis that once the lease is assigned the personal covenant disappears. Obviously the *Max Factor* case was not concerned with an option which was expressed to be granted to Max Factor whilst they were original tenant or after an assignment back to them and clearly I cannot see any good reason why if wording of that nature was inserted, the break clause should not be operable whether or not there has been an intervening assignment. However, bearing in mind the *Max Factor* decision was based on the premise that once a lease ceases to be vested in the original tenant the right to break disappears with the original tenant and would not resurrect when the lease was reassigned back to the original tenant, one has to be wary of this.

3. CASES ON CONSENTS

3.1 As one might expect, cases in this area tend to turn on their specific facts. However, it is worth looking at one or two cases that have come before the courts in order to glean some general principles.

3.2 Landlords very often look at an application for licence to assign as an opportunity to assess the state of repair of the premises and, if the premises are in disrepair, try to persuade the tenant to carry out repairs as a quid pro quo for the landlord granting consent. The tenant needs the landlord to grant consent and the landlord seizes the opportunity by saying that it will grant consent so long as the tenant remedies its breach of the repair covenant. One can imagine that if this is all that a landlord needed to do, then it would be relatively easy for the landlord to use repair clauses as a ground to object. If one factors into this the case of *British Telecommunications PLC* v *Sun Life Assurance Society PLC* **1995 EGCS 139**, the position would be even worse for prospective assignors. In *British Telecom* the Court of Appeal said that where a party accepts an obligation to keep the building in repair, the liability imposed by that covenant is absolute and if the building is not in repair at all times the covenanting party is in breach of covenant.

3.3 So, if there is an obligation to keep premises in repair then it is almost certain that at the date of application for licence to assign the tenant would be in breach of some or indeed, perhaps, many of the repair obligations. Probably for that reason courts have leaned against construing a refusal on grounds that the premises are in disrepair as a reasonable refusal. In ***Beale* v *Worth, King* v *Worth* and *Reynolds* v *Worth* 1993 EGCS 135** there was a consolidated appeal to the Court of Appeal in connection with a residential building and an allegation that application for licence to assign was being unreasonably withheld.

3.4 In these cases the refusal to consent was made on the grounds of a continuing breach of relatively minor repair covenants and indeed the evidence before the courts substantiating the allegations of breach was largely unfounded.

3.5 The Court of Appeal reiterated that a continuing breach of a covenant to repair did not necessarily lead to a reasonable refusal of a licence to assign. Everything depended on the seriousness of the breach. In the absence of an extensive long-standing breach where the landlord could not be satisfied that the proposed assignee would remedy it, the refusal may well be unreasonable and certainly a mere dispute over a minor aspect of the repairing obligations would not suffice.

3.6 Following the 1995 Act, one of the clauses that one is increasingly seeing landlords put forward in new commercial leases as one of the specific criteria for opposing licence to assign says something along the lines that the landlord is entitled to object to an assignment 'if the tenant is in breach of its obligations'. Sometimes this is qualified to refer only to repairing obligations and sometimes landlords put forward, or tenants negotiate, a dilution of such a provision so that it refers to 'material' or 'substantial' breaches. There is no reason why specific criteria of this nature cannot be inserted in new qualifying leases but I would urge extreme caution before a tenant accepts such a condition. Even watered down, these covenants can prove an enormous hindrance to assignment and certainly if a tenant does accept such a provision and there is no dispute resolution process, just the very delays that are unquestionably going to be occasioned whilst the parties try to sort out any dispute as to whether the premises are in disrepair, may well be sufficiently long to have the effect of quashing the deal if the proposed assignee does not want to wait around whilst the dispute is resolved.

3.7   When considering proposed clauses of this nature tenants should bear in mind that without such a clause the courts are not likely to uphold as reasonable a refusal to consent on the grounds of breach of covenant unless the breach is substantial and I would therefore suggest that such clauses which look to the past history should not be accepted as sensible provisions governing the tenant's ability to assign. The landlord should be looking to the future and deciding whether the proposed assignee is able and likely to comply with the tenant's covenants; he should not be looking to punish a previously recalcitrant tenant by preventing him from assigning.

3.8   It is dangerous for a tenant to be prohibited from doing what it requires (either assigning or, in the case of break clauses, determining the lease) because of some past breach. Arguably, this is not what clauses regulating assignment and determination are all about. Assignment clauses are designed to ensure that the landlord has a measure of protection to prevent it from having foisted upon it a tenant that is not capable of paying the rent and observing the covenants, and break clauses are drafted to regulate the basis upon which the party having the right to break should exercise that break. They are not there as an alternative means of enforcing compliance with obligations.

3.9   In the *Worth* case the Court of Appeal also made it clear that so long as the conclusion to which the actual landlord came was reasonably reached in all of the circumstances, it was not necessary for the landlord to prove that the conclusions were justified on their own merits. One must look at the circumstances through the eyes of the reasonable man. This was of course the third of the propositions enunciated in *International Drilling Fluids* referred to in paragraph 1.11.3 of this chapter.

3.10   I have already looked at *Dong Bang Minerva UK Limited* v *Davina Limited* in Chapter 1. One of the issues of this case concerned whether the landlord could consent subject to pre-conditions. It was made clear in this case that a consent may be subject to pre-conditions such as the right to approve the form of underlease (as long as those conditions are themselves reasonable) and a landlord should not delay and/or withhold consent on the basis that it does not wish to consent other than subject to conditions. It should give consent conditionally.

3.11 A further recent case is that of ***Barclays Bank PLC v Daejan Investments (Grove Hall) Limited* 1995 18 EG 117**. This case concerned Section 19(3) of the Landlord and Tenant Act 1927 and consent for change of use. This section provides that, save in cases where a change of use involves any structural alterations to the premises, 'no fine or sum of money in the nature of a fine, whether by way of increase of rent or otherwise, shall be payable for, or in respect of, such licence or consent'.

3.12 Section 19(3) allows the landlord to require payment of a reasonable sum in compensation for damage to, or any diminution in value of, the reversion or adjoining premises owned by the landlord and its expenses.

3.13 The landlords were seeking a variation in the lease providing for five-yearly upward-only reviews, an increase in rent, full service charge provisions and an option to break paying compensation to the tenant of £132,000. The question for the court was whether these considerations taken together amounted to a 'fine' as consideration for granting consent to a change of use.

3.14 The court held that all of these were a 'fine', including the break clause. It was clear that the requirement of a break clause was a 'fine' since, although payment would not be required to be made by the tenant, existing authority indicated that the term 'fine' meant any consideration and the landlords would obviously only operate the break (paying compensation to the tenant) if they stood to benefit. The requirement therefore amounted to a 'fine'.

3.15 Notwithstanding the above, the tenant failed in its litigation because consent was being sought in relation to a transaction which involved structural alterations. The alterations in question were the enlarging of front windows and it was accepted that these works were structural. Accordingly, Section 19(3) did not apply in any event and the tenants could not go ahead with the change of use.

3.16 You should remember that Section 19(3) only applies to a qualified/absolute user clause. It does not apply if there is an absolute prohibition on change of use. Also note Section 19(3) is only concerned with user and does not apply if there are structural alterations involved. There is no implied obligation in user clauses for the landlord to act reasonably: hence the status of a qualified/absolute clause – something not known in the field of alienation.

3.17 If a clause in a lease provides that change of use is not allowed without the landlord's consent, we have seen that there is no implication that the landlord must act reasonably; this is of course different to alienation and as I have said user clauses are not within the 1988 Act. This Act applies only to covenants against the assignment, subletting, charging or parting with possession. Accordingly, although a landlord cannot require payment of a fine or other consideration for grant of consent where it is provided that consent is required for a change of use and it is not specifically provided that the landlord must act reasonably – a qualified absolute clause – the landlord would be able to simply say no.

3.18 In the case of *Kened Limited and Another* v *Connie Investments Limited* **1995 NPC 84** the Court of Appeal had to look at a situation where the landlord was refusing an application for the release of sureties in circumstances where there was a right to do so if a reasonably acceptable alternative could be found. The refusal was held to be unreasonable. The alternative surety was registered in Luxembourg and the landlord's argument was founded in the main on this fact and the consequences flowing from it, primarily the difficulties in enforcing the surety covenants. This held little sway with the court. The court felt that mere enforcement of a judgment in Luxembourg was not a problem. This was possible without much difficulty and the need to do this was not sufficient to allow a landlord to refuse consent. Previous complications in registering a judgment abroad and then endeavouring to enforce it abroad would normally have been thought to have been justifiable for most landlords refusing consent, perhaps not so with members of the European Union.

3.19   Obtaining the landlord's consent to an underletting is important and tenants ignore any obligation to obtain consent at their peril. Although self-help (i.e. granting the underlease without consent) is something tenants sometimes resort to when the landlord is being difficult in delaying or withholding consent, this is a dangerous option.

3.20   *Fenston* v *Chestermark PLC*, an unreported case to the best of my knowledge, concerned an application for consent to sublet a shop in Oxford Street for the last three months of the lease. The landlords indicated an intention to consent but at the last moment the tenant asked that the sublease be granted to an associated company of the proposed subtenant. The landlords wanted time to think about this and, during that time, the proposed undertenant simply moved in. The shop traded in a market style and many complaints were received as a result of the loudspeaker system used to sell goods in an auction-type environment. The landlords obtained an injunction ordering the occupier to vacate and even though about one month had elapsed between the occupier taking occupation and the date that application for the injunction was sought, the judge did not think this was too long. The landlords were entitled to have time to investigate complaints before seeking injunctive relief. This case is a reminder of the dangers of taking the law into one's own hands.

3.21   Three further cases were considered and reported in October 1996 and it is worth mentioning each of those here. Firstly, in *Straudley Investments Limited* v *Mount Eden Land Limited* **1996 EGCS 153** the Court of Appeal was faced with a situation where the landlord was seeking to impose a condition in a licence to sublet that the rent deposit that was to be paid by the proposed subtenant be paid into an account held jointly by the landlord and the tenant.

The property demised by the lease in question allowed the tenant to sublet part and for the landlord to receive 12.5% of the rents received. The tenant had obligations to use its best endeavours to underlet at the best market rent and there were various obligations to comply with the accounting procedures.

3.22 The landlord was therefore very concerned to ensure that the tenant maximized its receipts as the landlord gained directly from this.

3.23 In the case in question, the landlord was concerned at the covenant status of the proposed subtenant and the landlord had also been concerned at the way in which its tenant had previously accounted for rent received under earlier sublettings. It was for that reason that the landlord suggested a condition that the rent deposit account be held in joint names. The tenant did not want that condition and alleged a breach of duty under the 1988 Act. The landlord's appeal was dismissed. The *International Drilling Fluids* guidelines (see paragraph 1.11) were considered and the court felt that a condition could not be reasonable if it related to matters foreign to the lease itself. The condition the landlords were seeking here fell into that category and it was effectively an attempt to seek a collateral advantage above the safeguards and security which were already available to the landlord, for example the ability to intercept rent payable under the lease, under the Law of Distress Amendment Act 1908. It was made clear by the Court of Appeal that although most reported cases on consents, including *International Drilling Fluids* itself, related to assignments, the guidelines were applicable *mutatis mutandis* to intended sublettings. The Court of Appeal wanted to add to those guidelines, firstly that it would normally be reasonable to refuse consent if the refusal is necessary to prevent the tenant from acting to the prejudice of the landlord's existing rights and secondly that it would normally be unreasonable to impose a condition which would increase or enhance the control which the landlord was entitled to exercise under the terms of the lease. Clearly landlords must look carefully at alienation clauses where the head lease rent is geared to receipts achieved by the head tenant; it is fundamentally important that the clause gives the landlord the protection it requires since it seems clear from *Straudley* that the court will not confer upon a landlord some additional security not contemplated by the lease.

3.24   *Blockbuster Entertainment Limited* v *Leakcliff Properties Limited* **1996 EGCS 151** was a High Court decision, again concerning licence to sublet and again reported in October 1996. The *Blockbuster* case concerned a freestanding unit in Watford which had been let in 1994 at a rent of £115,000 per annum subject to five-yearly upward-only reviews. It was a pyramid structure and quite difficult to compare with other premises.

Underletting was prohibited without landlord's consent and, again, consent could not be unreasonably withheld. There was a condition (as is quite often the case) that permitted under-leases should be at market rent and the lease allowed the land-lord to approve the market rent before the subletting.

The proposal was to grant an underletting at £75,000 per annum, some £40,000 per annum less than the rent Blockbuster would have to continue paying. The landlords refused consent notwithstanding, of course, that Blockbuster's obligations to pay such rent would continue in any event. They alleged that this would detrimentally affect the value of their reversionary interest and they did not think the rent of £75,000 per annum was the market rent. In making the application for unreason-able withholding of consent Blockbuster contended that the premises had been exposed to the market and a number of bids had been received including one at the same rental level as that made by the proposed subtenant, but for a purpose not per-mitted under the lease. The landlords were contending that even if £75,000 per annum was the open market rent, they were still entitled to withhold consent if, at the time consent was withheld, they reasonably believed the sum was not the open market rental value. I am not sure that it is terribly surprising that the High Court felt the landlords had unreasonably with-held consent. Clearly the best evidence of what a property is worth is the level of bids received in the open market. Evidence was quite clear in this case that the proposed rent was in a band of values comprising the open market rental value and the court gave short shrift to the landlord's argument that they were still entitled to object to the subletting on grounds that they believed the rent was not reasonable. On the construction of this particular lease, once Blockbuster had established that the rent was the open market rental value the landlords could no longer object merely on the basis that they reasonably believed that it was not. It was certainly not reasonable for the landlord to require the tenant to wait for the market to improve.

3.25 Mount Eden were involved in another case on consents at the back-end of 1996. The case of *Prudential Assurance Company Limited* v *Mount Eden Land Limited* **1996 EGCS 179** is potentially quite scary. The case concerned a 999-year lease of some premises in Oxford Street, London. The premises were let to the Prudential and the tenant was required to obtain landlord's consent before doing certain alterations.

Section 19 of the 1927 Act also deals with alterations. If the alterations covenant prohibits improvement to premises without consent, there is an implied obligation upon the landlord to act reasonably. Note that this requirement is only for improvements. If an alteration is not an improvement it is not covered by Section 19(2). The Section permits the landlord to collect its reasonable fees and, indeed, payment of a reasonable sum to compensate it for diminution on value of its premises. Also, if there is no addition to the letting value of the premises by virtue of the improvement then if it is reasonable to do so, the landlord can request an undertaking for reinstatement.

Plans were submitted and the tenants wrote to the landlords in January 1993 seeking licence to alter. The works in question were major works of replacement of the concrete cladding.

The landlords (who were Mount Eden's predecessors) arranged for their managing agents to write back in May 1993 confirming consent subject to formal licence being entered into by the Prudential. That letter was headed 'Subject to Licence'. The managing agents went on to say that if the tenants were to accept the position, they would arrange for the landlord's solicitors to prepare a licence. In September the Prudential confirmed that they had instructed their solicitors.

After that, it all went wrong. The landlords sold their reversion to Mount Eden and the question before the court was whether the managing agents' letter of May 1993 was a written consent for the purpose of the lease. The Court of Appeal upheld the judge's view that it was.

First of all the Court of Appeal said that just because a letter was conditional upon legal formalities being finalized this did not prevent the letter from operating as a consent within the meaning of the lease. That was disregarding the heading to the letter which was 'Subject to Licence'. One then had to look at whether merely heading a letter 'Subject to Licence' or 'Subject to Consent' was sufficient to negative any legal effect of such a letter and it was held that it was not.

In the case of *Venetian Glass Gallery Limited* v *Next Properties Limited* **1989 30 EG 92** the High Court looked at the phrase 'Subject to Contract' and its effect. The court felt that there was a distinction between using that expression in circumstances where two parties were strangers and in circumstances where there was a pre-existing legal relationship but the wording was used in relation to an act by one of the parties to that relationship.

Venetian Glass made it clear that where there are two parties who are strangers, 'Subject to Contract' would wipe out any legal effect. This is exactly what one comes across in cases where a vendor and a purchaser agree to do a deal 'Subject to Contract'. Until the contract is entered into there is no legal relationship.

However, where the parties are already in a legal relationship the heading would have to be read together with the text in order to discover the true intention of the writer and the Court of Appeal felt that this case was one where the only way in which one could reconcile the heading and the remainder of the letter was to find that the landlords had given conditional consent. Since the lease made it clear that any consent could be 'temporary or permanent, revocable or irrevocable or otherwise howsoever framed or qualified by the lessor', the letter fell within that category and comprised a conditional consent. The moral of the story is very clear and very worrying. Quite often one sees situations where tenants apply for consent and landlords believe that they have done all they need to do by simply stating in correspondence that it is 'Subject to Contract' or 'Subject to Licence'. It is clear that this may do no more than defer the obligation to give consent until satisfaction of the relevant condition. They are not magic words which will necessarily take away the legal effect of a letter.

If one truly wishes to ensure that no consent is given until the ink is dry on the formal licence to alter, and if one wishes to preserve the right to change one's mind as to whether consent will be granted until such time, then very clear language indeed will be required. This case concerns licence to alter but I would have thought the same principles would apply to any form of licence, whether it was a consent for assignment, use, alteration or anything else permitted in a lease so long as the appropriate consent had been obtained.

Surveyors acting for landlords must make sure that they do not unwittingly commit the landlord to the grant of consent when the licence is finalized – and do not forget that the *Prudential* case concerned a letter by the landlord's managing agents, not the landlords themselves.

3.26 Part I of the 1927 Act allows the tenant to carry out improvements and obtain compensation for them at the end of the term of the lease. This applies regardless of any prohibition in the lease. However, in order to obtain the benefits of this, the tenant must go through correct procedures both before carrying out the improvements, and also when seeking compensation. Where you are advising tenants who might be wishing to carry out alterations you should bead in mind Part I of the 1927 Act.

3.26.1 Leases frequently contain quite stringent restrictions on alteration, but at the same time impose obligations upon tenants to comply with all legislation affecting the subject premises. This can leave the tenant in the rather invidious position of being in breach of covenant and not being able to do very much about it. I would normally advocate a specific provision empowering a tenant to carry out any alterations which are required in order to enable the tenant to comply with its statutory obligations. Landlords sometimes resist this and perhaps it is not surprising that legislation also assists. There are provisions in the Fire Precautions Act 1971, Health and Safety at Work etc. Act 1974 and the Environmental Protection Act 1990 which water down the landlord's discretion to refuse consent to alterations and indeed in certain cases, compel the landlord to grant consent. There is also provision in the Disability Discrimination Act 1995 ensuring that the landlord cannot unreasonably withhold consent to alterations which are necessary in order to enable a tenant to comply with new duties imposed by that Act.

3.26.2 So if you are asked to advise in connection with alterations, it is necessary to look not only at the relevant lease, but also certain legislation.

3.27 *Hemingway Securities Limited* v *Dunraven Limited* **1995 9EG 322** was the first case to take the lead in formulating the law allowing a tenant to seek an injunction requiring a subtenant to surrender a sublease which had been created without consent. Previously it had been thought that the landlord was powerless unless he was prepared to forfeit the lease.

Hemingway is an exception to the general rule which normally prevents an injunction being granted for breach of an alienation clause. The tenant and the subtenant were both associated companies and therefore it was that much easier for the court to be persuaded to grant injunctive relief to the landlord; whether this would be quite so easy for an arm's-length sub-letting is not quite so certain, but I cannot see any compelling reason not to do so where the tenant and subtenant are both aware of the breach of covenant – which they almost certainly both would be whether or not they are related companies.

4. BACK-UP SECURITY

4.1 Before leaving the question of assignment, a few words about additional security where a proposed assignee may not be of sufficient covenant strength itself but might satisfy any concerns of the landlord if it produces a surety/bank guarantee/rent deposit deed or some other form of additional back-up security.

4.2 It is clear law that if a landlord is reasonable in refusing to consent to an assignment, that consent does not become unreasonable merely because the tenant produces a surety to guarantee the obligations of the tenant. For example, a landlord cannot be forced to take a newly incorporated insubstantial company with a share capital of £100 backed up by a substantial parent company guarantee. *Geland Manufacturing Company* v *Levy Estates* **1962 181 EG 209** and *Warren* v *Marketing Exchange for Africa Limited* **1988 2 EGLR 247** make this clear, although it might come as something of a surprise to many surveyors.

4.3 The position relating to guarantees is even more important in relation to assignments of new leases now that the 1995 Act is with us. Do not forget that Section 16 provides that only a tenant can be asked to give an AGA. A surety cannot be required to enter into an AGA and therefore, if a tenant assigns to a worthless covenant backed up by a substantial surety, then when that worthless covenant comes to assign the landlord will not be able to ask the person or company who was its surety to enter into an AGA. At that stage, the landlord will have lost the covenant of the surety (subject to the arguments which I have referred to in Chapter 1, above, as to whether the guarantee covenant itself can be made to last for such time as the worthless tenant is itself liable under an AGA.

4.4 For these reasons and also on the strength of *Geland* and *Warren*, landlords may well insist on sureties entering into licences to assign not as sureties but as additional assignees. This resolves these problems at a stroke.

4.5 There are, of course, many other forms of security that landlords often insist upon and tenants frequently grant as a way of supporting the covenant of prospective assignees. One of these is rent deposits.

5. RENT DEPOSITS

5.1 Rent deposits are a tried-and-tested method of securing the tenant's obligations. The assignee backs up the covenant that it gives to the landlord by depositing a sum of money in a bank account as additional security. This 'rent deposit' is then available to be used by the landlord if the assignee fails to pay the rent or observe the covenants or, even worse, becomes insolvent, requiring the landlord to re-let the premises.

5.2 Rent deposits are normally governed by a rent deposit deed and it is normal practice to provide for the tenant to top up the deposit if for some reason the landlord has been forced to take money out of the account following a breach of covenant by the tenant. For example, if the tenant deposits, say, three months' rent with the landlord and then fails to pay the next quarter's rent, one would expect the landlord to be entitled to take that quarter's rent out of the rent deposit and the rent deposit deed would normally provide, in circumstances such as this, that the tenant be obliged to deposit a further three months' rent with the landlord.

5.3   There was one relatively recent case, *Jaskel v Sophie Nursery Products Limited* **1993 EGCS 42**, which concerned this type of situation. The guarantor in *Jaskel* guaranteed the lease but did not give a guarantee of the tenant's obligation to top up the rent deposit. They had signed the rent deposit deed but, unusually, had not given any covenants in it and the Court of Appeal had no difficulty in holding that since there was no separate obligation by the guarantors in the rent deposit deed, they were not liable to top up the rent deposit and the landlord's argument that the documents comprising the lease and the rent deposit deed should be read together, was wrong. Landlords must make absolutely sure that if there is to be a rent deposit deed, and if there is also to be a guarantor, then the guarantor should give covenants sufficient to enable the landlord to enforce compliance with the deed by the guarantor. Quite frankly, this is relatively straightforward and one would expect that wherever a landlord was relying on a guarantor's covenant, the guarantor should guarantee all of the obligations of the tenant.

5.4   It is very important for landlords to ensure that rent deposits give them adequate security if the tenant becomes insolvent and there is a void between a disclaimer and a new letting. Where a corporate tenant goes into liquidation, the liquidator can disclaim the lease as onerous property. He does not need the approval of the tenant: he will merely disclaim and bring the lease obligations to an end. The position is much the same for a trustee in bankruptcy appointed following the insolvency of an individual tenant. The problem for landlords is that, technically speaking, once the lease has been disclaimed, no further 'rent' will become payable. Rent deposit deeds should cover this by allowing the deposited sum to be retained by the landlord in these circumstances. It is not terribly difficult to do this, so long as one makes it clear that the deposit is not just for non-payment of rent but for any breach of covenant and rent deposit deeds are often quite comprehensive in order to deal with this. Clearly the full circumstances in which recourse may be made to any rent deposit must be thought through very carefully.

5.5   The landlords simply must protect their position. They must make sure that if a tenant company goes into liquidation and the liquidator disclaims the lease, they can get their hands on payment of rent that would have fallen due following the disclaimer. For example, if there is a disclaimer on, say, 24 December and the September quarter's rent had been paid, then at that stage no further rent would become due. The December quarter's rent due only the following day is not due at the date of disclaimer and the landlord might then be faced with the unenviable prospect of not being able to get its hands on the December quarter's rent simply because technically there are no 'rent arrears'. In these circumstances the tenant would not have been in breach of its obligations to pay rent before the disclaimer.

5.6 If the rent deposit deed provides for money to remain in the ownership of the tenant (and this is unquestionably the norm) it is essential that the rent deposit is charged to the landlord. If the tenant is a company, that charge must be registered at Companies House within three weeks of the rent deposit deed if it is to be enforceable against a liquidator of the tenant.

5.7 Rent deposits are normally required from tenants whose covenant is still maturing and does not stand on its own. Tenants frequently want to ensure that there is a mechanism for the release of the deposit when their covenant has matured. They do not want a sum of money to remain on deposit with the landlord for ever but want the money back so that it can work for the tenant. Most rent deposit arrangements therefore provide for a return of the deposit at some stage, either on a lawful assignment or perhaps once the tenant passes some financial test showing that its covenant strength has improved. Where a rent deposit is repayable on assignment (and this is nearly always the case) the landlord must ensure that he is adequately able to vet the covenant being provided by the assignee. Leaving aside any specific criteria that might be imposed to cover this in a new lease, it is something for the landlord to consider when it is asked to consent to disposal of a lease to an assignee. That assignee may be a reasonable covenant if it is simply a question of comparing the assignee's covenant with the assignor's covenant. If in addition the assignment will give rise to a requirement by the landlord to repay the assignor the rent deposit, the landlord may want more from the assignee (for example, the landlord may ask the assignee to put up a deposit). The landlord must look at the covenant that it is giving up and compare it with the covenant that it is gaining. It must look at both packages and clearly one of the things to take into account may well be the fact that on assignment a landlord is giving up an existing rent deposit. Clearly, however, the landlord must always act reasonably and promptly if it is to avoid problems under the 1988 Act.

5.8   Assuming a rent deposit is to be repaid to a tenant once they pass a profit test of some sort or on assignment, tenants must make certain that there is a clear obligation to refund the balance of the rent deposit. They must make certain that the obligation binds not only the landlord but also successors in title. In 1987 the case of *Hua Chiao Commercial Bank Limited v Chiaphua Industries Limited* **1987 AC 99** had to consider a situation where an assignee of a reversion had not acknowledged the terms upon which a rent deposit was held following a transfer of the reversionary interest. The case makes it clear that a tenant must insist that arrangements surrounding rent deposits clearly provide for the funds to be transferred on a disposal of the reversion.

5.9   Rent deposits invariably provide for the tenant to receive interest. This is perfectly reasonable. The deposit is taken out of the tenant's cash flow as a way of providing security to the landlord and although the money is not there to work for the tenant, at least the tenant should be entitled to receive the interest earned on it. After all, the money does belong to the tenant. I should stress that it is important that the money continues to belong to him. This is a fundamentally important point. Under no circumstances should the ownership of the money pass to the landlord since this would leave the tenant with no control if the landlord were to become insolvent.

5.10   Negotiation of the rent deposit deed is important and many points need to be carefully thought through including:

5.10.1   Should the rent deposit deed apply to an increase in the deposit if there is an increase in rent on review?

5.10.2   What should happen if the rent is exempt on the date the rent deposit deed is granted, but subsequently there is an election?

In those circumstances, should the landlord have the ability to increase the deposit?

5.10.3 Should there be an increase of the deposit if it is a deposit of rent plus VAT and then there is a change in the VAT rate?

5.10.4 Who has the right to withdraw from the deposit and upon what basis?

5.10.5 What if the tenant's usual place of abode is outside the UK? In those circumstances, if interest is being paid to the tenant, the landlord may be required to deduct basic rate tax at source.

5.11 If the landlord wants an alternative form of security then it may ask the tenant to provide a guarantee by the tenant's bank. These have the significant advantage to landlords in that once the form of bank guarantee is agreed, the procedure for recovering the money from the bank may be simpler than recovering moneys under a rent deposit deed. Tenants also often find this proves to be an attractive alternative to a rent

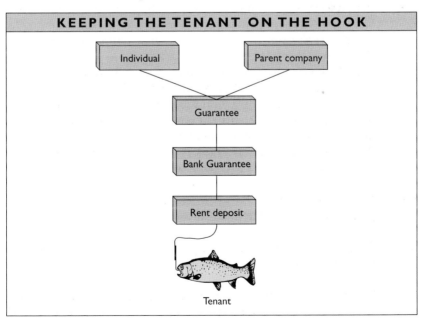

KEEPING THE TENANT ON THE HOOK

Individual

Parent company

Guarantee

Bank Guarantee

Rent deposit

Tenant

deposit deed, since they can sometimes persuade their bankers to put up a bank guarantee of, say, six months' rent without having to freeze six months' rent in an account. The bank may be prepared to put up the guarantee on payment of a fee and the advantages of this are obvious in that the tenant's cash flow is not so severely affected.

5.12   It is very important to keep the tenant on the hook (see the diagram on the previous page).

6.   ALIENATION AND UPWARD-ONLY REVIEWS

6.1   Tenants should beware of alienation clauses that prohibit subletting at less than the higher of passing rent and market rent. If such a clause prevents the tenant from giving a reverse premium to its assignee there may be problems for a tenant. Rents will be kept at an artificially high level and the tenant will be prevented from assigning.

6.2   In this example the rent that the landlord will be entitled to receive from the tenant is £100,000 per annum but if rents have fallen so that the market rent is only £50,000 per annum the tenant would only be able to obtain a rental of £50,000 per

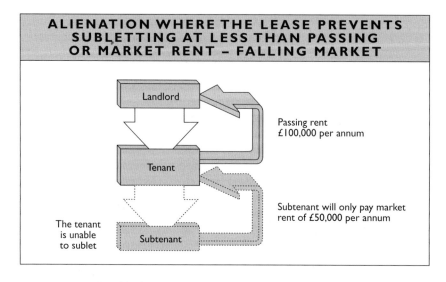

ALIENATION WHERE THE LEASE PREVENTS SUBLETTING AT LESS THAN PASSING OR MARKET RENT – FALLING MARKET

Landlord

Passing rent
£100,000 per annum

Tenant

Subtenant will only pay market
rent of £50,000 per annum

The tenant
is unable
to sublet

Subtenant

annum in the market-place. If the alienation clause in the head lease prevents subletting at less than the higher of passing or market rent and prevents the tenant from granting its subtenant a reverse premium, then effectively the tenant will not be able to assign. Clearly there will be little market for a subtenant to pay a rent of £100,000 per annum where this is double the market rent and the subtenant cannot obtain a reverse premium from its landlord. Tenants must be very careful not to accept provisions of this nature since clearly they do hamper their ability to dispose of their premises. For the same reason it is not terribly intelligent for landlords to insist on such a provision since this may well reduce the rent it can obtain on review; the tenant will argue that it is effectively prohibited from disposing of its premises in a falling market.

6.3 The position still needs to be addressed in a rising market.

In this situation the tenant wanting to sublet and being bound by a provision requiring settlings to be at the higher of passing or market rent will only be able to sublet at £100,000 per annum. This removes from the tenant its ability to sublet at passing rent and take any increased value in the premises by way of premium from its subtenant. Certainly in circumstances where a tenant wants to sublet rather than assign, perhaps keep an eye on its privity of contract liabilities, it may well want to

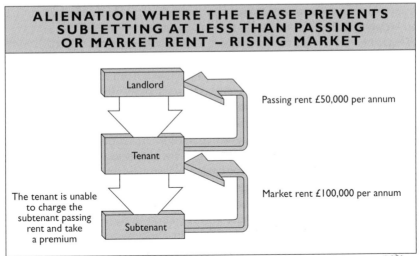

ALIENATION WHERE THE LEASE PREVENTS SUBLETTING AT LESS THAN PASSING OR MARKET RENT – RISING MARKET

Landlord

Tenant

Subtenant

Passing rent £50,000 per annum

Market rent £100,000 per annum

The tenant is unable to charge the subtenant passing rent and take a premium

LIVERPOOL
JOHN MOORES UNIVERSITY
AVRIL ROBARTS LRC
TEL. 0151 231 4022

take a premium from its subtenant and clauses of this nature may prevent it from doing so.

6.4   From the landlord's perspective, I think all that it should really be trying to prevent is subletting by a tenant at below market rent. It seems to me that there is no good reason why a tenant should be prohibited from subletting at market rent, even if this is less than the passing rent payable. True, there is the possibility that the intermediate tenant could go bust, leaving the landlord with the need to forfeit. In those circumstances the landlords might argue that they are prejudiced if the sublease is at a rental less than the passing rent under the head lease. I do not believe that this is the case since the sublease would disappear following forfeiture and, although the subtenant would have the right to apply for relief from forfeiture, it is unlikely that it would do so in circumstances where it would have to pay a higher rent than that which it would be obliged to pay in the market-place. In such circumstances the subtenant is likely to allow the sublease to be forfeit and then seek to renegotiate in an open market situation or move to alternative premises. There may be reasons why a subtenant would not do this, particularly, for example if the location was vital to its business but, by and large, I cannot see any good reason why a landlord should be entitled to insist upon sublease rents being at the higher of passing and market rent and there is of course the danger referred to above that this could prejudice the landlord on review.

6.5   It is important to remember that sublessees do not have an obligation to apply for relief from forfeiture and if a landlord seeks to forfeit the head lease the sublease will disappear unless the subtenant does make an application. Landlords must consider this before forfeiting head leases and in circumstances where a landlord is granting a right to a tenant to sublet, it might want to insist on the subtenant applying for relief from forfeiture in circumstances where the head lease becomes forfeit. Subtenants are unlikely to accept such a provision and again I suspect it would be unreasonable to demand this as a condition of consenting to an underletting unless the head lease alienation clause provided for its possibility. Clearly, however, where leases are being granted with the expectation that the head lessee will sublet and perhaps share in the sublease income with the head landlord, this is something that should be thought about at the time the head lease is granted and licences to sublet are issued. If the subtenant is not obliged to apply for a lease from forfeiture then a forfeiture of the head lease will cause subleases to disappear. The point needs to be addressed, particularly, by banks lending money on security of leasehold property investments. If the tenant investor cannot guarantee the continuance of subleases this may be a problem for its mortgagee. Imagine a situation, for example, where a head tenant has granted leases of five shops each at £100,000 per annum and raised finance in order to purchase that investment, secured on those leases. If rental values were to drop and the head tenant/borrower were to default in its head lease obligations, the head lease would be forfeit and it is quite possible that some or all of the subtenants would not seek relief from forfeiture. There would be little reason for them to do so, since by seeking relief they would have to pay a rent higher than the market rent. In such circumstances the security offered by the borrower to the lender would unquestionably be impaired and it is in circumstances such as this where the lender might insist upon a sublease containing contractual obligations by the subtenant to apply for relief from forfeiture if the head lease is forfeit. For these reasons, thought must be given to this type of provision in an alienation clause, particularly on leasehold investment purchases.

7.   CONCLUSION

7.1   Deciding what security to take is a very important process. It is important that it is sufficient to give the landlord the protection that it needs to underpin the covenant status of the tenant. It is also important in that it will help to act as a benchmark for what will be reasonable to seek when the tenant seeks to assign its lease. The fact that new leases do not confer privity does not diminish the importance of this task.

CHAPTER 4

BREAK CLAUSES

I.   GENERAL PRINCIPLES

I.I   Break clauses have become much more important in the recent
past. It has become fashionable in many property sectors for
tenants to require an option to determine their lease at some
stage before the contractual term is due to expire. This gives
added flexibility to tenants. Rather than take a short lease and
rely on rights to renew (which of course a landlord may oppose)
a tenant has the security of knowing it can stay in premises for
a lengthy period of time but, if it requires, walk away.
     A reasonably long lease containing a tenant's break is also
seen by landlords as better than a short lease. There is the perceived security of rental income over a longer period, albeit
subject to the possibility that the tenant might break early.
     Landlords have often taken the view that having spent a con-
siderable amount of money on its premises and in fitting them
out and perhaps having built up significant goodwill in the
premises, the tenant is relatively unlikely to want to break early.
Therefore landlords tend to be happier to grant a longer lease
with a break rather than simply grant a short lease and hope
that the tenant renews.

I.2   Landlords' break clauses are a different kettle of fish. There may
be any number of reasons why a landlord grants a lease with
the right to determine early. He may wish to redevelop the
premises, take the premises back for his own use or perhaps
simply re-assess what is to be done with the premises at some
time in the future. For example, in the early 1990s when the
office market was right back on its heels, landlords were
extremely keen to grant leases to tenants on almost any terms
imaginable, if only to have some rental income as a way of
funding mortgage debt. Lettings also help to defray the expense
of holding premises. If a property is let then the landlord can
pass on to the tenant the rates liabilities and the obligations to

122

maintain and repair. However, in these circumstances where perhaps the landlord's main objective is to have someone in occupation to cover the overheads, landlords very often let premises to tenants whose covenant would not otherwise be acceptable and at rents far below the desired level.

Even with the benefit of upward-only reviews, it is often a significant help to landlords to be able to determine a lease at some stage before the expiry of the contractual term and re-evaluate the situation. By then the market may have recovered, rents may have gone up considerably and the landlord may be in a position to replace a tenant who had been brought in as a quick-fix-it expedient with a more substantial covenant.

1.3   Tenant's break clauses are also attractive to lure tenants to take space in situations where there is little confidence in the market-place. In the early 1990s for the first time in many years, most sectors saw rentals dropping. Tenants were happy to commit to new premises on the basis that the rental was less than they might previously have been paying, but they remained nervous that the market had not yet bottomed out. They wanted the ability to walk away in a few years time if they were proved to be right and rentals were to drop even more.

1.4   Also, in the retail and leisure sectors, location is absolutely vital and again as shopping trends and leisure requirements change, it is not unusual for retail and leisure accommodation that was once in the best pitch to cease to be so. The high street best pitches may have moved as a result of a new in-town development, or it may well be the high street itself has fallen away completely as a result of some out-of-town development. In such a situation it is extremely helpful for tenants to have the right to determine their lease early and re-locate to the best pitch then available. Retailers will tell you time and time again, that the three prime ingredients that make up a good property, and all that really matters, is location, location and location.

1.5   There are many other business needs that drive the desire for one party or the other to negotiate a break. In July 1994 the Property Managers Association (PMA) carried out a survey amongst its members in relation to lease renewals. The survey showed that many lease renewals were negotiated with break clauses. Of the returns made to the PMA, which it has to be said were quite low, 46% of ten-year leases, 44% of fifteen-year leases, 57% of twenty or twenty-one-year leases and 30% of twenty-five-year leases had break clauses varying in each case between three, five and ten years.

2. BREAK CLAUSES AND THE 1954 ACT

2.1 It is very important to remember that there is a relationship between a break clause and the 1954 Act. Under the 1954 Act leases that are protected by it do not come to an end before they are determined in accordance with Part II of that Act.

2.2 Accordingly, where a break clause exists in a lease which is protected under the 1954 Act, the tenancy will not come to an end until it is terminated in accordance with the relevant provisions of the 1954 Act.

2.3 The effect of this is that if a landlord has a break clause and the lease is protected, then in order to exercise the break the landlord must serve a Section 25 notice on the tenant. For the tenant to determine such a tenancy, it has always been thought necessary for the tenant to serve notice under Section 27. I do not think that the requirement for a Section 27 notice is altered by the recent case of *Esselte AB and Another* v *Pearl Assurance* **1995 37 EG 173** which we consider in paragraph 2 of Chapter 6. This is not clear, however, and a court might hold that a tenant serving a contractual break needs merely to vacate the premises in order to prevent the 1954 Act from applying to the premises. In those circumstances a Section 27 notice would not need to be served. However, I think the better view is that a tenant should serve a Section 27 notice in order to avoid any argument that the contractual break clause has no effect on the tenancy which would then simply continue under the 1954 Act.

There is a further recent court decision illustrating that the tenancy continues under the 1954 Act after a landlord has served its break: *Willison* v *Cheverell Estates Limited* **1996 26 EG 133** which is also mentioned in paragraph 6.7 of Chapter 2. The landlord served its contractual break but the tenancy continued under the 1954 Act.

2.4 So, where a landlord is negotiating a break clause entitling it to possession if it requires the premises back for its own use or for redevelopment or some other purpose, it will have to prove the equivalent ground in Section 30(1) of the 1954 Act. For a landlord to simply give itself the right to determine if it wishes to develop or rebuild, the landlord will find that it not only has to satisfy the tenant that it has complied with the provisions of the contractual break clause, but also that it has proved the necessary grounds in the 1954 Act. It will need to convince a judge that the tenant should not be given a new lease on an application to the court made by the tenant under the 1954 Act following exercise of the break by the landlord. Remember the break will operate to end the contractual term and the tenant would be able to apply for a new tenancy; the landlord would have to object to the grant of that tenancy. If a landlord gives itself the right to determine 'in the event that the landlord shall wish to develop or reconstruct the building of which the premises form part', the landlord's opinion that the premises are ripe for redevelopment will not, on its own, be sufficient that the premises *are* ripe for development. The landlord will also have to prove that at the date of the hearing under the 1954 Act, it had the requisite intention, funding, planning, etc. and generally the wherewithal to carry out the development. It is therefore unquestionably advisable for the landlord to try and persuade the tenant to agree to a lease containing such a break clause being excluded from the 1954 Act. If this is done the landlord will have to do no more than satisfy the terms of the contractual break and that may be nothing more than writing to the tenant stating that it intends to redevelop.

2.5 The same principle applies, even more so, where a landlord wishes to determine a lease because it requires the property back for its own use. A contractual break in a lease excluded from the 1954 Act will require the landlord to say no more than that this is what it requires. If the lease is protected under the 1954 Act then again the landlord may be put to a stricter level of proof. It may even be impossible for the landlord to exercise the break at all. Section 30(2) provides that this ground of opposition to a tenant's application for renewal is not open to a landlord that has not owned its reversionary interest for at least five years. So, if a landlord buys the property and immediately grants a ten-year lease with an option for it to take the property back at the end of the third year of the term should it require the property for its own use, then if the lease granted is inside the 1954 Act and protected by it, the landlord will simply not be able to exercise that option. It will not be worth the paper it is written on.

2.6 Many other grounds for exercising a landlord's break would not be available at all if the lease was protected under the 1954 Act. For example, I mentioned in paragraph 1.2 above the fact that landlords sometimes grant leases merely in order to have the overheads paid for by someone else and, in those circumstances, to tenants whose covenant status might leave a great deal to be desired. There is no basis under the 1954 Act for a landlord to oppose renewal on the basis that it wishes to 'improve the covenant strength of the tenant'. In these circumstances, for a landlord's break to be effective, the lease would have to be excluded from the 1954 Act.

2.7 Obviously the question of whether a lease is excluded from the 1954 Act is one for negotiation between the parties. However, I think that if the parties have agreed the principle that a landlord is entitled to determine, it may often be a relatively straightforward extension to this principle for the landlord to persuade its tenant that the lease should be outside the 1954 Act. If a tenant is happy to allow its landlord to determine should it wish to redevelop, then the same tenant should really also be content that the landlord can exercise its break without fear of being tripped up by a failure to comply with statutory requirements imposed by Section 30 of the 1954 Act. This may not always be the case since the tenant may be anxious to ensure that the landlord's intentions are genuine. In these circumstances the tenant may well want the landlord to have to go through the process of convincing a judge. I must say, however, if I am advising a landlord who is proposing to grant a lease with a right to break given a desire for redevelopment, I would always advise the landlord to negotiate that the tenancy is excluded from the 1954 Act.

2.8 I suppose that if one takes this theory to its logical conclusion then one may as well simply agree that a landlord can break at a certain time in the tenancy 'for any reason'. This will stop the landlord from having to prove anything but give it the right to simply walk away early. I think this is a slightly different proposition for a tenant to accept than one where the landlord has to at least contemplate a redevelopment or resumption of occupation or some other agreed basis for taking the lease back. Perhaps the fairest compromise is for the parties to agree the basis upon which the landlord can exercise its right to determine but then to provide that the lease is excluded from the 1954 Act so that the landlord does not have to concern itself with both proving its ground contractually and also under Section 30.

3.   BREAK NOTICES AND THE 1954 ACT

3.1   So, we have seen that if a lease is protected by the 1954 Act then if a landlord wishes to exercise a right to determine, it must also serve a Section 25 notice; merely serving the contractual determination notice will be insufficient.

As you will see in Chapter 6 devoted to 1954 Act renewals, the normal way that a landlord brings a lease to an end is by serving notice under Section 25 of the 1954 Act. Does the landlord have to serve both a contractual break notice and notice under Section 25 or will one notice effectively deal with both requirements? There is plenty of authority for the proposition that a landlord's Section 25 notice may be sufficient to operate a contractual break clause in favour of the landlord (see *Scholl Manufacturing Company Limited v Clifton Slimline Limited* **1967 Ch 41** and *Keith Bailey Rogers and Company v Cubes Limited* **1975 31 P&CR 412**). One notice may combine both the statutory and the contractual determination, although one would have to check the lease carefully to ensure that this principle fits the circumstances of any individual case.

3.2   Where a tenant wishes to exercise a tenant's break, if the lease is protected under the 1954 Act, we have seen that both statutory and contractual notices should be served by the tenant.

3.3   The statutory notices that will need to be served will normally be under Section 25 (landlord's break clauses) or Section 27 (tenant's break clauses). We have seen that a Section 25 notice may be sufficient to operate as both the contractual and statutory notice. Remember that the reverse is not true and it is no use serving a contractual break and hoping that will satisfy Section 25. The statutory notice has to be in a prescribed form.

3.4 Section 27 does not require a tenant's notice to be in a specified form and therefore the contractual break can be made to satisfy Section 27 and when drafting a lease that contains a tenant's break, it is relatively straightforward to provide that no separate notice needs to be served under Section 27, so long as the form of contractual break notice complies with the requirements of Section 27.

3.5 Part II of the 1954 Act states quite clearly that protected commercial leases continue until determined under the 1954 Act. Therefore, if a tenant serves a contractual break in a protected tenancy I believe it must serve notice under Section 27. Without that the lease will continue. I acknowledge, as mentioned in paragraph 2 of this chapter, that there is the possibility that the *Esselte* case removes this obligation. Quite clearly no chances should be taken and notice under Section 27 should be served.

3.6 Section 27(1) of the 1954 Act requires the tenant to give at least three months' notice. So long as the contractual break requires at least three months' notice (and only in very short leases, and even then not that often, does one see break clauses requiring less than that) there will be no difficulty in complying with the requirements of Section 27. If the tenancy is continuing under the 1954 Act a notice may still be given by the tenant terminating the tenancy on three months' notice although, to comply with Section 27(2) in this situation, the notice would have to bring the lease to an end on a quarter-day. Under Section 24(2)(a) of the 1954 Act no such notice can be served until the tenant has been in occupation for at least one month.

3.7 Where a protected lease does allow the tenant to give less than three months' notice to break then the tenant does have the difficulty of making the decision whether to serve notice under Section 27. If it serves a Section 27 notice then, clearly, at the time it is able to give its contractual break notice it will only be able to serve notice under Section 27(2) and that will require the notice to bring the lease to an end on a quarter-day. It would not be able to serve notice under Section 27(1). My view is that a Section 27 notice should be served and the tenant should not simply vacate on the authority of *Esselte*. Accordingly, notice under Section 27(2) should be served in these circumstances. I do think, however, that this is a very unlikely scenario in practice and when negotiating a tenant's break, the tenant's advisers must ensure that any lease conferring a right to break on less than three months' notice is excluded from the 1954 Act in order that these problems do not arise.

3.8   Although decided before *Esselte*, the case of *Provident Mutual Life Assurance Society v Greater London Employers' Association* **1996 NPC 36** gives further weight to the principle that a tenant cannot simply vacate and cease business occupation and, by doing so, avoid the necessity to serve notice under Section 27. In *Provident Mutual* the tenant only gave two months' notice and the landlord was arguing that a Section 27(2) notice (three months' ending on a quarter-day) was necessary. It is arguable, however, that this case would no longer be followed after the decision in *Esselte* on the basis that the rationale for the decision (namely that once a lease is protected under the 1954 Act it remains protected forever) is no longer good law. The question is a difficult one. Certainly where a Section 27(1) notice can be served it should be, to avoid any problems. Where this is not possible, detailed and specialist advice should be taken very early on to ensure that no time is lost.

3.9   One can see, therefore, that when negotiating and drafting break clauses and actually serving the notice, it is very important to have one eye firmly fixed on the 1954 Act and its consequences and to make certain that the negotiations lead to documentation that quite clearly enables the party exercising the break to do so, satisfying all the statutory requirements at the same time.

4.   BREAK CLAUSES AS A DOWNWARD REVIEW?

4.1   The recession and decrease in property values not only fuelled the negotiation of break clauses in many leases but also set tenants and their advisers thinking about whether they could operate a break clause in a 1954 Act protected tenancy as a device to bring to an end the contractual term and promptly seek a renewal of the lease under the 1954 Act.

Imagine a lease with both a break at year five and also an upward-only rent review at the same time. If the market rent of the premises had decreased by the time the break was operable, then there may be very good commercial incentives for the tenant to operate the break and endeavour to renew the tenancy on more favourable terms. True, the tenant could operate the break and move elsewhere at a lower rent, but clearly this would often be less attractive than being able to stay put whilst reducing outgoings.

4.2   The potential stumbling-block to this tactic lay in Section 26(4) of the 1954 Act which makes it quite clear that a tenant cannot request a new tenancy after having already given notice to quit. It is clear from Section 26(4) that a tenant cannot serve a break notice and then, after that date, serve a Section 26 request for a new lease.

4.3   It is difficult to see how a Section 26 request could precede service of a break notice. Under Section 26, at least six and not more than twelve months' notice before the contractual expiry date must be given and, if the Section 26 request precedes service of a tenant's break notice, then when it is served it would be a misconceived notice since the date given for the expiry of the tenancy in the Section 26 request (between six and twelve months following service) would be before the end of the contractual term if the break clause had not yet been served.

4.4   Assuming that the above two principles are correct, then either a contractual break notice and Section 26 request would have to be served at exactly the same time or perhaps the Section 26 notice would have to act as the break notice on the authority developed in relation to Section 25 notices (*Scholl Manufacturing*). The major difference between Sections 25 and 26, however, is that a Section 25 notice is worded to bring the tenancy to an end whereas a Section 26 request is worded so as to request a new tenancy. It is not worded in such a manner as to break an existing tenancy.

4.5 The perceived wisdom therefore was that a Section 26 request would not be sufficient to operate a break clause and, if a tenant was to use a break as a downward review device, then the two notices under the lease and the 1954 Act would need to be served simultaneously.

4.6 The case of *Scottish Widows* v *Garston* **1996 1 EGLR 113** has now considered this subject and for the time being has effectively closed off the possibility that a tenant might use a break notice as a way of effecting a downward review. I say for the time being, simply because I understand that there are possibilities of a further appeal.

4.7 The contractual notice and Section 26 request were served at the same time but there was a deficiency with the break notice since it gave the wrong date of expiry. The tenants, who were a firm of lawyers, were therefore relying on the Section 26 request as effective to both bring the lease to an end and seek the new tenancy. The High Court held that the proviso to Section 26(2) of the 1954 Act made it clear that a Section 26 request cannot be served unless it relates to a date upon which a lease is due to expire by ordinary affluxion of time. The *Scottish Widows* case therefore clearly brings to an end any question of using a Section 26 request as a way of using a break notice as a downward review. I think this is correct and prevents misuse of break clauses. There is nothing wrong with determining a lease and seeking to renegotiate its terms. However, the parties are then at arm's length. I do not believe it is right for the tenant to be able to do this in the context of being able to force a new lease out of the landlord under the 1954 Act.

5. RELATIONSHIP WITH RENT REVIEW CLAUSES

5.1 We saw in paragraph 2 of Chapter 2 that a break clause must be considered in the context of a rent review clause. Strict time-limits imposed for exercise of a break clause may well have the effect of rendering time of the essence of the review clause itself.

5.2 The rationale for linking time-periods in a break clause with those in a review clause is relatively straightforward. Assume that a tenant has agreed a long lease with five-yearly upward-only reviews and breaks at the review dates. It may well have done so thinking that if the market rent for the premises rises beyond a level that it can afford, then it has the opportunity to walk away and seek smaller, less prestigious or just plain cheaper premises. The parties are effectively acknowledging that the tenant has no control over the level of rent which might be payable and, therefore, in order to protect itself it has the right to determine the lease and the long term obligations contained in it if, at review, it finds it cannot afford to stay. This is one of the prime reasons that tenants seek to negotiate break clauses where they are otherwise committed to long leases with upward-only reviews. Such a break is really of no help or relevance whatsoever if, in practice, the tenant cannot ascertain the level of rent that it will have to pay if it does not exercise the break and stays.

5.3 For that reason the courts have said that if a tenant's break notice must be served within a strict time-period, it would be quite wrong if the landlord could delay negotiating a rent review, forcing the tenant to make a decision regarding the break before knowing what the rental is going to be. If the rent review clause does not say that time is of the essence then so long as it does not specifically exclude this possibility, the court may imply such a term to prevent the landlord causing such an effect by delaying the review process.

5.4 I think that there may be many reasons in practice where this scenario is simply not thought through properly. Whilst a tenant might seek such a break at each review date with the intention of being able to look at its potential overheads and make a decision whether or not to stay, in fact it may negotiate lease documentation that simply does not give it this opportunity. It is not at all unusual to see rent review machinery where there is simply no way in which the tenant can possibly ensure that it will know what its new rent is going to be at a time when it is required to serve a break notice. It is so often the case that a break notice operable at the fifth year must be given as long as twelve months before the rent review date. The break which can be operated at the fifth year will nearly always require prior notice and whether this is twelve months or something as short as six or perhaps even three months where the notice has to be given before the fifth year of the term and where that is the review date, the tenant is going to be forced to make its decision to serve notice before it knows what the rent is going to be. If the tenant is truly trying to ascertain the amount of rent that it is likely to have to pay if it does not determine the lease, then this should be brought out in the negotiation process and the break should be operable by the tenant within a certain period following agreement or determination of the review.

5.5 Even where one can get over this hurdle and provide for a break clause to be operable within a certain period following the agreement or determination of the new rent, there is still a further complication. Given that the rent will have risen to a level beyond that which the tenant wishes to continue paying, the tenant will want to exercise its break. However, both parties will want a reasonable period of notice, the tenant in order to find alternative premises and the landlord in order to endeavour to find a new tenant. A deal will need to be struck between the parties as to who pays the increased rent during that period. The tenant will obviously wish to avoid any obligation to pay the difference between the existing rent and the new rent yet of course the landlord will, by definition, have proved the new rental level and will not wish to add to its misery of losing an existing tenant and having a potential void by not being able to recover the excess during any such notice period. Perhaps the best compromise would be for the parties to agree to split the difference during any notice period. The landlord will have seen an uplift in circumstances where the tenant had made it clear from the outset that it might want to walk away if rents went up too much and the tenant will for a short period have to pay something in excess of its initially agreed rental as the price for having had the benefit of having been able to walk away. This seems reasonable. When the landlord and tenant will have originally negotiated the lease they will have contemplated the possibility that rents can rise and the tenant's desire to negotiate a break clause, giving it the opportunity to leave will have been based on a desire to cap its responsibilities in relation to an increased rent, not to avoid any increase whatsoever.

5.6 Unless one operates a break which is clearly linked to the date that the rent review is agreed or determined, then there is certainly no guarantee for the tenant that it will know what its rental commitment is going to be at the time it wishes to determine. Clauses of this nature need to be very carefully drawn indeed and certainly many break clauses currently in circulation in the market-place do not give tenants the certainty that perhaps they may think they have: notice provisions in leases very often bear little relationship to the time-scales needed to give real, practical effect to this scenario. Whilst this type of clause might lead to what could be termed a 'floating break' it does have the benefit of certainty.

5.7   Since the courts have held that there can be a link between the time-periods in rent review clauses and break clauses such that rent review time machinery is impliedly of the essence, I would strongly advocate that if this is not the intention of the parties when they are negotiating a break clause, they should specifically say so in the drafting of the rent review clause. It is very easy to insert a paragraph stating that the time-periods in the rent review clause are not of the essence and this will avoid any kind of problem arising. There is little point in leaving these things to the whim of a judge to decide, given that the parties to the original lease negotiation can deal with the point quite simply.

6.   TIMING OF THE BREAK CLAUSE

6.1   If there is a break at year five, different consequences may flow simply from the way in which the clause is drafted. Let us take a tenant's break as an example, although the same issues arise where one is dealing with a landlord's break but in reverse. The tenant may be given the right to determine its lease on a named date or simply on 'the fifth anniversary of the term commencement date'. Assume that a twenty-five-year lease was granted on 1 September 1997 with the term commencing on that date. Is there a difference between such a lease that allows the tenant to determine 'on the fifth anniversary of the term commencement date' (lease A) and a lease which requires the tenant to determine on 1 September 2002 (lease B)?

6.2   If the clause reflects the wording in lease A then, assuming the tenant does not exercise the break and assuming the lease continues beyond the fifth year, the reference to a tenant break clause may be a factor in increasing the rent at reviews throughout the term of the lease. On each rent review, the landlord may be able to argue that on the fifth anniversary of the term commencement date of the notional lease which is being valued for the purposes of review, there is a right for the notional tenant to determine. If such an argument is valid (and it must be arguable at least that it does confer a benefit upon the tenant which would not exist if there were no break clause) then the rent may be higher than that which would apply for a notional lease without such a right. A clause such as this may also be a factor in negotiating the terms of any renewal lease, assuming that the lease containing the break clause is within the 1954 Act. Under Section 35 of the 1954 Act such terms are determined by the court in default of agreement between the parties. Section 35 says that in determining those terms the court has regard to the terms of the current tenancy, one of which, of course, is a tenant's break 'at the fifth anniversary'. If this is correct, then the tenant would have the advantage of being able to ask for the new lease to contain a tenant's break. This may be countered by the tenant having to pay more rent for such a new tenancy, on the basis that the lease may be worth more to a tenant with a break than would a lease without such a break.

6.3 If the wording of lease B is employed, the landlord would not have the rent review advantage referred to. Assuming the next rent review was in fact on 1 September 2002 it is difficult to see how the landlord could argue that the tenant had the benefit of a break clause that in practice can no longer be operated. The notional lease to be granted in 2002 would not have a tenant's break. However, on a renewal the court, in having regard to the terms of the current tenancy, would probably disregard the existence of the break clause which by then will have been and gone.

6.4 This analysis is somewhat strained since on any reading a rent review of lease A at the tenth anniversary of the term will be agreed or determined against a background that lease A itself no longer contains a break clause that is operable. Any third party determining the rent would therefore no doubt go out of his way not to increase the rent, merely because the notional lease has a break clause whereas in reality the break that was conferred by the actual lease does not exist any longer. The arbitrator or expert will no doubt be looking hard for the presumption of reality that we talked about in the rent review chapter. None the less, the point does need to be thought through. Say, for example, the relevant right to determine was at the tenth anniversary. Either one would use lease A wording and state that the break is on the tenth anniversary of the term commencement date or lease B wording and state that the break is operable on 1 September 2007. At the review in 2002 it will be necessary to determine whether the notional lease has a break in five years' time or in ten years' time. It is much easier to see that the lease A wording would give rise to the former construction whereas the lease B wording would give rise to the latter.

6.5   The 1995 Act introduces a potential complication to this type of analysis. As we saw in Chapter 1, former tenants now have the right to claim an overriding lease where they have received a Section 17 demand and where they pay up in full. If the lease has a break clause which has expired but is worded in accordance with lease A, does the overriding lease have that break clause inserted? The answer to this question is dealt with in the 1995 Act and is plainly no. Section 19(4)(b) of the 1995 Act makes it clear that where the break date has come and gone it will not be repeated in the overriding lease whatever the wording. The fact that there is legislation dealing with this, albeit only in relation to overriding leases, is one that cannot be ignored and I think assists a tenant in arguing that even where the wording employed is that set out in lease A, any notional lease on review should not be valued on the basis that the break subsists. The argument would run along the following lines using the wording of Section 19(4)(b) (adapted by the substitution of the words in italics for those in the section so as to refer to a notional lease in a rent review and not an overriding lease): 'the *notional* lease shall not be required to reproduce any covenant of *the lease being reviewed* to the extent that it has become spent by the time *of the review*'.

6.6   However, one might also argue that it is actually equitable to value the premises as if they have a break. Certainly if the notional term for the notional lease is the full length of the original contractual term, then since that was valued and the rental agreed originally on the basis that the tenant had a right to break at year five, why not so value the notional term at each review?

6.7 In any event, the 1995 Act wording does not really give any assistance in the situation that I looked at in paragraph 6.4 above.

6.8 These are interesting valuation questions but again ones that the careful draftsman can avoid by making it absolutely clear in the review clause that any right to break is disregarded on any review taking place on or after the break date.

7. WHEN CAN A BREAK NOTICE BE SERVED?

7.1 Break clauses invariably set out a time-scale for service of the notice triggering them. Again by way of example let us look at a tenant's break although, once again, if one is dealing with a landlord's break the same points arise, but in reverse. In a tenant's break a landlord would normally want to give the tenant a reasonably small window in which to serve his break notice. The hope might be that the tenant will miss his opportunity. It is not unusual to see the tenant having the right to determine not earlier than twelve or less than six months before a particular date. This is wording cribbed from the 1954 Act.

7.2 Time is normally expressed to be of the essence of the break clause. If a window like this exists then it is essential that the tenant ensures that the notice is served within this window. Everyone knows exactly when the lease might be determined and, assuming this is the case, the tenant must serve the break within the period given to him.

7.3 It is important to a tenant that he does not have the right to break on exactly six months' notice. This may be contrasted with a right to determine on 'at least' six months' notice. The former would arguably require service on a particular day and since the courts have been littered with cases where even given a reasonable window within which to serve a notice, the party serving it has got it wrong, it is clearly ludicrous for people to put themselves in the position of having to serve on a named date. This is emphasized by the fact that there may be difficult questions of interpretation as to the day upon which the notice can be served. If a lease is granted for a term of twenty years from 1 September 1997 and there is a break at the expiry of the fifth year of the term, where such break must be activated by a notice given exactly six months before that date it would be difficult for the tenant to know when to serve his notice. Is the expiry of the fifth year of the term 1 September 2002 or is it 31 August 2002? This will largely be a matter of interpretation and may turn on very fine distinctions in wording and circumstances.

7.4 One very good example of this arose in the case of *Meadfield Properties Limited* v *Secretary of State for the Environment* **1995 03 EG 128**. This case concerned an option to determine where a lease had been granted on 24 June 1984. The option to determine arose after ten years and the question before the court was whether the notice purporting to terminate the tenancy on 23 June 1994 was sufficient, or whether in fact the term commenced on 25 June 1984 and therefore did not expire until 24 June 1994. The judge in *Meadfield* held that the term did in fact commence on 24 June 1984 and therefore the term started on that date and expired on 23 June 1994. Accordingly the notice was valid. The decision turned on its own facts but is a reminder that practitioners must ensure that notices terminate on the correct date.

7.5 It is for these reasons that I always advocate giving a few days' grace when serving notices which are time critical. This may not be possible if the obligation is to serve a fixed period of notice expiring on a fixed date. For that reason one should negotiate a position allowing the server of a break notice to do so on giving 'at least' or on giving 'not less than' the relevant period of notice; in those circumstances he will simply be able to give, say, seven months' notice and ensure that he gets it absolutely right. If he has to serve on a particular named date the recipe for disaster is enormous. Sometimes this goes too far and one sees a break clause requiring service simply on not less than six months' notice but without a maximum period of notice. I do not think this is a terribly sensible way forward. For example, if one is dealing with a tenant's notice the landlord might be in the invidious position of receiving notice many years before the exercise of the break and this clearly will leave a cloud over the investment.

7.6 Another complication arises where a break is granted in a 1954 Act protected tenancy. It may be necessary for such a tenancy to be brought to an end by notice being served under the 1954 Act. A landlord would need to give between six and twelve months' notice in a Section 25 notice and, therefore, if a landlord is given a right to break on less than six months' notice it would still have to give six months' notice under the 1954 Act in any event. If he were able to terminate on more than twelve months' notice and, say, exercised a contractual break eighteen months before the end of the term then he would still have to serve a Section 25 notice some six months after he served that contractual break. For a tenant the position is slightly more complicated. We have seen in paragraphs 2 and 3 of this chapter that notice may need to be given under Section 27, although this is no longer clear following the *Esselte* decision and it may be possible for the tenant to vacate without serving any form of notice. If a tenant does need to serve notice under Section 27 then that notice must be at least three months (expiring on a quarter-day in certain cases). It is not often the case that a tenant is given the right to walk away from a tenancy on less than three months' notice but, again, if the lease is protected under the 1954 Act there will be no commercial advantage for the tenant being able to do so. Assuming that a Section 27 notice needs to be served he would still have to serve at least three months' notice anyway. There may even be a disadvantage. If a tenant serves a contractual break giving less than three months' notice and this merely has the effect of leaving the tenancy continuing under the 1954 Act, then a further notice under Section 27(2) of the 1954 Act may need to be served terminating the tenancy on a quarter-day. This in itself may extend the tenancy by perhaps up to six months. This could arise, for example, if a tenant had the right to give one month's notice to terminate the tenancy on, say, 29 August. If the tenant served that notice on 29 August and brought the contractual term to an end on 29

September and then realized that notice needed to be served under Section 27, at least three months' notice would need to be served and it would need to expire on a quarter-day. If that notice were to be served on 29 September then the lease could not be terminated until the March quarter-day, since the December quarter-day (25th) would be less than three months away.

7.7 This inter-relationship between the break notice and the 1954 Act is quite complicated and the *Esselte* decision adds to the complication since it does not expressly deal with break notices and, at the time that I am writing this book, the full transcript of the report has not been issued.

8. CONDITIONS FOR SERVICE

8.1 So, assuming that the break clause requires service within a certain period, what else is likely to be required before a tenant can serve his break?

8.2 Very often one sees landlords providing that the right to determine is subject to a condition precedent that the tenant shall have complied with all its obligations to pay rent and observe covenants contained in the lease. If a lease provides for this, then the tenant will not be able to exercise his right to determine the tenancy if he has not complied with the condition precedent. If the condition precedent says that the tenant must have complied with his covenants, that may well be sufficient to require full compliance with all of his covenants including his repair clause. If he has not kept the premises in the state of repair required by the lease then, even if the breach is relatively minor, he will not be able to exercise his right to determine.

8.3 It may seem intrinsically unfair that a tenant has no right to determine a tenancy in circumstances where, for example, there is a relatively minor breach of a repair clause, but I think it is important to emphasize that if this is what the parties have negotiated, then that will be the effect of their negotiations. I have seen many leases drafted by landlords containing such a condition precedent and I have seen many such leases accepted by tenants. I have also seen many leases where tenants have tinkered with the concept by agreeing to a condition precedent that would prevent exercise of the break if the tenant is in 'material' breach or 'substantial' breach of covenant. I do not think this is a sensible way forward for tenants and again I should emphasize that the position is exactly the same in reverse; I think it is equally shortsighted for a landlord to accept that it cannot exercise a right to break if he has not complied, or even substantially complied, with his covenants.

8.4 I should like to illustrate my concerns about break clauses geared to conditions precedent by looking at the case of *Trane (UK) Limited* v *Provident Mutual Life Assurance Association* **1994 EGCS 121**. Here the court had to consider the validity of the exercise by a tenant of a ten-year break option in a twenty-five-year lease of industrial premises. There were five-yearly reviews and the tenant had the right to break at the end of the tenth year. The tenant served notice in June 1991. It was accepted by both parties that at the date when the notice was to take effect, there were a number of minor tenant repairing breaches. It was also accepted that for the purpose of deciding whether or not the break had been validly exercised, the fact that the breaches may or may not have been minor was not relevant. The fact that there were breaches was sufficient on its own. In *Trane* the break clause contained the following proviso:

> Provided that the said lessee shall until expiration of such notice [i.e. the six-month break notice] pay the rents ... and observe and perform the covenants on its part ... and provided that [the tenant] shall upon such expiration deliver up vacant possession of the whole of the demised premises the term shall determine without prejudice to any right of action or remedy of either party hereto in respect of any antecedent breach of covenant or other obligation hereunder.

As I say, covenants of this nature are to be found in many commercial leases and tenants have no doubt signed them in the hope and belief that they have the right to determine. In *Trane* the tenant sought to argue that the wording was simply a restatement of its obligations contained in the lease but it was clearly accepted that if there was truly a condition precedent then there could not have been an effective break since the tenant was in breach of its repairing obligations, albeit not to any great extent.

8.5 Prior authorities supported the landlord's view that a condition precedent had been created. Despite very able and persuasive argument by counsel for the tenant, the judge was not persuaded and stated that the break clause was not operable. The judge was not impressed by the fact that the breaches concerned were minor or even that they may have occurred at the last minute. One will appreciate that a breach that occurs right at the end of the notice period would be almost impossible to control since it would not be capable of remedy before time ran out.

8.6 In *Reed Personnel Services PLC v American Express Limited* **1996 NPC 7** a tenant had failed to comply with a dilapidations schedule and lost his rights to break which were conditional on compliance with a repair clause. This was another case where the tenant had argued that there was little damage to the reversion but this did not obviate the necessity to comply with the condition precedent.

8.7 Accordingly, if one is advising a tenant who is seeking to break a lease which has a condition precedent, it is absolutely essential that, before seeking to terminate, a detailed due diligence of the tenant's obligations should be carried out in order to ascertain whether the tenant is likely to be able to operate the break clause or fail for want of compliance with a condition precedent. That is all a tenant can possibly do in those circumstances. If a tenant has committed a breach, but that breach has been remedied by the time the option is exercised, the tenant will not lose his rights.

8.8 When negotiating a break clause at the outset I think lawyers and surveyors have a duty to make absolutely sure that there is clarity and certainty. I cannot see any good reason why a tenant should ever accept that its right to determine is conditional on compliance with covenants. A right to determine should do no more than bring forward the end of the term. In the normal way, at the end of the term the lease does not continue if the tenant is in breach of repairing obligations. It comes to an end and the landlord has a right to serve a terminal schedule of dilapidations. The position should be exactly the same where the term is brought to an end prematurely by exercise of a break.

8.9   I hear landlords and their surveyors arguing that they must have the right to control operation of a tenant's break and inserting a condition precedent is a very good way of policing repairing obligations. I do not believe that this is the correct approach. Landlords can protect their position by reserving rights in respect of antecedent breaches and I do not believe that it is equitable for a lease break to be conditional on compliance with covenants. One thing has nothing to do with the other, and a tenant's break is designed to give him the certainty of knowing that he can bring his lease obligations to an end at a certain date. If the right to determine is conditional then he clearly does not have that certainty. How is a tenant supposed to run his business if he serves a notice to break, looks for alternative premises and then finds that the landlord is challenging the validity of the break on grounds of breach of covenant?

8.10   For these reasons I also do not believe that it helps to water down a condition precedent by inserting 'substantial' or 'material'. The person seeking to break will still not have the certainty required. It is perhaps reasonable for the tenant to be obliged to pay the rent but, if this is accepted by tenants, then they must make sure that the obligation applies only to the principal rent and not other payments reserved as rent (for example, service charges). If service charges are reserved as rent (as they frequently are) then surely it is not reasonable for a tenant to lose its right to break if it has not paid its service charge where there is some bona fide dispute.

8.11   It will be apparent from the above that I believe that since the commercial purpose of a tenant's break is to give the tenant the certainty of knowing when it can leave its premises and bring to an end its liabilities, the break clause ought be drafted on that basis. In case one feels that this is a bias towards tenants, I should say that I feel exactly the same where one is dealing with a landlord's break which is conditional on compliance with landlord's covenants. The basis behind my approach is purely and simply that the right to determine is inserted in order to give the party that has the benefit of the right the certainty of knowing that it can terminate early and I do not think that the wording should cloud that desire and need for certainty.

8.12   There is also an interesting side-issue. If a lease has a right for a tenant to break subject to compliance with a condition precedent, then would it be possible for the tenant to seek to rely on its own non-compliance with that condition precedent if after service of its notice it changes its mind and wishes to stay? The general principle is that the court will not allow a tenant to rely on its own wrongdoings when litigating, but I think very much will depend on the type of condition precedent and the wording of the condition precedent. If a tenant is obliged to keep the premises in repair and the condition precedent is compliance with its covenants, including a repairing covenant, then I suspect that a court would not allow a tenant to serve a break notice and then effectively withdraw it, stating that it has not complied with its repairing obligations. This would clearly result in a situation where a tenant will have profited from its own wrongdoing, namely non-compliance with repairing obligations. However, if the break clause were to require the tenant to do something new in order to exercise the break, for example, paying a premium or six months' rent and if the lease does not contain an obligation upon the tenant to pay that money but merely a provision stating that if it does not do so the tenant cannot operate the break, there may be an argument that even if the tenant has served a notice exercising the break subject to that condition precedent, it may effectively withdraw the notice by not paying the money. The landlord would have to show that there was an implied obligation to pay the money once the notice was served and whether it will be able to do this will depend on the wording of the documentation. You can see that this may give rise to all sorts of arguments and potentially allow a tenant to utilize the wording of the condition precedent as an option to serve notice and look around for alternative premises in the knowledge that, if it cannot find a deal that it wishes to accept, it can fail to comply with the condition precedent and then remain where it is. Again for reasons that should be self-evident from my earlier comments, I do not think a tenant should be allowed to get away with such a tactic but practitioners, both lawyers and surveyors, should exclude the possibility with careful drafting.

8.13 Clarity of drafting will resolve these issues and certainly if a tenant is having difficulty in negotiating a break clause where a landlord is insisting on inserting condition precedent wording, perhaps a tenant might use the threat that this could come back to haunt the landlord in the future as a way of persuading the landlord not to insist on drafting a clause in this way. I think both parties to a lease should be out to ensure certainty in relation to break clauses. They should not be seeking litigation.

9.   SOME CASES ON TIMING

9.1 We have already seen the *Meadfield* case (see paragraph 7.4) and its effect on timing. *Micrografix* v *Woking 8 Limited* **1995 37 EG 179** concerned a lease where a tenant had been given a break clause allowing determination at the fifth year of the term. The tenant had to give not less than twelve months' notice. On 21 January 1994 the tenants stated they were enclosing a notice determining the lease on 23 March 1995. That would have been sufficient, save that the notice itself stated that they were determining on 23 March 1994. The tenants applied for a declaration that the lease would in fact determine in 1995. They obtained their declaration and the court held the notice was valid.

9.2 The law is not terribly consistent in this type of case. In *Mannai Investment Company Limited* v *Eagle Star Life Assurance Company Limited* **1996 6 EG 140** the tenant had the right to serve a break notice expiring on the third anniversary of the term commencement date. It was agreed that this was 13 January 1995 and the tenant gave notice determining the lease on 12 January 1995. The tenant argued that this confusion was totally irrelevant since 13 January was the only date on which they could have terminated anyway. They went on to say that if this was not right, the notice did not take effect until that moment of time which was both the last moment of 12 January and the first moment of 13 January! The judge somewhat surprisingly found for the tenant on the second of those two grounds, but this was overturned on appeal. The Court of Appeal made it clear that the date was vitally important. It was essential to the operation of the break and the fact that it was clear what the correct date ought to have been was simply irrelevant. The fact that the wrong date was inserted whether by slip or not, was sufficient to make the notice invalid. The recipient was not required to guess what was in the tenant's mind.

9.3   I mention these cases purely to give some further weight to the need for landlords and tenants and their advisers to work together to ensure that once a break notice is to be served, it is served properly and timeously. It is so straightforward provided proper diary notes are made and provided there is sufficient time given for planning and consideration of the various issues. None the less, it never ceases to amaze me how people get themselves into the mess that these cases demonstrate. It is a fact that lawyers and surveyors are continually sued for negligence for failure to properly advise in relation to time-scales.

9.4   It is a theme of this book that clarity in drafting as well as careful and appropriate planning will very often avoid many of the pitfalls. The drafting and operation of break clauses is no exception to that.

10.   DRAFTING AND SERVING THE BREAK CLAUSE – A PRACTICAL SOLUTION

10.1   Many things can go wrong when one is drafting and serving a break notice. A number of the cases illustrate notices that are not in the correct form or not sufficiently clear, some show incorrect references to clause numbers or even wrong references to the parties or the date from which the break should operate. Perhaps this is more a problem for lawyers than surveyors, since it normally falls upon them to draft a break notice but I make no apology for referring to these issues in this book since I believe surveyors have a vitally important role to play. One way of helping to eliminate problems is for the form of the break notice to be appended to the lease. This will enable the party who is seeking to terminate the lease to simply draft a notice which has already been approved between landlord and tenant and is in a specified form. It is likely that there will be blank spaces in that form (hence the potential for disaster!) but one will have limited the opportunity for error since the basic format will be clear. One sees this approach in lease documentation where, for example, a form of memorandum of rent review is specified. Also, in loan documentation notices, drawing down loan advances nearly always have to be in a certain format appended to a schedule to the loan agreement. Most of the pain is therefore removed and I would strongly advocate this. If one adopts this approach with a careful diary system and a reasonable amount of care and diligence in the carrying out of the procedures, the room for error is considerably reduced.

10.2 If one does not want to go the length of actually drafting the break clause when negotiating the lease then, at the very least, when making diary notes these should not simply be a reminder of the date for service of the notice but should also set out exactly what is required. When one comes to exercise the break and look at the diary note, perhaps many years later, one will have the advantage of a contemporaneously drawn reminder of the procedures required.

10.3 Once the notice is drafted it needs to be served and again it is surprising how little thought is given to this. Most leases set out a procedure for service of notices and the party serving the notice should adopt that procedure. If there is no such procedure, reference may need to be made to statute. The Law of Property Act 1925 and the Recorded Delivery Service Act 1962 as well as Section 23 the Landlord and Tenant Act 1927 and Section 66(4) of the 1954 Act in relation to renewal leases all have something to say on service of notices. Once the correct procedure for serving the notice is adopted, contemporaneous evidence should be made and retained as to how the notice was served and perhaps even an affidavit of service sworn so that if any point is ever taken on service the party serving the notice has all the appropriate answers.

10.4 As I say, these points are mainly 'lawyer points' but I do think surveyors have a very important role to play in the service of notice and must liaise carefully with lawyers to ensure that the drafting and serving of the notice gives the party doing so the remedy that it seeks.

11.   PERSONAL BREAK CLAUSES

11.1   Break clauses, particularly those given to tenants, are often expressed to be personal to the original tenant. The negotiations between the parties will have been run along the lines that the landlord wants the security of a long term but acknowledges that its original tenant does not want the commitment to a long term. The landlord therefore gives it (but not its successors in title) the right to walk away at some stage in the future. What happens if that original tenant assigns its lease and subsequently becomes the tenant once again? Two cases have considered this scenario. You will see that I have also looked at these in Chapter 3, since they deal with alienation as well.

11.2   In *Oil Property Investments Limited* v *Olympia and York (Canary Wharf) Limited* **1994 29 EG 121** a lease had been granted to ICI Petroleum Limited. They changed their name to Enterprise Petroleum Limited (EPL). Back in 1987 EPL had assigned the lease to Olympia and York (Canary Wharf) Limited (O and Y). Following the administration of O and Y, the administrator sought to assign the lease back to EPL. The original rent was £360,000 per annum although this had risen to over £1 million at review and the lease was the subject of an upward-only review clause. The rent would therefore never be less than £1 million. By the time the matter came to court the property was heavily over-rented. The lease gave the original tenant, and only the original tenant, a right to determine the lease at the tenth year of the term.

11.3   In *Olympia and York* the Court of Appeal was asked to determine whether it was reasonable for the landlords to refuse consent for the assignment to EPL. The landlords were nervous that, once the lease was assigned back to EPL, they would have the right to break: no other tenant had or could get that right. Since this would leave the landlord in a position with a rental void of perhaps well over a year, in view of the time it would take to re-let the premises following exercise of the break and given the fact that the rental that they would ultimately achieve would no doubt be much smaller than the passing rent, the matter was of some importance to the landlord. The court dismissed the appeal. They held that the landlord would be severely damaged by the assignment, notwithstanding the fact that there was no objection to the covenant of EPL *per se*. According to the Court of Appeal, it was reasonable in these circumstances for the landlord to refuse to consent to an assignment. It is important to note that *Olympia and York* was premised on the supposition that once the lease was assigned back to EPL they could exercise the break.

11.4   Another case came before the courts in 1995. *Max Factor Limited v Wesleyan Assurance Society* **1995 41 EG 146** was a High Court decision concerning personal break rights. In this case Max Factor were granted a lease which contained a mutual break. The break was given to Max Factor only. Once again the original tenant had assigned the lease but, in this case, Wesleyan had already consented to an assignment of the lease back to Max Factor Limited. In June 1994 they sought to exercise the break. They contended that the break clause was valid and the society responded that the right to determine was no longer available since Max Factor had assigned their lease. They argued that they had lost their right to determine even though they had taken the property back as assignee. The court upheld the landlord's argument and determined that the break right was only vested in Max Factor whilst they had the lease vested in them as original tenant.

11.5   If *Max Factor* is correct, then when a tenant is given a personal right to break, it will lose that right on assignment. Furthermore, if *Max Factor* is right, it is difficult to see how *Olympia and York* is correct in enunciating a principle that it is reasonable to refuse consent to an assignment merely on the grounds that the assignee would be able to exercise the break. According to *Max Factor* the assignee could not do that in any event. None the less, *Olympia and York* is a Court of Appeal decision and unless overruled by a higher court, remains good law; a landlord can reasonably object to an assignment on the grounds that the assignee could operate a break, even though according to *Max Factor* if such a break is granted to the original tenant only, that tenant would not be able to do so when re-taking premises following assignment. For these reasons I suppose it is difficult to see why a prospective tenant would be keen on taking an assignment in any event; even if it persuaded its landlord to grant consent, according to the authority of **Max Factor** it could not operate the break anyway.

11.6 One final word on personal break clauses arises from the 1996 decision of **Brown and Root Technology Limited v Sun Alliance and London Assurance Company Limited 1996 NPC 183.** In this case the Court of Appeal, quite extraordinarily, allowed a tenant who had already assigned his lease to exercise a break clause that was only available to the original tenant. The facts were somewhat curious. The tenant had assigned the lease to its parent company with landlord's consent and, indeed, the assignment had even been registered with the landlord. Because the lease was for more than twenty-one years it was registered at HM Land Registry and the assignment itself should have been registered at the Land Registry. There was some dispute over stamp duty and for that reason the assignment was not stamped or registered.

11.6.1 At law, where you have an unregistered disposal of a registered title the legal estate does not move. It remains with the original owner. On the basis of these facts, the Court of Appeal held that the original owner could exercise the break clause available to it. Not surprisingly, the landlord had claimed that the break notice was invalid; so far as the landlord was concerned the lease had been assigned.

11.6.2 I have to say that I have very little time for this legalistic approach. The position would have been entirely different had the lease not been granted for a term in excess of twenty-one years. If that were the case, the lease would not have been registerable and the assignment need not have been registered.

11.6.3 However bizarre this decision seems to be, it is a Court of Appeal decision and must be respected, if only for this reason. If one is trying to ensure that a break clause is only available to the original tenant (and on the authority of **Max Factor** it does seem to be the case that once a tenant has assigned a lease with the benefit of a personal break he can no longer exercise that personal break), then the language must be clear to ensure that the break is no longer operable following assignment whether or not the assignment is perfected as a legal assignment.

12. BREAKS AND ORIGINAL TENANT LIABILITY

12.1 For leases that were granted before the 1995 Act came into force, original tenants remain liable throughout the term of the lease and, as we have seen in Chapter 1, many successor tenants also remain liable through direct covenants given to landlords in licenses to assign. For leases granted after the 1995 Act the concept of privity has disappeared but there is still a liability in certain cases for former tenants who have entered into an AGA. If a tenant has the potential of future liability after an assignment and if that tenant also has the benefit of a break clause which would enable it to bring its liabilities to an end, it must be very careful to ensure that it properly manages its property so that it does not assign its lease before the break clause is operable only to find that the assignee subsequently does not determine the lease and leaves the former tenant with a contingent liability for a period after it (the former tenant) would have been able to determine its liabilities under the lease.

12.2 If, for example, a tenant were to have taken up a twenty-five-year lease in 1995 with a once-only break at year five and that tenant were to assign its lease in 1998 (i.e. before the break was operable) the tenant would have to remain responsible under privity of contract for the entire duration of the term unless the assignee terminated the lease at the opportunity presented to it in the year 2000.

12.3 In this example the original tenant would have to carefully think through whether it should in fact assign its lease or try to dispose of its property in some other way. It could, for example grant a sublease to the prospective assignee and thus remain in control when it is given the opportunity to determine in 2000.

12.4 A further way of dealing with this problem would be for the tenant to approach the landlord when seeking licence to assign and try to persuade the landlord to include a provision in the licence releasing the original tenant from liability from the year 2000. The landlord would not necessarily be in any worse position, whilst the tenant would be able to ensure that its liabilities came to an end in 2000 in just the same way as it could have done had the tenant not relinquished control by the assignment.

Negotiating this type of situation can be a little tricky since the landlord will realize that if it simply refuses to release the tenant there is little the tenant can do other than to retain occupation of the premises or take a chance that it will be able to rely on the indemnity that it would obtain from the assignee. It may be possible to commit the assignee to determine but unless the assignee is looking for a very short occupation of the premises there is no great merit in the assignee taking an assignment in 1998 and committing itself to determine the lease in the year 2000. Equally, if it is not prepared to accept the possibility of the lease coming to an end in the year 2000, the original tenant's only hope is to obtain some form of release from the year 2000. Without that the original tenant's contingent liability will remain.

12.5   I have seen situations where this scenario is overlooked by tenants anxious to dispose of their lease liabilities as quickly as possible. Because privity can come back and haunt a tenant many years later I think that this situation needs to be very carefully thought through before one assigns leases that contain a tenant's right to determine. Similarly if one is negotiating a new lease with a break clause, I think it is essential that one agrees that any liability that the original tenant might have under an AGA should it assign the lease before the break becomes operable will come to an end on determination. This may be easier to negotiate against the background of the 1995 Act than it was previously and clearly this needs to be taken on board. The position is even more important given the effect of *Max Factor* and the fact that the tenant is not able to take a re-assignment in order to exercise a personal right to break.

13.   VACANT POSSESSION AND SUBLEASES

13.1   Where a tenant has an option to break, very often he is required to give vacant possession and if this is a requirement, then the tenant must make absolutely certain that it really does give vacant possession and, for example, it does not leave the premises cluttered up with equipment, tenant's fittings and the like: this might just give the landlord the argument that vacant possession has not been given.

13.2 The position of subtenancies also needs to be thought through. If a tenant has a right to break, it must make sure that it does not give any sublease to a tenant who might be protected under the 1954 Act. If that were the case, the tenant may be in difficulty in exercising its break, if it has an obligation to provide vacant possession. Questions about the subtenant's right to occupation will need to be asked. Having said that, where a tenant does have a right to determine and has created a subtenancy, that subtenant would lose the subtenancy if the tenant (his landlord) determined the head lease. This was clearly shown in *Pennell* v *Payne and Another* **1995 06 EG 152**. It is therefore very important that subtenants make certain that their landlord does not have a tenant's right to break in the superior lease.

13.3 Where a landlord has an option to determine it must make sure that it has control over potential subtenancies. Whilst determination of a head lease by the landlord would end any sublease, if the head lease were protected under the 1954 Act any subtenant in occupation would have a right to remain in possession against that head landlord unless, of course, the landlord could oppose renewal under one of the grounds in the 1954 Act.

14. CONCLUSION

14.1 Break clauses are very important in the commercial lease market-place. It is absolutely essential that their negotiation and implementation is carefully thought through in order to ensure that no nasty surprises are forthcoming. This is yet another situation where I believe it is essential that lawyers and surveyors work together; putting this negatively, it is perhaps one of the most clear-cut examples of the dangers that exist where they do not.

Many of the dangers can be circumvented by careful planning. Our two professions should work in tandem, ensuring that break clauses that are negotiated serve the purpose for which they are sought and that there is no legislative or drafting interference that prevents them from operating as required. The most important facet of the exercise of a break clause must surely be certainty. The person serving notice must do so in circumstances where he knows, for sure, that the lease will determine on expiry of the notice.

CHAPTER 5

KEEP OPEN CLAUSES

1. WHAT IS A KEEP OPEN CLAUSE?

1.1   Most leases contain user clauses restricting the type of use that can be carried out on the premises. Sometimes these clauses are phrased as positive clauses requiring the tenant to use the premises for specified purposes or even more clearly setting out detailed obligations to trade at certain times. Where the user clause states a requirement to use the premises, say, as a retail shop and the clause is phrased positively the question has been posed whether this involves a positive obligation to keep open so that such a clause can be distinguished from one phrased in the negative, i.e. 'not to use the premises other than as a retail shop'. It is not absolutely clear that phrasing a user obligation in a positive way does this and I believe that it is no more than a restatement of what is allowed as opposed to an obligation to trade.

1.2   There are, however, many leases where continuous trading obligations are intentionally imposed by landlords. 'To keep the premises open for retail trade during the usual business hours in the locality' is a phrase that one often sees in shopping centre leases where landlords are anxious to ensure that their tenants not only commit to paying the rent but also keep their premises open and thus help keep the shopping centre alive. It is clear that such a keep open clause does impose a positive duty to keep the premises open and if the tenant closes down he would be in breach of covenant.

1.3   Why, you may ask, would a tenant want to close down? After all, he has already committed to pay the rent and no doubt repair the premises, perhaps contribute to substantial service charges, rates liabilities and so on and so forth. Surely he would want the opportunity to trade from the premises? Whilst this is clearly the original intention when parties sit down to agree the form of lease, there may be many reasons why the tenant would not wish to continue trading even though he may have to continue paying the outgoings.

1.4   If trade at the premises is not going well then although the tenant would not be able to do anything about mitigating fixed costs it may well be that the variable costs involved in opening the property would add to the loss. If that is the case the tenant may well wish to cut his losses and close down, no doubt whilst looking to dispose of the property. It is in these circumstances that a tenant would not want to be bound by a keep open clause.

1.5   The other side of the coin also needs to be considered. If a landlord can obtain the rent and enforce compliance with the other covenants dealing with obligations to contribute to rating liabilities, service charges, etc. and also obligations to repair, why would the landlord care whether or not the tenant occupies? The fact is, even with the full and detailed responsibilities that would continue under a lease, landlords do want to see their premises occupied. Particularly in the retail and leisure sectors, yields unquestionably suffer where properties are left vacant.

2.   ARE KEEP OPEN CLAUSES ENFORCEABLE?

2.1   Until very recently the courts have shown a marked reluctance to enforce covenants of this nature other than by awarding damages for breach. If a clause contains an obligation to trade then, other than the damages option, the only other remedy really open to the landlord is to seek an injunction requiring the tenant to trade in compliance with his covenant. The courts have been most unwilling to go along with this, feeling that it is an intrusion to require a tenant to carry on a business even if he has obligated himself to do so.

2.2   A majority Court of Appeal decision has now thrown this issue open once again. In *Co-operative Insurance Society Limited* v *Argyll Stores (Holdings) Limited* **1996 9 EG 128** specific performance was awarded. Argyll operated a Safeway Supermarket in Sheffield and their unit comprised some 30% of the total letting area of the shopping centre. They were a key anchor tenant. Argyll were making losses and made the decision to dispose of the unit and, pending the disposal, close it. They made this decision in the full knowledge that by doing so they would breach the keep open clause. The landlords were quite anxious to keep the anchor unit open and even offered Argyll temporary rent concessions whilst doing so. They were ignored, the Safeway store closed and Argyll stripped out the unit. Evidence showed that it would cost about £1 million to reinstate it. The judges accepted that damages would normally be the appropriate remedy and cited *Braddon Towers Limited* v *International Stores Limited* **1987 1 EGLR 209** where the High Court somewhat reluctantly refused to grant an injunction. In this new case the court felt that there could be really no better circumstances for granting an injunction. The clause was clear and Safeway had flagrantly breached it in the full knowledge of the consequences. The court were moved by the fact that if an injunction was not granted here, where a responsible and substantial company, properly advised, had undertaken to keep the premises open and had breached that obligation, then probably it would never be appropriate for an injunction to be granted. As I say, this was not a unanimous decision of the court and the dissenting judgement made it clear that granting injunctive relief could expose the defendant to unquantifiable losses way out of proportion to the loss which his breach of covenant had caused. Injunctive relief is an equitable remedy and this did not sound equitable to the dissenting judge. However the Court of Appeal decision is now good law although this case has been appealed to the House of Lords. Anchor tenants must clearly be careful that if they agree to a continuous trading clause the likelihood is that, if they wish to close their unit, they could face claims for injunctive relief and an obligation to keep open and not merely damages as had been ordered in the cases of *Costain Property Developments Limited* v *Finlay and Company Limited* **1988 NPC 93** and *Transworld Land Company Limited* v *J Sainsbury PLC* **1990 EGCS 49**.

3. PRACTICAL POINTS

3.1   Assuming the court's position is shifting and the previous reluctance to grant injunctive relief is to become a thing of the past, tenants must be even more wary before they accept keep open clauses. Obviously anchor tenants are very important to shopping centre and leisure schemes since many of the other traders would simply not be able to operate unless the main traders were occupying and open to the public. An extension of that principal, certainly in shopping centres, has seen landlords seek keep open clauses from multiple retailers even where the amount of space they are taking is relatively small and clearly they are not a key tenant for the scheme on their own. The landlord's position has tended to be to seek such clauses in order to ensure that a number of tenants on any particular mall do not close down. It is rare however that the closure of any one individual tenant which is not one of the anchor tenants will give rise to much of a problem for the landlord. However, if the landlord can show damage then there is no reason why it should not be able to seek recompense from the tenant. Equally, on the authority of *Co-operative Insurance* it may even be able to ask the tenant to go back in and trade.

3.2   With the move towards turnover rents in shopping centre leases it is not difficult to see how a landlord could have a substantial loss in income if a tenant were to close down. Obviously the turnover from that individual tenant would be affected and if that tenant and perhaps one or two other tenants on the relevant mall were to close, the turnover of other units might also be affected and thus affect the landlord's income.

3.3   So keep open clauses are very much a live issue. Tenants should look very carefully before accepting them for the obvious reason that they are increasing their potential exposure. Certainly tenants should not face the possibility of being liable for breach of a continuous trading clause after they have parted with possession.

3.4   If an original tenant of a pre-1995 lease had covenanted to keep premises open and were to subsequently assign those premises, there is no reason why that tenant could not be made liable for a subsequent closure by an assignee. Clearly the tenant is likely to be very aggrieved by this because he will have little, if any, control over the subsequent assignee and any desire that it may have to close its unit. The overriding lease rights contained in the 1995 Act may help but I do think that a properly-advised tenant should ensure that it cannot be made liable under a continuous trading clause where any closure is by an assignee. The same applies in a new lease under the 1995 Act where an assigning tenant retains liability under an AGA.

3.5 If a tenant is forced to accept a continuous trading clause there are many other specific exceptions that may be negotiated. These may include:

3.5.1 A period of authorised closure pending a disposition of the unit or whilst carrying out lawful alterations;

3.5.2 Permitted closure if it is unlawful to trade or if the premises are damaged by one of the insured risks;

3.5.3 Closure if the tenant has underlet and the underlessee refuses to keep open; and

3.5.4 In small units, perhaps where there is a family business, closure during holiday periods.

One cannot really over emphasize the need to try and negotiate exclusions of this nature and, had the first been included in the *Argyll* lease, closure of the Safeway store would not necessarily have given rise to a breach or any claim for an injunction. As you will see in Chapter 6 on the 1954 Act, the *Esselte* decision now makes it clear that tenants need not serve a Section 27 notice if they are vacating at the end of the contractual term; it will be important that the tenant is not occupying the premises for this to be the case. This may leave the tenant in the position of having to vacate the premises and in this case the inter-relationship with a keep open clause will be vital. Perhaps the tenant ought to be allowed to vacate in the last three months of the term as an additional exception to cater for this.

3.6 Now that the court has demonstrated that it may well require tenants to open and trade from premises, I think that tenants should try and negotiate that their liability for breach of such a clause will give rise to damages only.

3.7   For existing leases there is little that can be done other than perhaps varying the lease and the landlord may be reluctant to do that for many reasons not least of which might be the fear of losing original tenant liability in some form or another on the strength of *Friends Provident Life Office* v *British Railways Board* (see Chapter 1, paragraph 10).

3.8   An alternative way of dealing with continuous trading clauses and potential breach of them would be to provide for liquidated damages if a tenant is in breach of an obligation to trade. Some shopping centres already include this, requiring the tenant to pay, say, two days' rent for every day that the tenant closes. Do not forget that if one inserts a liquidated damages clause of this nature, then if there is a breach and the landlord wishes to recover any such sums from any former tenant, it will be necessary for the landlord to seek to recover them within the six-month period inserted by Section 17 of the 1995 Act. This applies for both new and old leases. Of course any former tenant paying in full would have the right to an overriding tenancy.

3.9   This all needs to be very carefully thought through. If the tenant breaches a keep open clause which gives rise to a claim for liquidated damages and if that tenant is not the original tenant, then if the landlord seeks recovery of those liquidated damages from a former tenant by service of a Section 17 notice then, if that former tenant claims an overriding lease, the landlord may suffer a double jeopardy. First of all the landlord would have lost the occupation of the tenant that it was trying to protect. Secondly, if the former tenant has been able to obtain an overriding lease and if there was a continuing breach of covenant that enables it to forfeit the existing lease, then the landlord may not only lose the occupation of the tenant it was trying to make trade from the premises but the landlord may also lose the lease itself which was granted to that tenant. The position may become even more complicated if the former tenant, having forfeited the lease, goes back into occupation itself. (For more on Section 17 notices and overriding leases see Chapter 1, paragraphs 8 and 9.)

4. CONTINUOUS TRADING AND THE SUNDAY TRADING ACT

4.1 Section 3 of the Sunday Trading Act 1994 provides that any lease entered into before 26 August 1994 requiring a shop to open during 'normal business hours', or hours to be determined by someone other than the occupier itself, shall not be regarded as requiring the occupier to trade on Sundays save that this does not apply to the extent that the covenant is specific and relates to the sort of Sunday trading permitted before the 1994 Act.

4.2 The Act does not talk about lease renewals and one can only assume that a renewal lease granted after that date can require Sunday trading if Sundays are part of the normal business hours. This seems almost certainly the correct interpretation, since the 1994 Act does allow leases entered into before its commencement to require Sunday trading if there is a post-Act variation. Surely a lease renewal applies even more so. This is something that the parties would wish to take into account in considering the terms of the new lease on renewal.

4.3 A covenant not to trade on Sundays, whether made before or after the relevant date is unaffected by the Act. Accordingly, where one is negotiating a lease the position regarding Sunday trading ought to be specifically addressed. The tenant will no doubt require maximum flexibility but the landlord may also have an input since it may not want to be responsible for the provision of services etc. on Sundays.

4.4 Large shops may not trade for more than six hours on a Sunday between 10.00 a.m. and 6.00 p.m. and before trading they must give local authorities fourteen days' notice of their intended trading. A large shop is one having a 'relevant' floor area exceeding 280 square metres. This is not the same as the gross internal area. The Act does not restrict the opening hours of small shops and there are a range of exempted large shops which are also not restricted such as airport shopping, petrol stations and motorway service stations. It is worth just looking carefully at what the relevant area is. It excludes parts of a building which are not trading areas on other days. DIY stores and garden centres are not exempt, but they may not actually be within the definition of large shops anyway because external areas are excluded as are internal areas used as restaurants and not for the sale or display of goods.

4.5   Large shops also have restrictions in the Sunday Trading Act whereby the local authority (which regulates the enforcement of the Act generally) controls loading before 9.00 a.m. on a Sunday morning. Local authorities must be notified before any tenant trades on a Sunday. At least fourteen days' notice of intended trading must be given and it is worth emphasizing that even with the Sunday Trading Act, trading is not permitted on Easter Sunday or Christmas Day.

5.   COVENANTS RESTRICTING USER

5.1   It is not uncommon in retail and leisure schemes for landlords to enter into covenants restricting the type of users that will be allowed to occupy parts of a scheme, leisure park, shopping centre, etc. Tenants often perceive a necessity to restrict competition and negotiate a restrictive covenant. If this is done, then clearly landlords cannot let other parts of the affected scheme to a competing covenant; should they do so, unwittingly or not, they would be in breach and liable for damages.

5.2   Where there is a restrictive covenant prohibiting competing uses, obviously all other leases on the park need to prohibit the carrying out of such use and it is essential that time and effort is spent on ensuring that all of the covenants marry up.

5.3   Where there is a restriction prohibiting a certain use in order that the landlord can ensure that it can comply with a covenant to another tenant in which the landlord has said that it will not allow competing uses on the premises, then the rent review implications of the restrictive user need to be considered. The tenant who is not permitted to use his premises for a purpose which might otherwise be a suitable purpose may want to bring that into the equation on review, in order to endeavour to negotiate a discount to reflect the restrictive user and therefore minimized opportunities for alienation.

5.4   All of this needs to be carefully thought through where one is dealing with a leisure scheme, shopping centre, etc. where there are going to be competing users; a clear letting policy needs to be established and, once it is established, everyone must stick to it.

5.5   In 1996 the High Court had to consider a situation where a tenant was complaining about a competing user in adjoining premises in circumstances where the tenant's lease did not contain any restriction on user. The facts of *Romulus Trading Company Limited and Another v Comet Properties Limited* **1996 48 EG 157** are relatively straightforward. The underlease in question demised premises which were used as banking premises including the provisions of safes and safe-deposit boxes. Fifteen years after the lease was granted the landlords granted an underlease of nearby premises to a further tenant for a competing use. Proceedings were issued by the tenant who contended that by letting the nearby premises the landlords were breaching their obligation not to derogate from their grant as well as the express covenant which was contained in the lease and which required them to administer the building in accordance with the principles of good estate management. The simple question before the court was whether there was any reasonable cause of action. Did a good estate management clause require the landlord to take this sort of thing into account when letting adjoining premises? The answer was no and the application to strike out was allowed. *Romulus* clearly establishes that where there is no restrictive covenant then there is nothing to stop a landlord from leasing any part of his portfolio for any purpose whatsoever, whether competing or not.

5.6   I cannot say that I am terribly surprised at this decision and I think it would have been quite ridiculous had the court established any form of precedent which might require landlords to consider letting policy as part of a general obligation to administer a building 'in accordance with principles of good estate management'. The provisions that dealt with that in *Romulus* where contained in the landlord's covenant and I think anyone reading them would believe (as did the court) that they were inserted by reference to service charge, repairing obligations and the like. The judge quoted the two leading textbooks, *Hill and Redman* and *Woodfall* (see Recommended reading), and made it clear that the good estate management clause could not be strained to include consideration of letting policy. The court went on to say that even if administration were to include letting policy, the clause would have to be construed as the law stood when the lease was granted in 1978. This was enshrined in the decision of **Port v Griffith 1938 1 AER 295** and made it clear that where premises are let for a particular trade there was nothing to prevent the landlord from leasing an adjoining shop for the same purpose.

The court also looked at the question of derogation of grant. The concept of this is fairly straightforward, but the court did not feel it was appropriate. Again the **Port v Griffith** decision was considered by the court and held to remain good law. There were one or two cases where perhaps some form of derogation claim might have been able to get off the ground. These were quoted by the court but excluded. It is worth considering them. **Molton Builders Limited v City of Westminster 1975 30 P&CR 1821** found Lord Denning stating that where one person agrees to confer a particular benefit on another 'he must not do anything which substantially deprives the other of the enjoyment of that benefit: because that would be to take away with one hand what is given with the other'. Also **British Leyland Motor Corporation Limited v Armstrong Patents Company Limited 1986 AC 577** was a House of Lords decision concerning the manufacture of spare parts for British Leyland vehicles. Again the principle of non-derogation of grant was used in **British Leyland**. None the less the court felt that there was no derogation. **Port v Griffith** was still good law and on behalf of all landlords I am rather pleased that the court felt able to decide as it did. I think it would have been nonsensical to find that a landlord's ability to let its premises was constrained in this way. If there is to be a restrictive covenant against competing users, the parties should clearly negotiate it. As the judge quite rightly pointed out in **Romulus** there are circumstances where competing users are thought to be a good thing: one quite often sees competing users sharing the same mall or street. How could this situation possibly be tolerated if one had to always have one eye on the possibility that by allowing a competing user to share a mall or a street, one was potentially exposed to an action for derogation of grant.

CHAPTER 6

LANDLORD AND TENANT ACT 1954 RENEWALS

1. GENERAL PRINCIPLES

1.1   For over forty years business tenants in England and Wales have enjoyed security of tenure in their leases. This is different to their Scottish counterparts and I believe it is a unique position in Europe.

1.2   It is possible to exclude security of tenure and I shall look at that briefly in this chapter, but unless the parties have agreed to remove security, and have gone to the trouble of obtaining a court order ratifying those negotiations, business leases in England and Wales are protected under the 1954 Act.

1.3   The machinery of the 1954 Act and procedures required to be carried out under it in order to retain protection are complex. They invariably require certain notices to be served in specified or prescribed forms and it is necessary to issue proceedings in court in order to renew a lease, and all of this within stipulated and strict time-limits. The courts have been unrelenting where parties have missed those time-limits or have failed to serve the right notices or even when notices have been served but have been misconceived. For these reasons I make no apology for the emphasis in this chapter on the need for clarity, certainty, precision and, once again, the need for lawyers and surveyors to work together in order to protect their clients and retain the rights that the legislation has given them.

1.4   A significant proportion of negligence claims against both solicitors and surveyors arise out of 1954 Act renewals, missed time-limits and the like. Indeed, lawyers are now finding that their professional indemnity insurance deductibles increase substantially following claims made for notices etc. served out of time. Indeed the Solicitors' Insurance Indemnity Fund has now introduced a system of penalty deductibles whereby the excess on solicitors' insurance is significantly increased in respect of a claim arising from failure to do various things, including serve notice or issue an application under the 1954 Act. The purpose of this is to encourage lawyers to implement practice-management systems leading to a prevention of such avoidable actions.

1.5   Tenants jealously guard the protection that has been given to them by the 1954 Act and there may be a world of difference between two leases of the same set of premises granted on exactly the same terms but one excluding security of tenure. As an illustration of just how valuable the right to security of tenure is, take the case of *Ricci* v *Masons* **1993 38 EG 154**. Here the court was concerned with a case where a tenant was out of time and no longer protected under the 1954 Act as a result of lawyers not complying with appropriate time-limits. The landlord was prepared to grant the tenant a new lease in this case, but only subject to obtaining a court order excluding security of tenure. The tenant was not faced with losing the right to remain in the premises but merely the lack of any guarantee of protection at the time this new lease would ultimately come to an end. The tenant was suing his lawyers for damages on the basis that the excluded lease would not be as valuable to the tenant as would have been a protected lease. This loss of protection sometime in the future was valued at £100,000, since these were the damages that the lawyers were ordered to pay the tenant to compensate him.

1.6   The concept of 1954 Act protection is therefore very important and a key part of business lease negotiations.

2.   WHEN DOES THE ACT APPLY?

2.1   Section 23 of the 1954 Act confers protection where the property comprised in a tenancy is occupied by the tenant for the purposes of a business. We shall look at the concept of occupation a little later but, first, a word or two on the position where the tenant simply vacates. What would happen to a 'protected' lease if the tenant were simply to leave? The matter had not been adjudicated by the courts until 1990, many years after the

1954 Act was passed. Before 1990 one school of thought was that if a tenant simply left the premises after the contractual termination date, or any later date substituted by a Section 25 notice, then the tenant could hardly be said to be 'occupying for the purposes of a business' and since Section 23 only applies to tenants who are occupying, the tenant would lose protection and cease to be entitled to a new lease.

2.2 In the case of *Longacre Securities* v *Electra Acoustic Industries Limited* **1990 06 EG 103** the Court of Appeal had a different view when it had to determine the date upon which the 1954 Act were to cease to apply. Here the court was concerned with a tenant who no longer wished to stay in the premises and the case concerned the date upon which the tenant's liabilities would cease.

2.3 In *Longacre* the contractual term of the lease was due to end on 25 March 1988. Early in March the landlord served a Section 25 notice terminating the lease in March 1989. The tenant responded with a Section 27 notice giving three months' notice expiring on 24 June 1988. The tenant vacated before 25 March 1988. The question before the court was whether the expiry date was 25 March 1988 (the contractual termination date), 24 June 1988 (expiry of the Section 27 notice), or 1 March 1989 (the termination date in the landlord's Section 25 notice).

The court selected 24 June 1988. They said that once the 1954 Act applied, automatic continuation applied until notice was served either under Section 25 or Section 27. The position seemed to have been settled in 1990.

2.4 In 1995, *Esselte AB and Another* v *Pearl Assurance PLC* **1995 2 EGLR 61** seemed to clarify the need for notices in situations where a tenant vacates before the contractual termination date. Here the tenant vacated in February 1993. They had served a notice but the notice was insufficient and did not satisfy the demands of Section 27(1). In January 1993, the tenant, fearing this, served a fresh notice but this time under Section 27(2) because the three months' notice that needed to be given spanned the contractual termination date. Three months from January takes you to April and, since the next quarter-day is 24 June, the tenant's notice served in January terminated the lease in June. They served this without prejudice to their contention that they were not in occupation and could quit at the end of the contractual term without notice and obviously their concern was to prevent the need to pay the rent between the end of the contractual term and 24 June. The High Court reiterated the need for notices and therefore, even if no Section 25 notice or Section 26 request has been served, stated that the tenancy continues until a Section 27 notice validly brings it to an end.

2.5   Most practitioners thought this was settled law but *Esselte* was taken to the Court of Appeal where it was reversed. The Court of Appeal decision is reported at **1996 EGCS 178**. The Court of Appeal said that *Longacre* was wrong and where a tenant vacated before the contractual termination date the tenancy would simply come to an end. The Court of Appeal considered the three Sections: 23, 24 and 27. Section 23 stated that Part II of the 1954 Act applies to a tenancy where the property is occupied for the purposes of a business and Section 24 provides that a tenancy to which Part II applies cannot come to an end other than in accordance with the provisions of that Part of the 1954 Act. Section 27 states that where a tenant under a tenancy to which Part II applies gives notice, Section 24 does not have effect. The Court of Appeal felt that reference to a tenancy 'to which this Part of this Act applies' referred to the present and should not be construed to mean 'a tenancy to which this Part of this Act applies *or has applied*' (writer's italics). The Court of Appeal made it clear that the Section showed that occupation was essential and, since the Section was expressed in the present tense, it could not be construed to include the past. The Court of Appeal acknowledged that, if this conclusion was correct, it was contrary to *Longacre* but drew attention to the case of *Morrison Holdings Limited* v *Manders Limited* **1976 1 WLR 533**, which the court felt dealt with a similar issue to the one considered in *Longacre* and should have been referred to in *Longacre*. The Court of Appeal felt that, had it been referred to in *Longacre*, the court would have been bound to follow it. Normally the Court of Appeal will not reverse its own decisions. It will normally feel bound by previous Court of Appeal precedents. This is not the case where those precedents are formed without taking into account relevant cases and because *Morrison* and also *I and H Caplan* v *Caplan (No. 2)* **1963 1 WLR 1247** had not been considered in the Court of Appeal hearing of

Longacre and since they concerned the same topic (i.e. that the tenancy must be one to which the 1954 Act *currently* applies) the Court of Appeal felt free to ignore the *Longacre* decision.

2.6 After *Longacre* practitioners felt it was wrong to advise a tenant who did not wish to retain protected premises that he only had to leave. The authority of *Longacre* required service of a notice with the appropriate pre-planning. The Court of Appeal in *Esselte* has now made it clear that if a lease comes to an end and prior to the contractual termination date the tenant vacates, that is all that is necessary and no notices need be served.

2.7 So where you are advising a tenant who does not wish to renew a 1954 Act protected tenancy it seems, on the authority of *Esselte*, that the pre-planning that one was advising tenants was so necessary following *Longacre* is no longer needed. All the tenant needs to do is actually vacate.

2.8 For the tenant to be off the hook, it is clear that he must no longer occupy the premises for the purposes of a business and if one is advising a tenant to vacate in order to avoid the 1954 Act applying in circumstances where the tenant does not wish to renew, then it is important that the tenant does not occupy and that all vestiges of occupation are removed. Occupation does not always require physical occupation or trading and I think tenants need to be absolutely sure that they are no longer occupying or they may have some unpleasant surprises awaiting them. If the tenant cannot satisfy the test that it is not occupying, then clearly pre-planning is needed and the advice that would be given to a tenant is exactly the same as the advice that was being given after *Longacre* and before the Court of Appeal decision in *Esselte*. In these circumstances, for example, if a lease was due to come to an end on the September quarter-day, it is now clear that prior to 29 September the tenant can cease occupation, stop Section 23 applying and no notices need to be served. If it fails to do that, notice can be given under Section 27 only up to 29 June. After 29 June notice can still be given under Section 27 but only under subsection (2) of that Section and this will require the Section 27 notice to end on a quarter-day. So, if in these circumstances the tenant were to serve Section 27(2) notice on 30 June, this notice could not end the tenancy before 25 December. At least three months' notice would have to be given and this must end on a quarter-day. One will appreciate therefore that if one is looking at a lease where the contractual termination date ends on 29 September, then if that date comes and goes and the tenant is still in occupation for the purposes of a business, the lease will need to be terminated under Section 27(2) and it is self-evident in these circumstances that if the notice is served only after the September quarter-day, as it is almost certainly likely to be, the lease could not end before the March quarter-day.

2.9   These issues concerned tenants greatly before the Court of Appeal decision in *Esselte* but now it is clear that so long as the tenant ceases to occupy and Section 23 no longer applies *before* the contractual termination date, everything will be all right. Bearing in mind the fact that it is not always clear which day a lease terminates on, and given the need for the tenant to vacate before the end of the term, tenants should not leave their departure to the last moment.

2.10   The previous position needs to be considered in the light of leases where there is a continuous trading clause or a keep open clause (for more on this see Chapter 5). If a tenant has signed up to a keep open clause then arguably it cannot cease occupation for the purposes of a business without breaching that clause. Accordingly it may not be able to take advantage of the Court of Appeal decision in *Esselte* without exposing itself either to an action for damages or perhaps even a claim for injunctive relief. The court might feel that the landlord would be entitled to damages if the tenant breached such a clause in order to vacate so that it could take advantage of the *Esselte* decision; I suppose that if a court did feel that this was the correct approach, the level of damages might well be the amount of rent between the earliest date that the lease could have been brought to an end under Section 27 (without the tenant breaching the continuous trading clause) and the contractual termination date. For this reason, I think that it is still important to consider whether a Section 27 notice is needed and it is not always good advice to simply tell any commercial tenant who wants out that all he needs to do is vacate before the contractual termination date and his worries will be over. Pre-planning is still very important and, certainly, landlords and tenants need to give some thought to what needs to be done in order to ensure that the 1954 Act does not continue liabilities in circumstances where a tenant does not wish to renew a lease.

2.11 Once a tenant has applied for a new tenancy, the position shifts. Section 27 notices are replaced by Section 64 of the 1954 Act which alters the termination date in the Section 25 notice or Section 26 request to the date three months after the date the application to the court is finally disposed of. If the tenant discontinues then Section 64 operates, although it is not absolutely certain whether this excludes Section 27. Clearly if the application to the court is made after a Section 26 request the tenant cannot serve a Section 27 notice because this is prohibited by Section 26(4). However, he can discontinue the application to the court. Where the application has been made following service of a Section 25 notice and where the tenant no longer wishes to continue, it is not clear whether he needs to serve a Section 27 notice or whether the proceedings will come to an end pursuant to Section 64. I think to be absolutely clear, notices under both Sections may need to be served. The tenant should take advice early and make sure that all proper notices are served. Lawyers and surveyors should be pro-active in informing their clients of these requirements as early as possible.

2.12 Section 24(3) adds a further complication. This section states that where the tenancy is continuing but the tenant ceases to occupy the landlord may serve notice under subparagraph (a) of that Section. The notice required is between three and six months and brings the tenancy to an end. Once the landlord serves that notice the tenant cannot save the day by going back into occupation. This is made clear by Section 24(3)(b). I cannot see anything in Section 24(3) that prevents service of that notice after a Section 25 notice or Section 26 request has been made although the *Caplan* case makes it clear that this Section does not apply once proceedings have been issued. From then onwards only dismissal of the application under Section 64 will be sufficient.

2.13 It is reasonably understandable that a landlord should be able to bring the lease to an end if the tenant has vacated. The tenant may not do anything to bring the lease to an end and therefore it is logical that there should be a mechanism for the landlord to be able to serve a notice in order to terminate the landlord/tenant relationship where the tenant vacates. The landlord has that right under Section 64 once proceedings have been issued but, before then, certainly Section 24(3) may help.

2.14 Tenants who want to rid themselves of premises must therefore be absolutely sure that they have served the appropriate notice and if they have not done this they may well retain a continuing liability. Those tenants who are seeking to renew must make sure that they do not render themselves vulnerable to attack by ceasing to occupy. If Section 24(3) applies, then once the tenant has ceased to occupy, Section 24(3)(b) will prevent him from going back into occupation after service of a notice. Similarly, under *Caplan* an application may be made by the landlord at any time for dismissal of the proceedings if the tenant no longer occupies. Occupation is therefore vital if the tenant wants to retain protection although if he does not, ceasing to occupy will not end his lease obligations.

2.15 The inter-relationship between the various Sections is quite difficult to fully comprehend and the Court of Appeal decision in *Esselte* asks as many questions as it answers.

Where one is confronted with a tenant who wants to vacate and bring an end to his responsibilities, I think the following is now good law:

2.15.1 Where no notices are served all the tenant needs to do is vacate prior to the contractual termination date;

2.15.2 Where a Section 25 notice has been served and that notice specifies the contractual termination date as the expiry date then the tenant needs to do nothing. So long as he does not serve his counter-notice within two months, or if he does, so long as he does not make application to the court within the two-to-four-month period, he will have no right to apply for a new tenancy and his lease will come to an end on the contractual termination date;

2.15.3 If the tenant receives a Section 25 notice, does everything necessary to protect his position and then changes his mind and decides not to stay, he must simply withdraw his application for a new tenancy and the lease will come to an end either on the date specified in the Section 25 notice or, if the tenant has left it too late, three months after the withdrawal if this is later. This is set out in Section 64;

2.15.4   Where a Section 25 notice has been served and the termination date is beyond the contractual termination date, the tenant probably need not serve a Section 27 notice. If he simply stops occupation that will almost certainly be sufficient. This is not absolutely clear and Section 27 notices may still be used in these circumstances. Nothing will be lost so long as the Section 27 notice is served at least three months before the contractual termination date. Personally I am not sure that it is necessary to serve a Section 27 notice in these circumstances although I have seen it argued that one should do this in order to make the tenant's position clear.

If a tenant remembers to do this, nothing is lost by doing so but I would certainly not advocate serving a Section 27 notice where less than three months remain between the date the tenant gets round to serving the notice and the contractual termination date. In these circumstances notices would need to be served under Section 27(2). These notices must end on a quarter-day and for the reasons set out above this is clearly not a good idea; and

2.15.5   If the tenancy is already continuing, a tenant can serve a Section 27(2) notice and I think he must continue to do this. I do not think that *Esselte* allows the tenant to merely cease occupation. Whilst a landlord cannot serve an effective Section 25 notice on a tenant who is not in occupation and similarly a tenant could not serve a Section 26 request or apply for a new tenancy, I do not think it is correct that the tenant merely ceasing to occupy will bring the tenancy to an end. This would effectively render Section 24(3)(a), referred to above, redundant. Section 27(2) notices apply to tenancies 'continuing ... under the 1954 Act'. This, of course, begs the question whether they are continuing if the tenant is not in occupation but I do think it would be somewhat ridiculous if Section 27(2) notices were not needed in these circumstances. My strong advice to any tenant who is the subject of a statutory continuation is not to simply vacate and hope for the best. A Section 27(2) notice should be served.

2.16 What happens where a Section 25 notice is served during the statutory continuation? For the reasons set out in the immediately preceding paragraph, I do not think that the tenant can get out of his liabilities by merely ceasing to occupy. I think he must serve a Section 27(2) notice, although this is not clear law.

2.17 This is an extremely and, arguably unnecessarily, complicated area of law and one which has changed recently. It seems to me ridiculous that such a straightforward procedure should have evoked conflicting decisions in the courts; even more so since there was legislation on the subject for over thirty years following enactment of the 1954 Act. I only hope that prospective reform of the 1954 Act clarifies these issues. Until then, legal advice on individual circumstances must be sought and as early on as possible.

3. WHAT IS OCCUPATION?

3.1 Most of what we were talking about in paragraph 2, above, deals with the situation where the tenant is desperate to vacate and bring his liabilities to an end. The question of what constitutes occupation needs to be considered in the context of tenants who are endeavouring to prove a right to a renewal lease. We have seen that the 1954 Act requires that the premises are occupied for the purposes of a business. There are many cases that have considered what qualifies as occupation. Clearly a unit does not have to be physically occupied by its tenant at all times in order to qualify but there is no clear set of guidelines that one can advise a tenant to follow in order to qualify. It is relatively straightforward where one has occupational premises like a shop, office accommodation, etc. but there are greater difficulties where one is faced with what might conveniently be called 'passive occupation'. It has always been thought that the electricity companies, for example, have protection under the 1954 Act in relation to leases of substations. Clearly the electricity company itself does not occupy although the substation site is no doubt 'occupied' by equipment. In

Wandsworth LBC v *Singh* **1991 62 P&CR 219** the council had a lease of park-land. Again there was no physical occupation although the council used their own staff to inspect and manage the park and the court held that the council had protection. The council's control and supervision were sufficient to confer occupation.

3.2 What happens in situations where the tenant seeking renewal 'occupies' the property as a business of a landlord running serviced accommodation or a market? The House of Lords decision of *Graysim Holdings Limited* v *P and O Property Holdings Limited* **1995 4 AER 831** concerned Wallasey Market. This was an enclosed market hall where Graysim were tenant and themselves sublet units to stallholders who operated the stalls. It was clear on the facts of *Graysim* that each of the units were separate entities: the stallholders had their own shutters and secured their own units. The House of Lords had to decide whether any part of the premises were 'occupied' by Graysim and they decided that they were not. The unit holders had protection and the court held that there could not be dual occupation. The subtenants who did have protection were the only people that did so and Graysim did not occupy for the purposes of a business.

3.3 It is clear from Section 23 that the tenant seeking the protection of the 1954 Act must be in occupation for the purposes of a business. It is equally a question of fact whether they are truly in occupation and, although it will not always be necessary for physical occupation, where there is no physical occupation the matter must be considered with great care.

3.4 Since *Graysim*, careful advice must be given to clients who hold leases where their business is running markets, business centres or serviced accommodation. They may well not have the protection of the 1954 Act when their lease comes to an end and I think it is fundamental to make certain that any licences or leases granted to the people in physical occupation do not confer any statutory protection. If this is not done, certainly the holder of the head lease faces the prospect of not having the right to renew at the end of the contractual term. A tenant taking an assignment of an existing lease in order to run a market, serviced accommodation, etc. from the premises must make sure that it has the right to renew at the end of the term. If there is any doubt about this, as a result of the occupational lessees/licensees having protection, that tenant must clearly know the risks before acquiring the lease and purchasing the business if it is to avoid any nasty shocks later on which might adversely affect the value of its business.

3.5   The 1954 Act makes special provisions for partnerships and companies and, in particular, if there is a group of companies as defined under Section 42, then even if the tenancy is vested in one company where occupation of the property is by another, the tenant would not lose the right of renewal on the basis that it does not occupy but its subsidiary or holding company does.

3.6   The question of occupation is one that necessarily involves a careful consideration of the facts of each individual case.

4.   LIABILITY OF THE ORIGINAL TENANT AT THE END OF THE TERM

4.1   *City of London Corporation* v *Fell* and *Herbert Duncan Limited* v *Cluttons*, jointly reported at **1993 4 EG 115**, were decisions handed down in 1992 concerning Section 24 of the 1954 Act. Was the original tenant liable during the continuation period? At first instance the *City of London* had said no and *Herbert Duncan* had said yes.

4.2   In both cases the original tenant had assigned the lease which was continuing under the 1954 Act. Claims had been made against the original tenant for rent arrears.

4.3   The Court of Appeal backed the decision in *City of London*; the original tenant could not be liable for rent payable during the period of holding over. The court felt that, for the purposes of the 1954 Act, the tenant could only be the person who had the right to renew under the Act. The original tenant no longer held the land. On this basis, of course, it follows that where the original tenant has assigned the tenancy, before the end of the contractual term, the tenancy which continues under Section 24 of the 1954 Act can only be the tenancy of the assignee. The contractual obligations of the original tenant are not independently continued. Indeed the original tenant is not in occupation and to that extent, as we have already seen, the 1954 Act does not apply to him.

4.4   The court refused to express an opinion as to whether the contractual obligations of the original tenant would have ceased and not have been continued under the 1954 Act had there been no assignment. It was clear that the court would lean against such a construction but since the matter was not fully argued and was not directly relevant to the appeal, the court refused to give an opinion.

4.5   In *Herbert Duncan* there were two additional features. Firstly, a definition of 'the term' which included periods of holding over and extension and secondly, an interim rent award by consent between the landlord and the tenant.

4.6   If the term was defined to include periods of holding over the court felt that the original tenant should be liable for payment of the contractual rent during that period. This was not inconsistent with the decision of *City of London* since all the original tenant was being asked to do was comply with its contractual obligations. Interim rent was a different matter. The court felt that this was the subject of a contract between landlord and assignee since under Section 24A of the 1954 Act interim rent applied only in relation to a tenancy to which the Act applied.

4.7   The original tenant had no part of the 1954 Act proceedings and therefore should not be responsible for paying any interim rent awarded under them.

4.8   So if a landlord wants to make the original tenant liable for the rent during the holding over period then he must define the term to include that holding over period. If he wants to go further and get an increased rent for that period and be able to recover any arrears of such increase from the original tenant then it is no use trying to rely on Section 24A. He must ensure that the rent review clause itself contains a last-day review. Without that, the original tenant who has assigned would no longer be liable for any increased rent during the holding over period.

4.9   So once again tenants must be wary of the last-day or penultimate-day rent review since on the authority of *Herbert Duncan* this may fix the original tenant with liability which would not arise if there was merely an interim rent application. Extra vigilance is needed where the landlord has defined the expression 'term' to include periods of holding over and simply states that the rent is to be reviewed 'every five years of the term'. Wording of this nature may well create a last-day review without the tenant even realizing.

4.10   As we saw in Chapter 2, *Willison v Cheverell Estates and Another* **1995 EGCS 111** also looked at whether a rent review clause would survive termination of the contractual term of a lease. There was no express definition of 'the term' to include statutory continuations and, therefore, the landlord failed but the court left open the question of whether this would be the same had the landlord defined the expression 'term' to include extensions.

4.11   These points will no doubt reduce in importance over the years as original tenant liability is finally eroded. However, pre-1996 leases will be with us for many years to come and, therefore, we have not seen the end of this quite yet. Similarly, new leases under the 1995 Act might still leave the original tenant with the same kind of problem if there has been only one assignment during the term and the original tenant has retained liability under an AGA.

5.   SOME SECTION 25 NOTICE PROBLEMS

5.1   We have seen in Chapter 4 all sorts of problems where notices have not been properly served. I want to emphasize here the need for absolute clarity in service of Section 25 notices. This is the landlord's once-only opportunity to terminate the tenancy and the landlord must simply get it right.

5.2   First of all, if the landlord says it is not going to oppose renewal it is no good changing its mind later and trying to oppose renewal. Once it has said that it will not, it cannot change its mind. The landlord will not get a second bite at the cherry. If the tenant does what it needs to do to retain protection (including remaining in occupation) then if the landlord has said that it will grant a new tenancy it will have no option but to do so. It is essential, therefore, that the landlord decides whether it is happy for the tenant to renew and if it is not, whether it can prove one of the grounds in Section 30 of the 1954 Act.

5.3 The notice must describe the premises carefully. If a tenant is left in any doubt as to the premises to which the notice relates, the notice may be void. A small error is unlikely to invalidate a notice and this was illustrated in *Safeway Food Stores* v *Morris* **1980 254 EG 109** where a garage that the premises had the benefit of was not referred to but the notice was none the less valid. However, in *Herongrove Limited* v *Wates City of London Properties PLC* **1988 1 EGLR 82** a failure to mention storage facilities on a different floor invalidated the notice. While no hard-and-fast rules can really be given, once again I think the overriding principle with Section 25 notices is for them to be carefully considered by the client, its lawyer and surveyor acting in unison as a team. It is necessary to look at the lease, assignments, notices of change of name or ownership and any information that may be given in response to a Section 40 notice and it may even be necessary to look at the premises themselves. Where a company is concerned, the registered office address should be checked and the notice should be carefully proofread for errors before sending it. The landlord should be careful to date and sign the notice and, of course, the notice must also be properly served. A careful consideration of the notice provisions in the lease and any relevant statutory provisions dealing with service, including Section 66(4) of the 1954 Act which incorporates into the 1954 Act the methods of service set out in the 1927 Act, will need to be undertaken and all the points about service referred to in Chapter 4 above should be looked at.

5.4 The notice must not terminate the lease too early. At least six months' notice must be given and if a few days grace is not given in the notice, one might fall foul of this. The old chestnuts of whether a five-year lease commencing on 25 December expires on 24 or 25 December five years later apply just as much to service of the Section 25 notice as any other notice. Given the six-to-twelve-month window, plenty of time should be allowed so that the server of the notice has sufficient breathing space. If one is six months away from the contractual termination date and just getting round to serving a Section 25 notice I think it is prudent to allow a few extra days to take care of the problems of ascertaining on what day the notice was served and on what day the lease actually expires, etc. If the contractual termination date is 25 March and one is serving a Section 25 notice on 25 September, surely it is better to bring that lease to an end, say, at the end of March and thus avoid taking any risk that the notice might terminate the lease prematurely. In a rising market the landlord obviously wants to bring the lease to an end as soon as he can in order to get a higher rent but, even in this situation, it is unlikely that the loss of a few days higher rent is too great a pain to compensate for the risk of serving a notice that is invalid. Remember that if a Section 25 notice fails to give at least six months' notice, it is an invalid notice.

5.5   Any grounds of opposition must be set out in the Section 25 notice. The form of a Section 25 notice contains a statement as to whether the landlord wishes to oppose renewal. This requires a deletion of either the word 'will' or the words 'will not'. This should be dealt with carefully, although in the past the court has forgiven a failure to delete one of these alternatives (*Lewis v MTC Cars Limited* **1975 1 WLR 457**). If the landlord does wish to oppose, it must set out clearly the grounds for opposition. *Nursey v P Curry (Dartford) Limited* **1959 1 AER 497** emphasizes that the landlord cannot amend afterwards. Perhaps it could withdraw the notice and then serve a new one but it is not absolutely certain that a landlord can do this. Certainly if one is in doubt as to which ground under Section 30 one wishes to rely upon, it is possible to add in more than one ground. It is clear, however, that one should not overdo it. It would be very rare indeed that a landlord could reasonably argue a prima-facie case on every ground and a notice citing every ground is almost certain to be void. In *Stradbroke v Mitchell* **1991 3 EG 128**, an agricultural tenancy case, the landlord served notice to quit with no honest belief in its grounds, and failed. Arguably therefore, if one cites every ground in Section 30, unless one honestly believes that they all exist, which is hardly likely, there is a danger of the notice failing.

5.6   In *M and P Enterprises (London) Limited* v *Norfolk Square Hotels Limited* **1994 1 EGLR 129** the court had to consider whether four separate Section 25 notices relating to separate properties within a single tenancy were valid. The reversion had been severed between four landlords and the four defendant landlords owned the two hotels that were the subject of these proceedings. One of these comprised four adjoining buildings and the other was situate on a separate site. The four notices related to different buildings and one related to two. Each notice was accompanied by a letter which referred to all five properties and all four notices cited Section 30(1)(g) as the ground of opposition. On the same day the tenant served four notices under Section 26 requesting a new tenancy of all five properties. These notices were received by the landlords after service of the Section 25 notices and the landlord didn't respond to the Section 26 requests.

5.7   The question was whether the various notices were in respect of the whole of the premises and, for that to be the case, the court felt the notices must be capable of being read as a single notice. Separate notices at the same time would not have been sufficient.

5.8   The court felt that the reasonable tenant (as had the actual tenant) and any reader of this case (including me) would be confused. The reasonable tenant would be under the impression that he was being invited whether or not to serve counter-notices in relation to each of the separate properties. Therefore the Section 25 notices were invalid. In this case all was not totally lost because, since the Section 25 notice had arrived after the Section 26 request, the landlords had complied with the requirement contained in Section 26(6) to give notice to the tenant that the application would be opposed. They could still, therefore, rely on Section 30(1)(g).

5.9   Section 25 notices must be in a prescribed form and since this contains blanks that need to be completed there are numerous opportunities for error! If a Section 25 notice is received and the recipient believes it is misconceived it is sensible to serve a counter-notice without prejudice to the contention that one does not accept validity of the notice. If one does not do that and one is not absolutely right then one could lose protection. In *Smith* v *Draper* **1990 60 P&CR 252** the landlord served a bad Section 25 notice but then served a Section 25 notice again without prejudice to its contention that the first one was valid. The second one was clearly valid and although the first was held to be bad the tenant had done nothing to serve a counter-notice in relation to the second. The tenant lost the chance to renew as a result of that.

6. TENANTS' COUNTER-NOTICES AND TIME-LIMITS

6.1 Once a Section 25 notice is served upon the tenant then, within two months of the landlord giving the notice, the tenant must indicate whether it wishes to give up possession. Whilst the Section 25 notice must be in a prescribed form, the tenant's counter-notice does not have to be in any form but it is important to make sure that it complies with the relatively straightforward requirements of Section 25(5). The safest course of action is merely to follow the wording in the section.

6.2 It seems to me that a great deal more thought generally accompanies service of the Section 25 notice than the tenant's counter-notice. Perhaps this is because the counter-notice does not need to be in prescribed form. I have come across many counter-notices that are not served by recorded delivery or registered post, or where the tenant's surveyors or lawyers serving the notice do not keep a record of service or even a photocopy of the signed counter-notice. Don't forget there is a two-month window, and only a two-month window, for service of these notices and it is important that they are served in time and that the tenant can prove this.

6.3 So assuming that a Section 25 notice has been served and the tenant then serves its counter-notice it must make an application to the court. Another trap for the unwary is that the court application must be made within a period of not less than two months nor more than four months after the Section 25 notice. There have been many situations where a tenant receiving a Section 25 notice immediately does what is necessary to protect its position by stating within two months that it does not wish to give up possession but then either forgets to make the application or does so too early, perhaps not realizing that it must wait for at least two months after the Section 25 notice, before it can apply to the court. Again, careful planning and lawyers working together with surveyors should be able to avoid these straight-forward pitfalls but it is quite extraordinary how often one comes across problems arising from mistakes made in not com-plying with these relatively straightforward requirements.

6.4   Where a tenant has instigated the renewal process with a Section 26 request the landlord must serve notice under Section 26(6) setting out whether it wishes to oppose renewal and then again the application to the court must still be made by the tenant.

6.5   So far as service is concerned one must be careful of what is called 'the corresponding date rule'. In *Dodds* v *Walker* **1981 1 WLR 1027** an application to the court was made on 31 January 1979. The Section 25 notice had been served on the 30 September 1978. In *Dodds* the Court of Appeal held that the application was out of time because the corresponding date in January was the 30th. If a notice under Section 25 is served on 31 December, when will the counter-notice have to be served? Clearly two months, on a corresponding date basis, takes one to 31 February but, even in a leap year, there is never such a date and therefore one must simply take the last date of the month as the corresponding date. The tenant's counter-notice would then have to be served by 28 February and not, say, 3 March. So even allowing for the problems that the gap between service of the Section 25 notice and the first date for application to the court might cause, it is essential that notices are served in accordance with the corresponding date rule.

6.6   I am not going to say very much in this book about who the competent landlord is for the purposes of the 1954 Act. If he is not a freeholder then the competent landlord must have a ten-ancy not expiring within fourteen months or a tenancy which will continue because the head tenant has not been given notice to end it during that period. It is obviously essential that the notices are served on the appropriate party and Section 40 of the 1954 Act is designed to enable information to be obtained so that the notices are served on the right people and clear and careful advice needs to be taken in relation to this. Again this can be quite complicated and early consultation between the client, the surveyor and the lawyer is highly recommended.

7.   1954 ACT COMPENSATION

7.1   Compensation is payable where a tenant is deprived of his right to renew a statutorily protected business lease on grounds (e), (f) or (g). Ground (e) applies where there are complicated lease structures, ground (f) is the redevelopment ground and ground (g) deals with the structure where the landlord requires the property back for its own occupation.

7.2   It is not always possible to exclude this compensation and certainly where the tenant has been in occupation for five years or more, whatever the lease says, he will be entitled to compensation. Where the occupation for business purposes has lasted for five years before the date the tenant is to quit, any agreement to exclude or reduce compensation is void under Section 38(2), 1954 Act.

7.3   Compensation is geared to rateable values. Obviously, rateable values do not always keep pace with inflation and from time to time a multiplier is applied to the relevant rateable value in order to help the compensation provisions keep their value in real terms. The change of rating system, with the move to uniform business rates (UBR) gave the opportunity to remove the old multipliers and base compensation by reference to the new rateable values.

7.4   Before moving on to look at exactly what the figures are, I should mention that a tenant who has been in occupation for fourteen years or more gets twice the amount of compensation than that payable to his shorter-term counterpart. It is worth remembering that the tenant must have occupied for fourteen years and it is interesting that in the case of *Department of the Environment* v *Royal Insurance PLC* **1987 54 P&CR 26**, the lack of occupation for a few days after the lease was granted was critical. This period did not count towards making up the fourteen-year period.

7.5   Prior to the new rating system, the appropriate multiplier was three and accordingly a tenant deprived of the right to renew on grounds (e), (f) or (g) would have been able to receive three times the rateable value. The longer-term tenant (i.e. one who has been in occupation for fourteen years or more) would have a multiple of six applied to the rateable value.

7.6 With the advent of UBR and the rating revaluation, legislation was introduced for Section 25 notices and Section 26 requests served on and after 1 April 1990. This legislation replaced the old rateable values and their multipliers with the new rateable values and a multiplier of one (or two for the tenant who had been in occupation for fourteen years or more) of the rateable value.

7.7 So the current position is that in relation to post-1990 Section 25 notices or Section 26 requests, the multiplier is one or two times the new rateable value. For old Section 25 notices and Section 26 requests that are still continuing (and obviously there are not likely to be many such in existence now and the number is dwindling all the time) the multiplier is three or six.

7.8 In addition, there are transitional provisions which apply where properties contain a mixture of residential and commercial property. If the transitional provisions apply then one takes the rateable value as at 31 March 1990 rather than that which exists at the date of the Section 25 notice or Section 26(6) application. The four conditions are as follows:

7.8.1 The lease in question must have been entered into before 1 April 1990, or the contract of the grant of the lease must have preceded that date;

7.8.2 The notice given under Section 25 or Section 26 must be given before 1 April 2000;

7.8.3 The tenant must give notice to the landlord that he wants this special basis of compensation to apply. This notice must be given not less than two months nor more than four months after the landlord's notice is served; and

7.8.4 There must have been a rateable value shown in the valuation list on 31 March 1990. An assessment of rateable value at that date is insufficient.

7.9 If all of these conditions are satisfied the multiplier is eight (or sixteen for the fourteen-year tenant). Accordingly, compensation will be eight times the rateable value as at 31 March 1990 or sixteen times such rateable value rather than one or two times the later rateable value.

7.10 Needless to say, the tenant and its advisors must carefully consider whether the tenant would benefit by claiming the transitional relief. This is merely an arithmetical calculation. The tenant should simply ascertain whether the compensation that it would obtain by multiplying the rateable value in existence on 31 March 1990 by eight (or sixteen as appropriate) would give a higher level of compensation than multiplying the new rateable value by one (or two). If it would then be appropriate, notices must be served and within the relevant time-period.

7.10.1 It is clear from ***Busby and Another* v *Co-operative Insurance Society Limited* 1994 6 EG 141** that these transitional provisions apply purely to mixed commercial and residential property. This County court decision is based on what appears to have been Parliament's intention although I do not myself agree with the decision and indeed, before the matter came to court, I had received correspondence from the Department of the Environment that appears to back up my view. There were conflicting views in various correspondence in the *Estates Gazette* including an article written by Finers partner Katherine Miller and myself (see Recommended reading) but the matter has now been decided by the court and one must work on the basis that the transitional provisions only apply to business premises where there is a residential element. None the less I have still been involved in negotiations where landlords have been persuaded that the transitional provision apply to pure commercial property. Therefore, perhaps despite the law, this is something that tenants might want to bear in mind when negotiating compensation.

7.11 Because of the prospect of doubling of compensation, some thought should be given to the structure of lease acquisitions. If a tenant is proposing to take an assignment of a lease then, if it is possible for that tenant to acquire the business rather than just the premises and there are no commercial reasons why it should not do so, then it may be better for the assignee to acquire the business rather than merely the lease of the property. This may give the tenant the requisite fourteen years occupation by the business to which it has succeeded. Obviously a very careful decision needs to be made here and in particular the tenant must not do this unless it is commercially sensible when looking at the deal in the round. However, assuming that there are no commercial disadvantages if, for example, one is dealing with a fifteen-year lease where one is advising a tenant proposing to take an assignment five years from the end in circumstances where it might be possible for the landlord to oppose renewal on grounds (e), (f)or (g), then if the assignor has been in occupation since the outset clearly if the assignee can acquire the business and in a manner sufficient to enable it to acquire the rights to double compensation, then this might be a sensible piece of pre-planning.

8.   VAT AND 1954 ACT RENEWALS

8.1   Whilst I deal with VAT briefly in Chapter 7, I wanted to raise just a small point which is really more for lawyers to address, but where help from surveyors would not go amiss. As you will know, rents are exempt from VAT unless the landlord has made an election to charge VAT. The problem arises where a landlord has elected to charge VAT between the date of the grant of an old lease and the date of its renewal. It is absolutely essential that the terms of the new lease provide for VAT to be paid on rent. This is because of Section 89(2) of the VAT Act 1994.

8.2   Normally where a sum is referred to as 'the price' then that sum is deemed to include VAT. If one goes into a shop and a book is marked at £5 the shopkeeper cannot ask for VAT on top of that unless it is clear from the price sticker that VAT is to be added. The same with a property. However, if the VAT treatment is altered by virtue of a change in the law or according to Section 89(2) of the 1994 Act, a landlord's election, then VAT can be added. So if a lease does not refer to VAT and after the grant of the lease the landlord elects, the landlord can still add VAT to the rent. The problem with the scenario that I have envisaged in paragraph 8.1, above, is that the election will have taken place between the date of the grant of the old lease and its ending. That would be sufficient to allow VAT to be charged in relation to the rent under the old lease but not under the new lease unless VAT is specifically referred to. By the time the new lease is granted the election will already have been made and then there is no change in the tax treatment under the new lease. Imagine the following situation:

8.2.1　In 1992 a lease is granted and the demise reads as follows: 'the landlord demises the premises for a term of five years from 1 July 1992 at a rent of £100,000 per annum';

8.2.2　In 1993 the landlord elects and for the remainder of the term the tenant pays £100,000 plus VAT (i.e. £117,500);

8.2.3　In 1997 there is a 1954 Act renewal and a deal is struck at £120,000 per annum plus VAT for five more years. The landlord employs Sloppy Surveyor and Partners and Lazy Lawyer and Co. to negotiate and document the renewal;

8.2.4　Sloppy Surveyor and Partners write to Lazy Lawyer and Co. as follows: 'We have agreed terms for the renewal of the lease for a further five years at £120,000 plus VAT, please draw up the lease and arrange for the enclosed account to be paid on completion';

8.2.5　The lawyers cannot be bothered to do the drafting and simply photocopy the old lease and amend it as follows: 'the landlord demises the premises for a term of five years from 1 July ~~1992~~ 1997 at a rent of ~~£100,000~~ £120,000 per annum'. They complete and render their account; and

8.2.6　Since the new lease will not have mentioned VAT then for the period between 1997 and 2002 the tenant will pay £120,000 and not £120,000 plus VAT. The landlord's net income is therefore

$$£120,000 \times \frac{100}{117.5}$$

Bearing in mind many renewal leases are drafted by close reference to the terms of the old lease, this is definitely one to watch out for. It is essential that a clause allowing for VAT to be charged is inserted.

9. EXCLUSION ORDERS

9.1 As you know, it is possible to exclude Sections 24 and 28 of the 1954 Act provided that the parties make application to the court and that they do so before the lease is granted. The order must pre-date completion of the lease. This was made clear in *Essexcrest Limited* v *Evenlex Limited* **1988 55 P&CR 279**. The tenants obtained a new lease here because the court order was held to be invalid. In this case the lease was completed and about a month later the court order was obtained. The legislation makes it clear that the order applies to parties 'who will be' landlord and tenant and in the situation in *Essexcrest* the tenancy had already been created. It was not right therefore to talk of the landlord and tenant as people who would be landlord and tenant: they already were. Landlords must never fall into this trap and the court order must almost certainly precede the date of occupation and unquestionably the date of the lease itself. Certainly if the lease is granted on, say, 1 July 1997 with the term commencement date geared to the previous quarter-day, i.e. 24 June 1997 (as is often the case), the court order must precede 1 July. I do not think it needs to necessarily precede 24 June 1997 unless the tenant has been allowed into occupation earlier. It is disastrous for the term commencement date and completion of the lease to precede the court order. Ideally the court order should come first and although there is still an argument where the term commencement date precedes the court order which is then succeeded by completion, I believe this should be all right.

9.2 It is clear that if there is an agreement for lease and a court order in relation to that, the very fact that the agreement is not followed by the formal grant of the lease after the order is made does not mean Part II of the 1954 Act applies to the agreement. This was made clear by the case of *Tottenham Hotspur Football and Athletic Club Limited* v *Princegrove Publishers Limited* **1974 1 WLR 113**. This is not a particularly important case but as a staunch Spurs supporter I felt unable to write a book of this nature without reference to my beloved team!

9.3 Before a landlord and tenant can enter into an agreement for the tenant to surrender a lease protected under the 1954 Act, it is necessary for the parties to obtain an order of the court authorising the agreement to surrender. The application for the exclusion order is undertaken in much the same way as an application to exclude a tenancy from protection under the 1954 Act. It is clear that if the parties move direct to a surrender of the lease either by way of deed or simply by way of surrender by operation of the law, there is no need for a court order. If, however, there is to be a contract for the surrender, then it is that contract that needs to be excluded under Section 38 of the 1954 Act.

9.4   Section 43 lists various properties that are excluded from the 1954 Act. Agricultural tenancies, mining leases, service tenancies and leases for less than six months are excluded. Licensed premises used to be excluded. That was changed by the Landlord and Tenant (Licensed Premises) Act 1990.

10.   TERMS OF A NEW TENANCY

10.1   Generally speaking, where there is a renewal the parties will agree the terms of the renewal tenancy. Where they do not do so then it will be for the court to decide the terms. Rent will be determined pursuant to Section 34 of the 1954 Act and the length of the term will be geared to the length of the previous term with a maximum of fourteen years pursuant to Section 33, 1954 Act. Section 35 of the 1954 Act states that all other terms 'shall be such as may be agreed between the landlord and the tenant or in default of such agreement as may be determined by the court; and in determining those terms the court shall have regard to the terms of the current tenancy and to all relevant circumstances'.

10.2   *O'May v City of London Real Property Company Limited* **1982 1 AER 660** was a House of Lords decision which concerned the extent of the court's discretion in determining the terms of a new lease under Sections 33–35 of the 1954 Act. In *O'May* the landlord wanted to ensure that it had a 'clear lease' with all responsibilities for outgoings, maintenance, repairs, etc. to be borne by the tenant. The tenant was to pay a service charge and to be compensated by a reduction in the proposed rental.

The first instance decision (which found for the landlord) set out four tests as follows:

10.2.1 Has the party demanding variation of the terms shown a reason for doing so?

10.2.2 If the party demanding the change is successful, will the other party be adequately compensated by consequential adjustment of the rent under Section 34, 1954 Act?

10.2.3 Will the proposed change materially impair the tenant's security in carrying on his business? and

10.2.4 Taking all relevant matters into account, is the proposal fair and reasonable between parties?

These four principles were not overruled by the House of Lords although it seems clear that at each stage the court is to consider its overriding discretion and that this is not to be simply applied as a final separate test. The specific guidelines in Section 35 of the 1954 Act (looking at the terms of the current tenancy) were to be given some weight. Lord Hailsham (the then Lord Chancellor) stated that the court must begin by considering the terms of the current tenancy: the party seeking the change should fulfil the burden of proof to persuade the court that the change is reasonable. Lord Hailsham went on to say that one should look at the comparatively weak negotiating position of a sitting tenant requiring a renewal, particularly in conditions of scarcity. Perhaps this in itself is no longer of such great weight.

10.3 Since *O'May* no new principles have developed for the fixing of terms to be inserted in a lease and each case has tended to simply turn on its own facts; the overriding principles of Sections 33–35 and the *O'May* tests have ruled the day.

10.4 In 1992 two decisions received a great deal of property press coverage. They were consolidated applications by Boots The Chemist Limited and Thorn EMI, each under Part II of the 1954 Act and each case related to applications for a new tenancy of shops in the Elephant and Castle Shopping Centre. The cases are *Boots The Chemist Limited* v *Pinkland Limited* and *Thorn EMI PLC* v *Pinkland Limited* **1992 28 EG 118**.

10.5 Each case raised different issues and it must be borne in mind that they are no more than a County court decision. None the less, since the main principles have been outlined in *O'May* one can expect little more than lower court decisions in relation to the actual terms of new leases and, to that extent, they provide useful guidance. Furthermore, the cases certainly raised the profile of whether the landlord would be entitled to insist on the rent review clause in a new tenancy under the 1954 Act being upward-only.

10.6 In the *Boots* and *Thorn* consolidated action the county court was asked to consider the length of term and whether the new lease should contain a number of clauses that were not present in the leases which were to be renewed. These included:

10.6.1 An obligation to trade;   *clauses for renewal of lease*

10.6.2 An upward-only rent review clause; and

10.6.3 An assumption of a full-length term as the hypothetical term to be considered at review.

10.7 It should be remembered that the case is a County court decision and therefore doubtful as a strong precedent but it is an indication of the way the courts might approach the consideration of terms to be inserted in a new lease. Other more recent authorities certainly indicate that this decision has paved the way for upward/downward reviews in negotiations.

10.8 The dispute over the length of the term concerned Thorn only. In opening, the judge was told that a new ten-year term had been agreed but after presentation of the evidence Thorn stated they only wanted a three-year term and contended that they were bound by an agreement to take a ten-year lease since the lease had not been completed. Needless to say, the landlords argued strongly that they had conducted the case upon the supposition that a ten-year term had been agreed and that this compromise bound both parties. Thompson, J agreed that the agreement constituted the framework upon which the case had proceeded and stated that the landlords were entitled to conduct their case on the basis that there was no issue as to the length of the lease. The tenants could not have the benefit of both worlds and, assuming no agreement for a shorter term could be struck, it was held that the tenants would either have to discontinue the proceedings or apply under Section 36(2) of the 1954 Act for revocation of the court order if ultimately they found it unacceptable.

10.9   Upwards and downwards rent reviews

10.9.1   The issue of upwards/downwards rent reviews only concerned Boots and it was agreed between the landlords and Boots that although the old lease did not have rent review provisions the new lease should contain provisions for review at five-yearly intervals. The question between the parties was whether the review should be upwards-only or whether it should equally be possible for rent to be reviewed downwards as well. The court ordered a rent review clause that was capable of reviewing rent upwards and downwards.

10.9.2   This was not the first decision of this nature but it was widely quoted as fresh and compelling authority for upwards and downwards rent reviews in landlord and tenant renewals. *Stylo Shoes Limited* v *Manchester Royal Exchange Limited* **1967 204 EG 803** was a case heard in the High Court, where the judge made it clear that what was 'sauce for the goose was sauce for the gander'.

10.9.3   Accordingly the County court judge did not feel constrained to order an upward-only review. The judge said he had no means of knowing whether the decline in rental values over the past two years was merely a 'bear phase in the continuing bull market or whether it is the beginning of a new bear market, indicating that the long bull market has now come to an end'. The judge therefore felt that to be fair and reasonable to the parties it would be 'appropriate to incorporate in the new Boots lease a provision for the rent to be reviewed downwards as well as upwards'. The judge went on to say that if we were now beginning a bear market 'rents which can only be revised upwards will wreak the same sort of injustice upon tenants as that which has been suffered by landlords in previous decades when leases contained no provisions for rent review at all'.

This judgment originally hit the headlines as authority for upward and downward rent reviews on renewals. It must be carefully borne in mind that in both *Stylo* and this case the existing lease did *not* contain a rent review clause and clearly on the *O'May* principles the landlords would be in a much stronger position if there were an existing upwards-only rent review clause. Do not forget that the *O'May* principles require the tenants to show that the existence of the upwards/downward review clause will not unduly prejudice the landlords. Whilst the judge made it clear that if the current decline in rental values was merely an aberration the landlord would not be prejudiced, clearly this is not correct in terms of investment values and guaranteed rental income flow.

10.9.4   *Blythewood Plant Hire* v *Spiers Limited (In Receivership)* **1992 48 EG 117** is a case going the other way and perhaps helps to emphasize how *Pinkland* does not create any real precedent.

10.9.5   Judge Diamond QC was faced with a landlord who wanted to grant only a five-year tenancy (with a review on the penultimate day of the term) and a tenant who wanted a fourteen-year tenancy. It was decided that the applicant should be granted a ten-year term and the only matter that remained to be discussed was the wording of the rent review clause which it was agreed would operate on the fifth year of the term.

10.9.6   The wording of the clause was agreed subject to the question of whether there should be power to review the rent upwards and downwards or only upwards.

10.9.7   It was contended that an upward/downward clause would have an immediate adverse impact on the value of the landlord's interest whereas from the tenant's point of view there would be little immediate benefit. In these circumstances, the judge did not order a two-way clause and said he 'did not gain any assistance' from the adage that what is sauce for the goose is sauce for the gander.

10.9.8   *Forbuoys PLC* v *Newport Borough Council*, **Judgment on 21 October 1993, reported in [1994] 24 EG 156** is another County court decision on upward/downward reviews in renewal leases.

At the end of a twenty-one-year term, the tenant had applied under the 1954 Act for the grant of a new tenancy. The terms of the new tenancy had all been agreed, save for the provisions of the rent review clause. The new tenancy was to be for a term of nine years at a rent of £4,600 per annum subject to review every three years. The landlord contended that the rent review should be upwards-only whereas the plaintiff sought an upwards/downwards clause.

The tenant submitted (and its submission was accepted by the court) that all recent authorities showed that an upwards and downwards rent review clause was more appropriate in modern conditions. Only a landlord could benefit from an upwards-only clause, whereas there were benefits to both the landlord and the tenant from an upwards and downwards review.

The court relied heavily on the doctrine that under the 1954 Act the court must be 'fair and reasonable in all the circumstances'. It came to the conclusion that a rent review clause on an upwards-only basis would be unfair to the tenant and could not possibly be seen as being fair and reasonable in all the circumstances.

10.9.9 It is worth noting that in a 1994 Property Managers Association (PMA) Survey 33% of renewed leases taken out for periods in excess of ten years had upward and downward reviews and perhaps more interestingly, in each of those cases the previous lease had an upwards-only review. Obviously the PMA survey is based on lease renewals where the PMA member made a return to the PMA and indeed the returns were quite small and therefore this is not necessarily characteristic of the market in general, but it does seem to be a very high percentage and is something that should be borne in mind in lease negotiations, especially given the fact that judicial comment in most of the recent cases has tended to favour upward/downward reviews.

Where there is no previous rent review clause obviously there is no precedent for a rent review clause and the County court in *Thorn* was therefore asked to consider whether at each review date the new lease should be for a notional term equal to the then unexpired residue or for the whole of the term of fourteen years that Thorn had agreed to take.

10.9.10 The court did express some concern at the wording of the notional term provisions. The notional term was to be 'equal to the term hereby granted'. This wording is almost identical to the wording in the rent review clause in *Lynnthorpe Enterprises Limited* v *Sidney Smith (Chelsea) Limited* (see Chapter 2). The judge said that this wording effectively meant 'residue' but he urged the parties to choose a more sensible set of words. This is undoubtedly a correct piece of advice.

10.10 Positive trading covenants

10.10.1 In the *Boots* case the question of whether a positive trading covenant should be incorporated was discussed. Do not forget that until recently the courts have been reluctant to enforce positive trading covenants and have held that the landlord's proper remedy for breach of such covenants lies in damages. Boots were renewing leases of various premises within the shopping centre. The oldest lease did not have a positive trading covenant but other leases that they had taken and which were the subject of the proceedings did and the parties were agreed that there would be one new lease encompassing the whole of the premises. The court was satisfied that Boots had not discharged the burden of proof that (according to *O'May*) was for them to discharge. Accordingly the covenant was inserted and bound parts of the premises that were not previously the subject of that covenant.

It does seem that the inclusion of such a keep open clause is an onerous clause to foist upon a tenant; perhaps the matter would not have been resolved in this way if the clause had not appeared in some form in the old lease documentation. As we saw in Chapter 5 a keep open clause was enforced by injunctive relief in *Co-operative Insurance Society Limited* v *Argyll Stores (Holdings) Limited* 1996 9 EG 128. The *Boots* decision was of course before that and whether the County court would have ordered a continuous trading clause had the case come to court after *Argyll* is anyone's guess. Certainly prior to the *Argyll* decision it was generally thought that the court would not order injunctive relief and therefore, perhaps, the County court would have been a little more reticent before ordering a keep open clause to bind parts of the premises that were not bound by such a covenant prior to the renewal.

10.11   Length of the term

10.11.1 *Rumbelows Limited* v *Tyneside Metropolitan Borough Council* was an unreported case noted at **1994 13 EG 102** in the Southport County court where the tenant wanted a five-year tenancy and the landlords wanted to grant fifteen years and not less than ten under any circumstances. The tenants were concerned that they could not predict the future and were not anxious to take on long-term privity obligations.

10.11.2 The landlords' argument was that a five-year lease would affect the investment value of the property, particularly because there would be no upward-only review at the end of the fifth year but merely the ability to apply for an interim rent. The court felt that the tenants' arguments were valid and ordered a five-year tenancy.

10.11.3 The original term which was being renewed here was twenty years and, although this was a factor to be taken into account, the context of the original lease was that it was necessary for that length of term in order to finance the development.

10.11.4 In *Merseyside Glass Limited* v *J D Williams* noted at **1994 44 EG 103**, an original nine-year lease was the subject of renewal proceedings. The tenants wanted a three-year lease and inevitably the landlord wanted to grant a longer lease. The judge felt that it was for the tenant to persuade the court that a change from nine to three years was reasonable and it was not for the court to protect the tenant from market forces. A lease for nine years was ordered although the tenants were given a right to break at the sixth year.

10.12   By way of further reminder, I would mention that the 1995 Act contains consequential amendments to the 1954 Act. Section 34 and Section 35 allow the court to take into account in determining the rent and other terms any effect that is to be had on the rent or those terms by the operation of the 1995 Act.

10.13   Just before we leave the question of what terms should go into a new lease, it is perhaps worth considering the somewhat unusual case of *Amarjee* v *Barrowfen Properties Limited* **1993**

30 EG 98 where the court was asked to consider the terms of a new tenancy to be granted under the 1954 Act in circumstances where there was no previous written tenancy agreement. The tenant had occupied premises as a furniture warehouse on a yearly tenancy and apart from the rent of £35,000 per annum, none of the terms had been reduced to writing. The landlord now owned the freehold of the entire parade of shops of which these premises formed part and the other premises in the parade had been let on formal leases. The landlord served a Section 25 notice determining this yearly tenancy and indicating that an application for a new tenancy would not be opposed although the parties agreed that the new tenancy should be for a term of fourteen years with five-yearly rent reviews. There were points upon which they disagreed and these included the following:

10.13.1 Service charge – the plaintiff tenant wanted to be responsible for internal repair of his own premises and to pay a service charge relating only to his premises and those immediately adjoining. He agreed to pay a fair proportion of the cost of the common sprinkler system, fire-escape and routes and car-park. The defendant landlord wanted the plaintiff to contribute to a common service charge for the whole parade.

10.13.2 Insurance – the tenant wanted to insure his own premises; the landlord maintained a common insurance policy for the parade.

10.13.3 Rent review – the tenant wanted upward or downward reviews; not surprisingly the landlord contended that the reviews should be upward-only.

10.13.4 User – the tenant wanted the rental benefits of a user clause restricting use to furniture or carpet retailing; for the exact opposite reason the defendant wanted a wide user clause.

10.13.5 Alienation – the tenant wanted the freedom to sublet or assign part of or all of the premises and to be released from any liability on any assignment. Not surprisingly, the landlord did not agree.

10.13.6 Alterations – the tenant wanted the right to carry out any alterations with the landlord's consent not to be unreasonably withheld on condition that he reinstated at the end of the term. The landlord wanted to limit permissible alterations to non-structural ones.

There were fundamental differences, therefore, between the parties as to the terms of the new tenancy and it was left for the court to determine the terms under Section 35. Although *O'May* makes it clear that the party proposing a departure from previous terms has to show that the change is fair and reasonable, *Amarjee* differs significantly from *O'May* and other cases cited in argument in that there was no previous lease. There was no previous written agreement of the terms under which Mr Amarjee occupied the premises and this left the judge with the unenviable task of deciding what terms should be inserted. He had a very wide discretion indeed.

10.14 In the circumstances Judge Beddard took account of the other leases on the parade, of expert evidence provided by the parties and of the state of the property market in general in order to reach his decision on the final terms. He appears, however, to have relied on his own feelings in deciding upon the relevant weight of these factors in assessing each point at issue. It is important to emphasize that this case does not really set out any significant precedent but it is interesting to see how a court addressed the issues where it was not privileged to be able to see the terms of the previous tenancy.

10.14.1 Given a parade of shops, the judge saw no practicable alternative to the tenant contributing to a service charge for the whole parade. He took into account the common features such as the sprinkler system, rear access, car-park and fire-escape routes.

10.14.2 Again, the judge considered that for the tenant to insure his own premises would not be practicable and he noted that normal commercial practice in such a situation would be for the landlord to insure the entire parade and recover the cost from the tenant.

10.14.3 The judge accepted the tenant's argument for upward/downward reviews. He noted that the other leases in the parade were upward-only, but also noted that almost all of these were granted during a buoyant property market. Uniformity in the leases was not held to be a sufficiently strong requirement. In a declining or stagnant property market there was no reason to have upward-only reviews. The judge pointed to the fairness of such a review clause in a declining market despite the possibility of disputes between the landlord and tenant. Perhaps this is not surprising given the other cases on this issue.

10.14.4 The judge also accepted the tenant's argument that the user clause in the new lease should restrict the user to a general furniture and carpet warehouse. Once again, he was unimpressed with the argument that wide user clauses in the other leases in the parade meant that the same should be imposed in this lease. The judge did specifically point out that if a previous lease had contained an open user clause, the judge would not have considered imposing a restrictive one. In these circumstances where the plaintiff used the premises only as a furniture and carpet warehouse, he saw no reason for this not to continue. Previous case law on this subject was distinguished on the ground that it dealt with the modification of existing leases rather than their non-existence.

10.14.5 The tenant had argued for a release on assignment. The judge noted again that other leases in the parade did not include such provision. In this case, however, the judge appeared to believe that the tenant's claim was based on the belief that the property market was so slanted in favour of tenants that landlords had to accept almost anything which the tenant wanted. The judge did not accept this and noted that such a release would have a detrimental affect on the value of the landlord's investment. He therefore refused the release.

10.14.6 The question of alterations is a useful illustration of the way in which the judge used the practicalities of the situation facing him in order to make his decision. He noted the potential problems if one tenant could make structural alterations when this privilege was not available to other tenants whose premises were part of the same structure. He therefore again, accepted the landlord's argument and allowed non-structural alterations only.

The final score therefore was landlord (4) tenant (2)!

It also fell to the judge to determine the rent to be reserved by the new lease. The judge strongly indicated that he preferred the evidence of the landlord's expert witnesses and that he simply did not believe the tenant's surveyor's contention that a rent very similar to the 1985 rent was still fair. He therefore accepted the figures put forward by the landlord's surveyor, although he reduced the rent by $12\frac{1}{2}\%$ because of the restrictive user clause and then added $2\frac{1}{2}\%$ to take account of the upward/downward rent review. Having made these calculations he settled on a rent of £59,000 per annum with a 10% deduction to £53,100 for the interim rent.

10.15 I must emphasize again that this case is no precedent for the terms of a renewal lease. The case does, however, illustrate the risk of allowing a tenant into occupation without a written statement of terms. It also emphasizes again the considerable discretion of the judge in determining the terms of the renewals under the 1954 Act. Given that uniformity of lease covenants is often very important to property investors, this case can be construed as unfortunate in that the landlord ended up with one lease which differed, notably in the inclusion of upward/downward rent reviews and a restrictive user clause, from the others in the parade. The argument that leases in such developments should be uniform obviously had little impression on the judge, unless it was backed up by sound arguments based on the practicability of administering the development.

The further risk for the parties in these circumstances is that the court will fix the terms of a new tenancy and will do so in the context of the market that exists at the time the matter comes before the court. There will then be written terms of a lease which, when that lease comes to be reviewed, will have some considerable weight in determining the terms of the renewal of that lease. Under *O'May* it will be for the party seeking a change from those terms to justify any further alterations.

11.   REFORM OF THE 1954 ACT

11.1 There has been much criticism of the 1954 Act and the traps that it sets for the unwary in relation to the time-scale for service of notices, making application to the court and the like. Back in

1992 the Law Commission published a report in which it recommended reform of the 1954 Act. Until recently it had been thought that the Law Commission's report was not going to see the light of day but in July 1996 the Department of the Environment issued a consultation paper stating that the recommendations made in the 1992 report should be implemented almost in their entirety.

11.2 Whilst none of the reforms recommended in the Law Commission's report entitled *Business Tenancies – A periodic review of the Landlord and Tenant Act 1954 Part II* have yet hit the statute book it is perhaps worth pausing to consider one or two of the proposals.

11.3 Contracting out

11.3.1 The Law Commission proposed that court orders no longer be required in relation to the exclusion of the effects of the 1954 Act on leases and the approval of agreements for surrender.

The Law Commission recommended that no application to the court be necessary but that a statement in a prescribed form should be endorsed on the lease explaining the general nature of the tenant's statutory rights and the consequences of his giving them up. A sort of health warning. The recommendations extended to obtaining a signed declaration by the tenant again endorsed on the lease stating that the tenant has read and understood the terms of the agreement and statement.

The Government has effectively accepted these recommendations although the consultation paper invited comments on whether the health warning should be given at an earlier stage in lease negotiations.

I am not sure that that in itself is of enormous importance and certainly I think that the procedures would be far simpler and better if a health warning replaced the current court order procedures. The current procedures are no more than effectively a rubber-stamping exercise and considerable time and energy would be able to be saved by replacing the court order procedure with notices and health warnings on the lease. The Government felt that the very process of applying to the court deters some parties from acting unscrupulously but accepted the general thrust of the Law Commission's argument that the courts do not settle any issues and a health warning would suffice. They were concerned that the health warning should be given early on. There must be some merit in this so that tenants do not find that they have the loss of renewal rights foisted upon them at the very last moment. Equally, sometimes transactions proceed on a fast track and to require a health warning perhaps a month before completion would not be appropriate. It is also suggested that the declaration that the tenant has read and understood the terms of the health warning should be witnessed by someone independent of the landlord. The Government suggested the same procedures for agreements to surrender.

11.4 The Section 25 procedure

11.4.1 The Law Commission recommended that either party should be able to apply to the court for a renewal of a tenancy and that the Section 25 notice procedures could be simplified so that a landlord could start proceedings to terminate a tenancy without any renewal. It was suggested that the Section 25 notice should include the landlord's proposals for a new tenancy. This was something else considered in the consultation paper. There is concern that tenants seeing the terms on a Section 25 notice may feel that these are the terms to which the landlord is legally entitled, rather than an opening gambit and therefore the Government suggests a health warning for this too. The notice would explain that the proposals are merely a preliminary indication; the landlord should not be bound to offer those terms nor the tenant bound to accept them. If there is a disagreement the terms would, as now, be determined by the court. The notice should also advise the tenant to obtain professional advice. One of the Law Commission's recommendations included the abolition of the need for a tenant's counter-notice or even the requirement to make application within the timescale that currently exists. This would undoubtedly give rise to the possibilities of delay and the Government acknowledge this in the consultation paper. It may be, for example, that the landlord would have to wait up to a year until it could be certain of the tenant's intentions. The tenant might do nothing at all and then simply apply to the court the day before the date specified in the Section 25 notice. The tenant would therefore be able to hold over for a longer period. Notwithstanding all of this the

Government was minded to accept the Law Commission's proposals, since they undoubtedly simplified the procedures of the 1954 Act and since the Law Commission had made proposals for changing the basis of interim rent payments, the landlord might be able to minimize any disadvantage where the tenant was simply seeking to maximize the holding over period. It was not suggested that landlord's counter-notices be abolished.

11.5 Section 27 notices

11.5.1 The Law Commission recommended the Section 27 notice procedures be simplified so that the three months' notice could terminate on any day whenever served. This is a particularly interesting point. In the consultation paper the Department of the Environment made one or two additional proposals for legislative reform and one of these concerned Section 27 notices. The consultation paper was premised on the fact that the courts required tenants to serve Section 27 notices and the Government felt that this was a good thing and that the 1954 Act should be amended to make it clearer that tenants of fixed term tenancies need to give notice. Given the Court of Appeal decision in *Esselte*, this is no longer valid. Whether it is or it isn't I can see enormous merit in the 1954 Act stating clearly whether or not it is necessary for a tenant to give notice when it wishes to vacate. I do hope that any reform of the law makes it clear, when and in what circumstances, tenants must serve statutory notices to vacate.

11.6 Length of term

11.6.1 The Law Commission recommended that the term of a new lease could be up to fifteen years as opposed to the present fourteen years.

11.7 Interim rent

11.7.1 The Law Commission proposed reforms relating to interim rent. Interim rents were introduced by the Law of Property Act 1969 and primarily were brought in in order to protect a landlord during negotiations. The 1969 legislation was framed against the background that rents were generally rising and that it was right to protect the landlord and give him a higher rent during those negotiations. In a falling market, of course, this assumption does not hold good. Where a tenant is negotiating a renewal lease and the current market rent is less than that which was payable prior to the expiry of the old lease, the tenant must carry on paying the rent under the old lease even though this is higher than market rent. Only a landlord can make an application for an interim rent and clearly there would be no commercial reason for him to do so in these circumstances. Accordingly the tenant must simply carry on paying the inflated rent until he can get a new lower rent imposed in the 1954 Act renewal process.

11.7.2　The Law Commission recommended that either landlord or tenant should be able to apply for an interim rent. This would eradicate, at a stroke, the unfairness which enables a landlord to drag out the statutory renewal procedure ensuring that a tenant continues to pay a contractual rent which exceeds the current market level.

11.7.3　The Law Commission also recommended that where there was a subletting of part of the premises the court should be directed to have regard to the rent payable under the subtenancy.

11.7.4　One of the reforms relating to interim rent was that this should equal the rent ordered under the new lease. This would apply, for example, where the tenant occupies the whole of the premises, the landlord does not oppose a renewal and the lease is subsequently granted in relation to the whole of the property currently leased. Under the Law Commission's proposals, the rent would simply be back dated to the date of the Section 25 notice or Section 26 request. Clearly where there is a long period between the notice and the completion of the renewal procedure, this might unfairly prejudice one of the parties and the Government felt that, in view of this inequity, there should be a slight modification so that in these circumstances instead of being equal to the initial rent under the new lease, the interim rent should be set by reference to values current on the date from which that rent became payable. This would obviously give rise to additional work for valuers but it was suggested that this is something that should be implemented given that it would eradicate any unfairness where there was a lengthy period between the Section 25 notice (or Section 26 request) and completion.

11.8 Ownership of a business

11.8.1 The Law Commission recommended alterations whereby individuals owning a business would be treated as equivalent to any company tenant when assessing the qualification for statutory protection. There are current complications where the property and business are in separate ownerships and the Law Commission recommended various amendments effectively treating the business owner as the person entitled to the renewal, even if the lease was actually held in a group company or through an individual whilst the business was operated by a company etc. The general tenor of these amendments was to look through any corporate veil and treat as one person an individual tenant and his business and similarly with regard to landlords.

11.9 Information notices

11.9.1 The Law Commission recommended revised provisions relating to notices requesting information. The current provisions of Section 40 allow parties to serve notices in order to obtain information but there are no teeth behind Section 40. The Law Commission recommended that there are revised provisions designed to increase the level of information that can be obtained and the Law Commission suggested that some force be given to these provisions so that failure to comply could give rise to an action for breach of statutory duty.

11.10 Compensation

11.10.1 The Law Commission recommended a consequential amendment to the compensation provisions so that they apply where a landlord wants to oppose renewal, not because it wishes to carry on a business from the premises but because a company under its control wishes to do so. One of the suggested amendments that appeared in the consultation paper and which arose due to representations received by the Government was that there should be a variation in compensation if, subsequent to its calculation, there is a variation in the rateable values. At present compensation is based on the rateable value in force when the landlord's notice under Section 25 (or Section 26(6)) is served and if after that rateable values were to change the argument runs that the compensation should change. Whilst this may be an anomaly, the implications of changing the law to give effect to this does require careful attention and this was noted in the consultation paper. Take, for example, the position of a tenant who has received compensation and then following a reduction in rateable value is required to repay it, having already spent the proceeds. Clearly this needs to be carefully thought through and whilst the current system may not be absolutely fair, it does benefit from certainty. Whilst this is not a common problem, the consultation paper invited responses on this.

11.11 The period for consultation expired at the end of September 1996 and nothing has been issued by the Department of the Environment at the time I am writing this. However, it does seem that after lying relatively dormant for some considerable time, the Law Commission's 1992 recommendations might, after all, lead to legislation.

CHAPTER 7

POT-POURRI

This last chapter deals with a number of unrelated items that I believe are worthy of mention in a book of this nature. Some of these such as VAT, service charges and repairs are detailed subjects in their own right and there are books dealing with these subjects to which you can obviously refer for more detail (see Recommended reading). Once again the issues that I have referred to in this chapter have been chosen primarily because they are thought provoking and concern matters which I believe it is sensible to raise in the minds of surveyors advising clients.

It is important to stress that like all the other chapters in this book, the items dealt with in this chapter are not comprehensive treatises on their relevant subject matter.

A.   SERVICE CHARGES

I.   GENERAL

1.1   Many commercial leases contain obligations upon tenants to pay service charges. The landlord provides the service and the tenant pays the cost. The interests of the landlord and tenant can often be diametrically opposed. The landlord wants to keep the building in pristine condition for the benefit of his investment and particularly because the landlord is not picking up the tab. The tenant has little control since in some cases he may not even want the services that the landlord wishes to provide and in other cases, whilst the tenant may want the service, he may well not want it at the cost that the landlord proposes. As with any situation where someone is responsible for spending somebody else's money, there are dangers of abuse. Even where there is no abuse there may be a certain ambivalence about the landlord controlling the purse strings where he knows that he does not have to contribute to the expenditure; this ambivalence often leads to disputes between landlords and tenants surrounding the amount of money being spent on certain services.

This has caused escalating service charges to come under the microscope more and more often. There is no direct legislative control and the whole basis upon which service charges may be levied is simply governed by the deal struck between the parties and encompassed in the lease.

1.2   In 1995 a paper was produced by the British Council of Shopping Centres, British Property Federation, British Retail Consortium, the ISVA, the PMA, the RICS and the Shopping Centre Management Group entitled *Service Charges In Commercial Properties – A Guide to Good Practice* (The Guide). You will see later on in this part of this chapter that I have referred to the Guide. It is, however, important to bear in mind that this Guide is no more than a guide, it has no legal weight; this merely emphasizes the need for careful and considered negotiation of the items that make up the service charge clause in the lease and as perhaps you may be tired of hearing by this stage of this book, careful and considered drafting!

1.3   Service charge clauses can deal with a number of items and perhaps the neatest way of looking at service charges is to split them into two main categories as follows:

1.3.1   Repair items – by this I mean service charges dealing with external or structural repairs where the tenant has the direct repairing obligation for the interior of his unit but his liability to repair the exterior of the building or the structural elements of the building is dealt with by way of an indirect contribution towards those repairs which are carried out directly by the landlord. To take a simple example, if there is a situation where the tenant occupies the whole of a building on a full repairing and insuring (FRI) lease, then he would normally be liable to repair by way of a direct repairing liability. Where he merely takes one floor in the building, it would be normal for the landlord to retain responsibility for the exterior and structure of the building and the tenant holding an FRI lease of space within that building would find that his repair obligation is dealt with by way of a liability to pay service charges. In both these cases, the tenant is considered to have an FRI lease. The only difference is that his repairing obligation in the former is a direct repair obligation, whereas in the latter it is a liability to pay money to the landlord who keeps the building in repair.

1.3.2   All other services – wider service charges have developed over the years, whereby the tenant is responsible through a service charge clause to contribute to a number of diverse and often contentious items. This may include the provision and equipping of buildings with security systems. It may include installation of air-conditioning. It may include items such as marketing and promotion expenditure where the tenant could argue that the inclusion of such matters is entirely for the benefit of the landlord in improving the investment value of the building. It may include landscaping, tarmacking and improving roads and many other items that go towards management of a building. Wider service charges may also include the provision of traffic management systems, telecommunications and even refurbishment and improvements and many other services which the tenants perhaps do not want and certainly do not want to pay for.

1.4   The dichotomy is a simple one. The landlord wants to make sure that he is in control of the expenditure that needs to be made and that he is reimbursed for that expenditure. He wants a 'clear lease' with all the liabilities to contribute towards the maintenance of the investment passed on to the tenant. The tenant, whilst acknowledging that he must keep his part of the building or development in repair, wants to make absolutely certain that it is not his purse from which the landlord improves the investment. The tenant may feel it is quite wrong that he should contribute towards costs on other parts of a building where he does not feel he derives any benefit and even if the tenant feels that the relevant expenditure is in relation to items where he does take some benefit, the tenant might feel that too much is being spent or even if he thinks it is the right amount, he may simply not have budgeted for the expenditure.

1.5   If one looks at repairs, the major issue between the parties will turn on whether the costs that the landlord is asking the tenant to contribute to represent costs of repair or improvements. In a direct repair covenant the courts have made it clear that a tenant who is responsible for keeping a building in good and substantial repair is not liable to improve it. The tenant is responsible for all direct repairs but it is not responsible for improvements in the building. There have been cases concerning what constitutes

an improvement as opposed to a repair, but if one can get over
that problem it is not difficult to translate the distinction into
service charges. I think most tenants would accept the principle
that they ought to be responsible through the service charge to
contribute towards the costs of repairs and maintenance of the
whole building, shopping centre, leisure park, etc. Most tenants
would not accept that they should be responsible for improving
the investment value of the building in question.

2.   A CASE STUDY

2.1   Bearing in mind the large sums of money that are often disputed, there has not been a huge amount of litigation relating
to commercial lease service charges. However, there was a case
in July 1996 where the High Court considered a service charge
dispute and gave some guidance in relation to service charges
concerning repair items. *Postel Properties Limited* v *Boots The
Chemist* **1996 41 EG 164** concerned the service charge provisions of the leases of the Milton Keynes Shopping Centre. The
shopping centre had a huge area of flat roofs which, as the
judge pointed out, extended to something over twelve acres or
seven football pitches. These had been constructed in 1975 and
1976 with a maximum life expectancy of twenty years. Over the
years they had been the subject of various patch repairs. The
building surveyors looking after the centre had formed the
view that it was now time for a phased replacement, even
though some parts of the roof had never failed. The question
before Mr Justice Kennedy was whether the replacement programme was premature and whether the landlords ought to
have continued with the patch repairs. Furthermore, the court
was asked to consider whether the landlord could recover the
costs of certain upgrades in the specification. Were these
upgrades sufficient to lend weight to an argument that in fact
they were improvements giving back to the landlord something
different in character and better than that which he had given
to the tenants in the first place?

2.2   In the *Postel* case (where Boots were merely a representative
tenant) all the tenants had covenanted to pay a service charge
amounting to a proportionate amount of expenses reasonably

and properly incurred and the landlords had an obligation to keep the centre in good and substantial repair. They also had an obligation to do so in an economic and efficient manner.

2.3   The court did not uphold the tenant's complaint that the replacement was premature and that the new roof covering was of an unnecessary higher specification. When the landlord's surveyor had made her survey after walking the roof and took the decision that a phased replacement was more economic than continuing with patch repairs, she did so in the context that the roof covering was within five years of attaining its maximum life expectancy and that this life expectancy itself was perhaps optimistic, given that the roof now housed tenants' plant, causing local damage and clearly in circumstances which were not envisaged when the original roof had been constructed.

2.4   The judge felt that it was justifiable to upgrade the roof materials, including the replacement of a one-inch fibre board with a fifty-millimetre (two inch) polyurethane (described as PUR) board. Technology had advanced and these new materials were the right materials to use if there were to be a phased replacement. The court may have been influenced by the fact that building regulation controls had moved onwards so that the material in question was one that would now have to be used if one were constructing a new flat roof. This standard would now be needed if one were to comply with requirements in relation to insulation, but it was also clear that the new building regulation controls were not retrospective and the particular roof replacement could have been carried out without this material without infringing any legislation. No insulation standard was enforceable in relation to this replacement.

2.5   The judge carefully examined the evidence in relation to the material used and concluded that the higher specification was justified. One specific item was disallowed. This related to priming of troughs and the judge disallowed this since he did not think it was a reasonable repair. The landlords sought to include it as *de minimis*: the costs were no more than 1.4% of the total £1.6 million repair exercise. The judge rightly said that it was not a permissible answer to an unjustifiable claim to say that it was *de minimis*. This was a separate exercise and not a chargeable item. It is therefore worth remembering that if one is dealing with an irrecoverable item of service charge, then however small that might be, it is irrecoverable. The fact that it is small will not enable the landlord to gloss over the irrecoverable nature of the item and then charge it to the tenants.

2.6 So far as the windows, frames and cladding were concerned, the tenants were not objecting to the work nor were they objecting to the need for the work to be carried out. They simply said that had the landlords implemented a proper maintenance programme when they bought the centre, work would not have been necessary, since proper maintenance of the areas would have prevented the problems from arising. The judge accepted that there was no satisfactory explanation for the delay in setting up the maintenance programme and clearly during the delays the rusting had become worse. This did not, however, stop the works in question from being chargeable works and the tenants had to pay for them.

2.7 I think that the *Postel* decision is a sensible one. It does not really create any novel statements in law but certainly the judgment is a common-sense judgment underlying the rights for a landlord to carry out a maintenance programme in this way. It does emphasize the need for tenants to specifically exclude the cost of improvements in any way shape or form if they want to ensure that there is absolutely no question of them having to pay for something different to that which they had when they took the lease in the first place. Whilst it may well be good practice in building terms to replace thirty-five millimetres of insulation with fifty millimetres of insulation just because that is the accepted norm at the time of the replacement, some might argue that this should be at the tenant's discretion where he is paying for the work. If the tenant was carrying out direct repairs he clearly could have utilized the thinner materials, since this would not have contravened any legislative requirements and therefore tenants may well argue (as indeed Boots did in this case) that they should not have to contribute towards the higher costs of the better materials.

2.8 Just before leaving the question of repairs, a word about inherent defects. Where a service charge clause is being put together in relation to a new building, tenants are obviously concerned to ensure that they are not responsible to contribute towards inherent defects in the construction of the building. It is quite normal for tenants, particularly anchor tenants and others taking large amounts of space, to receive the benefit of warranties from the original contractors and professional team, but tenants very often seek to go further and exclude from the service charge, certainly for a fixed period, any liability to pay through the service charge for any costs in remedying inherent defects. Needless to say, landlords will be keen to avoid such an exclusion from the service charge since, unless they can recover under a contractual claim that they have against the contractors, they will be left to fund the difference between the cost of repairs and the amount of service charge that is recoverable. The landlord will argue that if it is not possible for him to recover under the building contract or via the professional, perhaps due to their insolvency or maybe because they did not breach their contract or duty of care, then it should not be the landlord, but the tenant, who should pick up the tab.

2.9   This is a debate that will always rage in relation to new leases, but at the very least I would urge tenants to require landlords to exhaust all remedies against all contractors and professionals before levying any charge under the service charge. There is no reason why the landlord should not agree to do this provided that the costs of so doing are themselves a service charge item, since then the landlord is merely acting as the tenant's agent in seeking to recover from the really guilty party against the background that if he can't, he will not have to pay himself. Many tenants will accept that they have the ultimate liability to pay the service charge if the landlord is not able to recover the amount from the contractor or the relevant professional within a certain period. Tenants will have difficulties in persuading the landlord that it should bear any shortfall since this is clearly inconsistent with the institutional requirements for a clear lease.

3.   COLLECTION

3.1   Should service charges be paid as rent? Very often a lease provides for the service charge to be paid by way of additional rent. This gives the landlord all the remedies that go with the obligation to pay rent, including forfeiture for non-payment without the necessity of serving a Section 146 notice and including distraint.

3.2 It is rarely easy for a tenant to persuade the landlord that the obligation to pay the service charge should not be recoverable as rent but I do think that there are certain problems with this approach. The principal rent is a fixed item which can be budgeted for and where both the landlord and tenant know exactly what sum is due and when. Service charges are intrinsically different. There may be a fixed quarterly sum on account of service charges where the landlord and the tenant can again know exactly what sums are due and when; but unquestionably, balancing payments are different. Here there will be a need for the tenant to investigate the expenditure and perhaps do its own due diligence on vouchers, receipts, etc., and arguably it is simply not appropriate for the landlord to require the tenant to pay by way of additional rent. Balancing payments are a one-off payment at the end of each year and do not have the characteristics of the principal rent, or indeed even advance payments on account of service charge. I would therefore suggest that when one is negotiating service charge clauses for tenants, one tries very hard to persuade the landlord to take a slightly different approach in relation to non-payment of balancing charges. If there is a bona fide dispute between the parties I cannot see that it can be right for the landlord to have all the remedies that go with non-payment of rent.

3.3 The same point arises if, for example, there is a break clause which requires the tenant to have paid 'the rent' before exercising the break or if there is an alienation clause in a new lease under the 1995 Act stating that one of the circumstances that allows the landlord to withhold consent is where the tenant has not paid 'the rent'. In either of these situations, if the expression 'rent' includes service charges and there is a bona fide dispute in relation to service charges and perhaps in particular the balancing payment, the tenant may be prevented from exercising its break or assigning the lease as the case may be. This cannot possibly be right. The landlord can easily protect its right to recover any sum deemed properly due following resolution of the dispute and caution is needed before tenants sign up to leases providing for this.

4.   INSURANCE THROUGH THE SERVICE CHARGE

4.1   Insurance is often a service charge item and perhaps not sufficient thought, time and effort is given to considering whether the liability to pay insurance should be included in the service charge or separately. Tenants need to make sure that the landlord can only recover the reasonable and proper costs of insuring and, whilst this may include periodic insurance valuations, clearly there should be some cap on the number of occasions that the landlord is entitled to charge his tenant for an insurance valuation. It is important that the landlord can evaluate the cost of rebuilding in order to make sure that it is insuring for the full replacement cost and therefore insurance valuations are necessary but arguably a landlord should not be in the position of being able to require its tenant to pay for this valuation more than, say, once every three years.

4.2   In considering an insurance clause the landlord needs to make sure that it has a full indemnity from the tenant for the insurance costs.

4.3   Again questions of value for money arise since the tenant will be paying the costs of insurance. Once again insurance payments, whether part of the service charge or not, are frequently reserved as rent and once again they represent a one-off item which cannot be strictly budgeted for, although obviously the tenant will have a rough idea of the amounts that it is likely to be called upon to pay and, generally speaking, insurance costs are likely to be manageable costs.

4.4   In *Havenridge* v *Boston Dyers* 1994 49 EG 111 the landlord was entitled to be indemnified for such insurance sum as he properly expended or paid. There was no reference to the sum being reasonable and it was clear that the landlord had no obligation to shop around for the best quote. In this case the court ordered the tenant to pay an insurance premium which was way in excess of that which the tenant could have obtained itself. There was no implication that the landlords had to act reasonably. In this case the landlords had in fact claimed over £15,000 by way of premium and whilst the tenant had paid under protest, they felt the appropriate premium was in the region of £3,000. They actually had received a rival quote.

4.5 One might have felt that the case of *Finchbourne* v *Rodrigues* **1976 3 AER 581** may have assisted the tenant but the court did not feel it was right to imply an obligation upon the landlord to act reasonably.

4.6 The court also looked at the Supply of Goods and Services Act 1982 which states that in contracts for the supply of services there is an implied term that the party contracting will pay a *reasonable* charge if the consideration for the service is not determined by the contract. In *Havenridge* the court felt that this was not appropriate because the consideration was determined by the contract; the clause provided for the consideration to be the money properly paid and the 1982 Act was of no help. The court felt that because the word 'reasonable' had been used elsewhere in the lease, there was a deliberate intent not to use it in relation to the payment of insurance premiums. Practitioners may think that the omission of the word 'reasonable' was not such a deliberate act but merely some form of omission, but perhaps an analysis of this nature helps to emphasize how judges look at the wording and how important it is to get the wording absolutely right.

4.7 Insurance can be expensive particularly if the landlord decides that come hell or high water it is going to insure against terrorism, subsidence, settlement or other matters where the cost might be substantial. In those circumstances tenants should try to have some form of input so that they can hopefully control the outflow of money.

5.   NEGOTIATING SERVICE CHARGES

5.1 In truth there is no substitute for a very detailed negotiation on each and every head of service charge expenditure. The sums of money that are at stake in relation to service charges can often be huge and can represent a substantial amount of a tenant's property overhead. The debate is sharpened by the fact that this amount of overhead is outside the control of the tenant.

5.2 It is absolutely essential that the drafting is clear and concise and that it reflects what the parties need and intend. Tenants must be very careful indeed not to be tempted to simply kotow to the oft used argument by landlords that the service charge 'is in standard form and is non-negotiable'. If a landlord really does say that and no amendments are made whatsoever, then it may even be necessary now to look at the European Directive on unfair contract terms that took effect at the end of 1994 and which imposes reasonable criteria for standard non-negotiated contracts. Arguably the Directive does catch property transactions and although one might take the view that commercial documentation, where the terms are negotiated, may be outside the ambit of this type of legislation, where a landlord really does prohibit any amendments to a service charge, perhaps one might be able to obtain some comfort from the directive. Assuming that one does not wish to rely on that, service charges must be properly negotiated and I would canvass the need for service charges to be dealt with as a preliminary issue. Very often they are ignored by surveyors in the negotiation process and are at best dealt with in lease meetings. Equally often the service charge clause appears at the end of the lease and might run to several pages in a schedule at the very back of the lease. If the lease is some sixty or seventy pages long and full of tenant's covenants and obligations, it is not difficult to see that the tenant's surveyor and solicitor may well not be in the best negotiating frame of mind when they come to deal with service charges at the end of a long meeting and, if one then considers that landlords will very often take a robust attitude stating that the service charge is in standard form, it is clearly not the best time to deal with service charges. This may seem a very simplistic argument, but I have seen many negotiations heavily weighted in the landlord's favour and I am convinced partly for these reasons.

5.3 It is for that reason that I advance the suggestion that service charges are dealt with as a preliminary issue or, at the very least, early on in the negotiation process. If they are left to the end it is often much more difficult.

6.   THE SERVICES

6.1   The service charge clause must reflect the services that the tenants need and require and the drafting must be clear and concise in doing that. There will obviously be some issues where landlords cannot negotiate separately for individual tenants without risking a shortfall, but if the service charge clauses are properly drafted, it is entirely appropriate for attention to be paid to the needs of individual tenants and for the needs of the tenant group as a whole. This can all be done against the background that the landlord must not be left in the position of having to pick up a shortfall. There is no reason why negotiation cannot take place on an individual basis. I should like to identify some specific areas that could be looked at.

6.2   Tenants should ensure that their landlords are required to obtain estimates before incurring service charge expenditure. Ideally the obligations to carry out the services should contain an obligation upon the landlord to carry them out in a cost-effective or reasonable and efficient manner. Wording of this nature was included in the *Postel* decision. Tenants are entitled to insist that if they are having to pay for the cost of services carried out by someone else, they are entitled at least to require those services to be carried out properly and cost effectively.

6.3   Tenants should consider whether it is reasonable to require a cap on service charges. This is an ideal way for tenants to limit their service charge exposure, particularly during the early years of a tenancy. One must balance the requirement for a service charge cap against the landlord's argument that this may well leave him with a service charge shortfall if the costs of providing the services exceed what is anticipated. Limits on service charges are not likely to be acceptable to landlords granting a twenty or twenty-five-year institutional lease. There are, however, situations where I would unquestionably urge that a tenant negotiates a cap. For example, if one is taking a reasonably short-term lease, I think it is intrinsically unfair that a tenant should have to pick up substantial service charge bills.
    Quite often when taking space in a building for a short period of time a tenant's surveyor or solicitor is confronted with

the requirement to pay a service charge and the service charge clause itself may run for many pages. It may well be more efficient and certainly more cost effective to simply accept what the maximum contribution should be and insert a cap rather than seek to negotiate a lengthy service charge clause. Over the years I have found that landlords have a relatively open door to this type of approach and it does commend itself in giving the tenant certainty in the amount of money that it is likely to have to spend in the short period of time that it is going to be lenient. One does need to be careful, however, in negotiating a cap on service charges. It is quite important to ensure that a landlord is not discouraged from providing services that a tenant might want and a cap on service charges can have this effect. Imposing a cap on a landlord must be considered against the obligations that a tenant puts on his landlord.

6.4   Tenants should avoid the obligations to pay towards capital expenditure, refurbishment, renewals, improvements, etc. These are classic items where a landlord may be seeking to recover from the tenant sums that really should not be service charge items.

Many years ago when negotiating a lease in a shopping centre I debated the service charge clause long and hard with both the landlord's solicitors and surveyors. They would not budge and merely repeated the need for the service charge to be uniform and in standard form. We failed to make much headway and I pointed out to the landlords that, as drafted, the service charge would enable the landlord to completely refurbish the shopping centre and charge a proportion of the cost to my client. The landlord retort was that whilst this was correct, they simply would not do this in practice. We did make some headway after getting to this stage in the negotiation, but it is a graphic illustration of how difficult service charge negotiations can often be. I suppose one can always fall back on the argument that if one is left with a service charge that really is onerous and can leave a tenant in this kind of position, then this may have an adverse effect on rent review. Whilst this is no doubt true, it is very much a fall-back position and I do not think it is an approach that should commend itself to practitioners as a serious alternative to sensible negotiation.

6.5   Check staffing costs and the like. Service charge provisions often entitle the landlord to charge back to tenants the costs of renting accommodation, uniforms, etc. for staff and this is something that may well aggravate tenants and should be dealt with directly if it is to be excluded.

6.6   Tenants should look carefully at obligations to contribute towards new services. One often sees a requirement to contribute towards the cost of the provision of services or equipping a shopping centre and this may well involve the tenant in paying for the setting up of services. Landlords will normally accept that the tenant should not be responsible for any costs of the original development but clearly, over the life of a lease, new services may become appropriate and it might be reasonable for the landlord to charge back the provision of these services. One will need to look at this in the context of any sweeping-up clause. Where all the services are properly identified as they should be, it is normal and probably reasonable for there to be some form of sweeping-up clause since it is not possible to identify all services that might be required in a set of premises over the life of a lease which might be as long as twenty to twenty-five years. However, tenants must ensure that where new services are introduced through sweeping-up clauses, they should be similar in character to the existing services. The tenant must remember that he is signing up to contribute towards costs which are simply incalculable and in doing that, unless he is in an extremely weak bargaining position, that tenant should try to ensure that the sweeping-up clause provisions are reasonable and are linked back to good estate management and perhaps even the approval of a majority of the tenants, if not the tenant negotiating the clause itself.

6.7   Landlords will readily accept that the costs of rent collection are to be excluded from service charges along with the costs of negotiating rent reviews. These are items that have nothing to do with the service charge itself, but relate to individual units in a building or a development and they should not form part of the service charge. They are a landlord overhead.

6.8   Tenants should also make sure that service charges do not allow the landlords to recover service charge costs in relation to unlet space or where the services were incurred or rendered before the date that the tenant occupied the premises demised by the lease.

6.9 Promotional costs represent an item that needs to be very carefully thought through in relation to leisure and retail developments. Landlords often want to include promotional costs but tenants must make certain that they are not simply contributing towards the promotion of the centre in circumstances where they are already undergoing their own extensive promotion campaigns. This is an area of particular concern to multiple retailers who have their own marketing and promotion budgets and in some cases very clear and identified targets for promotion and marketing. Contributing towards the promotion of an individual shopping centre may well give them no benefit whatsoever and in some cases it might even detract from their own marketing. The Guide talks about promotion and states that 'the funding of promotional activities is recognized as a shared cost to be borne by both owners and occupiers and, in such cases, consultation is considered appropriate'. Over the years and perhaps because of the introduction of the Guide, landlords have become a little more receptive to the tenants' objections that are frequently heard in relation to promotion expenditure and it is quite normal where promotion and marketing is charged through a service charge for the expenditure in relation to those items to be sanctioned by a committee of tenants.

6.10 Management charges need to be considered very carefully. It is obviously right and proper for tenants to be required to contribute towards management costs but the amount of these must be carefully monitored. Landlords will frequently want the right to undertake the management themselves and to charge their own costs of so doing in lieu of a fee paid to surveyors. I acknowledge that this is no doubt anathema to most readers of this book! The tenant's concern should merely be to ensure that they do not pay twice, once to a surveyor's firm and once to contribute towards the landlord's overhead costs. If the landlord chooses to manage in-house then that is no doubt a decision for it to take and in those circumstances the tenant should be responsible for paying the costs of management. If the landlords choose to manage by way of external surveyors (which is normally the case) then they should not be able to charge their own overhead expenditure as well.

The cost of management is a frequently disputed item. Market rates tend to change over the years and I would therefore simply suggest that tenants limit their liabilities to pay a reasonable and proper amount rather than a fixed percentage of the service charge itself. It does seem ironic that management costs are often linked to the size of the service charge bill since this is hardly an incentive to keeping costs down. The Guide states that the management fee should be reasonable for work done. Value for money is no doubt the order of the day. Management itself is quite a tricky issue. Tenants must make sure that the building is properly managed and this is best achieved by giving the management surveyors proper recompense for their management. I do not suppose many readers of this book will disagree with that. Tenants might also find that they can improve their position by providing for the managing agents or the landlord itself to owe a duty of care to the tenant in providing the services. This direct link may help although, so far, I have to say, there are very few situations where I have ever seen this applied in practice.

6.11   Tenants should ensure that all income coming to the landlord arising from common areas is credited to the service charge account. If part of the service charge area is taken away to provide, say, a kiosk for one of the motoring organizations or a barrow for temporary traders, etc. then it is arguable that the income from this should be credited to the service charge account rather than merely be taken by the landlord as additional rent. The argument of course runs along the lines that the landlord is creating income out of an area which was previously a common area and in those circumstances ought to share that with its tenants. This raises a much larger issue, namely whether landlords should ever be entitled to take away part of the common parts and create units on the part taken away. This is becoming quite a big issue in leisure and retail parks where landlords seek to maximize their income by creating units on part of a car-park or common areas and tenants must watch this very carefully, not just in the context of service charges but in negotiating the demise and rights granted in the lease.

6.12   Once one has properly identified all the service charges it is important to fix the percentage of service charge on a proper basis. Tenants should be responsible for paying reasonable and proper amounts on account of service charge. This is yet another concept highlighted in the Guide. The use of the word 'reasonable' is particularly important in view of the case of *Havenridge* (see paragraph 4.4). Most tenants will resist service charge percentages being fixed by reference to rateable values since these may change with rating revaluations. Floor areas may well be a better way of calculating service charge percentages. In certain cases the proportion of service charge payable may need to be geared to usage. Clearly, for example, if a parade of shops exists underneath a substantial office building, it would be quite unreasonable for the tenants of those shops to be required to pay towards the costs of the lift in the office building. This is a defined and clear example of a situation where a tenant has no use of a service and should therefore not contribute. There will be other situations where the tenant's use is more intensive and perhaps puts more pressure on the service charge and in those circumstances it is arguable that a tenant should pay a greater proportion. For example, in a leisure scheme where there is a nightclub open until the early hours of the morning, it might well be arguable that the nightclub tenant should pay a higher proportion of the costs of security. It may also be perfectly reasonable for the entire cost of security between, say, midnight and 4.00 a.m. to be borne by the nightclub; after all, no one else on the leisure scheme will derive any benefit whatsoever from that. These are difficult areas, not least because when negotiating leases with differentiations of this nature, the landlord must be absolutely certain that it does not leave itself in a position where it cannot make an 100% recovery. I have seen situations where, for precisely that reason, tenants have been forced to pay unreasonably for items where they patently derive little or no benefit. I have also seen difficult situations where a tenant, perhaps on the edge of a scheme and deriving only some of the benefit from common services within the scheme has not been able to persuade the landlord to reduce the service charge. A great deal of thought needs to be given to this. If you are representing a restaurateur who is within a shopping centre but who fronts onto an area outside the shopping centre, should that tenant pay a service charge simply geared to the size of its unit, compared to other units on the scheme? This restaurateur might keep the unit open when the shopping centre is closed and indeed it is quite likely that this will be so. A great deal of its trade may derive from outside the scheme. Weighted service charges provide some of the answers to this, but careful thought and negotiation is needed.

6.13 Sinking funds are an item which continue to cause dispute. Landlords want to make sure that whoever the tenant might be at any time during the life of a lease that tenant has sufficient funds to pay for any services that might need to be carried out as a one-off. If there is significant plant and there has been no sinking fund created for the replacement of that plant, then clearly when it fails and needs to be replaced the service charge is likely to shoot up. The provision of a sinking fund allows for this to be provided for over the life of the lease. It is like a saving scheme. The tenant's perspective of course is that he might contribute towards the sinking fund for many years and then find that it assigns the lease, having derived no benefit from that contribution. Equally tenants must make sure that any sinking fund is protected from the insolvency of a landlord and does not simply become the property of the landlord's trustee in bankruptcy or liquidator. The Guide talks about sinking funds and makes it clear that moneys held in a sinking fund should be held in an interest-bearing account accruing interest to benefit the fund itself. The Guide also makes it clear that the account might also be a trust account separate from the landlord's own money.

6.14 Tenants must ensure that all service charge accounts, invoices, etc. are open to full scrutiny. The tenant must be able to make its own investigations to ensure that sums have been properly paid. As I have said earlier, service charges are often paid by the tenant making payments 'on account' and subsequently a balancing charge being levied. Leases nearly always provide for the tenant to promptly pay any balance that is due following the reckoning at the end of the service charge year but equally leases quite often provide that where the reckoning shows that the tenant has paid too much through the service charge 'on account' payments, the balancing credit due to the tenant is merely credited against the following year's advance payments. I think tenants should resist this and insist that the sums are paid back and with interest. It is illogical that a tenant who has paid too much should have to wait for a refund. The landlord will have estimated the amount due 'on account' and by definition will have got it wrong. He ought to immediately reimburse the tenant. It is illogical for the tenant not to be in a position to demand his money back with interest immediately.

6.15 Service charges will always cause problems between landlords and tenants. There is a clear difference of approach and this will often lead to dispute. However, there is no reason why service charge clauses cannot be drafted in a reasonable fashion so that landlords can make certain their buildings are properly looked after and tenants make certain that there is proper value for money.

7. A THOUGHT ON REPAIRS

7.1 Normally where there is a full repairing lease of self-contained premises there is no need for a service charge and service charges are not used. The tenant has a direct repair responsibility. This has its limitations. As you will see later in this chapter in Section G, if a tenant breaches a direct repair obligation, there is a limit on what the landlord can recover. The level of damages is limited to the diminution in the value of the landlord's reversion. Furthermore, if the landlord wants to forfeit the lease for breach of a repairing obligation he must serve notice under Section 146, Law of Property Act 1925 and where the Leasehold Property (Repairs) Act 1938 applies, there will be further constraints on the landlord's rights to enforce the repairing obligation either by damages or forfeiture.

7.2 If, however, the tenant's obligation to pay for repairs is through a service charge these issues do not arise. The landlord has the obligation to carry out the works and the tenant has the obligation to pay the cost through the service charge. There is no limitation on the amount that can be recovered and, where the service charge is reserved as rent, there is no need for a Section 146 notice.

7.3 For that reason I have often wondered why landlords granting self-contained leases do not provide for the repairs to be dealt with through a service charge rather than directly. I have to say, however, that where I have suggested this in the past, landlords and their surveyors have never been terribly keen on dealing with leases in this way and have cited management issues as reasons why they would rather go the direct repair route. Whilst I know this is an unusual suggestion, I think there are reasons to commend it and perhaps you might want to think this through in relation to certain types of building from time to time.

8. VAT

8.1 Where a tenant is responsible for paying a landlord's solicitor's or surveyor's costs the costs are billed to the landlord and marked 'payable by the tenant'. The service is provided by the surveyor or the solicitor to the landlord and in those circumstances because the service is not supplied to the tenant, the tenant, who is the person paying the costs cannot recover the VAT on those costs. Whilst he might be in receipt of an original invoice, he is not entitled to a tax invoice and cannot recover the VAT. When negotiating for a tenant who is responsible for paying a landlord's costs one should try to persuade the landlord's solicitors to accept the amount of costs net of VAT and for them to bill their client direct for the VAT. So long as the landlord can recover the VAT he should be happy with the situation.

8.2 The question of VAT on service charges generally needs to be addressed. If the property is exempt and the landlord has not waived the exemption in relation to the lease in question, then the service charges will follow the VAT status of the lease and tenants will not be able to recover VAT which forms part of the service charge. In such circumstances it might be beneficial for the tenant to insist upon services being provided direct to it by a third party so that it can recover VAT. Without that there may be a problem in tenants recovering VAT on service charges in relation to exempt buildings.

B.   EXCESSIVE DEPOSITS

I.   **THE LEVEL OF DEPOSIT**

1.1   Land transactions are normally structured by the vendor receiving a deposit from its purchaser on exchange with the balance of the purchase price payable on completion. I think that in a chapter such as this it is probably sensible to mention a few words about the level of deposit that can and should be taken.

1.2   It is quite normal in land transactions for the deposit to be 10% of the purchase price, or less in some cases. The point of such a deposit is to give the vendor a level of comfort that the purchaser will proceed with the purchase and complete on time. If the purchaser does not do this then, after service of a notice to complete making time of the essence, the vendor may forfeit the deposit.

1.3   Effectively the 10% deposit is a form of liquidated damages for breach of contract. Normally in contract law where there is a provision for liquidated damages, there is a presumption that such provision is an unlawful penalty unless the liquidated damages are pitched at a level where they are a genuine pre-estimate of the loss that would be suffered by the vendor, should the purchaser breach the contract. In effect the 10% deposit, the traditional level of deposit on a property sale, is an exception to this rule. Clearly, however, if the label 'deposit' is attached to a liquidated sum that is in fact a penalty this special treatment may not apply. The deposit would have to be reasonable.

1.4   This was highlighted in a decision of the Privy Council in 1993. In **Workers Trust and Merchant Bank Limited v Dojap Investments 1993 2 AER 370** the Privy Council had to consider whether forfeiture of a 25% deposit was an acceptable course of action. In this case the deposit was taken in relation to a Jamaican auction sale and whilst it was common ground between the parties that, apparently, in Jamaica auction deposits often exceed 10%, the Privy Council were not persuaded that this meant that a 25% figure was reasonable. They held that the deposit could not be forfeited and the whole amount (not just the excess over 10%) was recoverable.

1.5   So, where a deposit is negotiated at a level higher than 10% this must be justifiable or, in fact, seeking a higher deposit may back-fire on the vendor. It may not provide any security to the vendor whatsoever. It may be far better to agree a 10% figure which can be easily forfeited rather than seek a higher figure, perhaps potentially giving a greater level of comfort, but which ultimately may be held to be an unreasonable penalty with the consequence that none of it may be forfeited. One example of where this needs to be thought through carefully is in relation to residential developments where the developer might agree to take the prospective purchaser's land in part-exchange. Assuming the sale of the new property being developed is at a higher figure than the part-exchanged land being bought back, the vendor will no doubt want a deposit. Should that deposit merely be 10% of the equality payment, or would it be reasonable for the purchaser to have to pay 10% of the full purchase price that he is paying for his new house without giving credit to the value of the part-exchanged property? If the latter, the contract should specifically and clearly state that this is the intention and understanding of the parties.

2.   NEW PROPERTIES

2.1   This is the same in situations where on acquisitions of new property a purchaser is to pay an additional deposit at some stage during the construction process. It is not unusual for vendors to seek additional security from purchasers. They might take a 10% deposit on exchange and then ask for a top up when the development reaches a certain stage. Careful consideration will need to be given to whether this is a reasonable course of action and more importantly a genuine pre-estimate of the vendor's loss if the purchaser does not proceed. If it does not the vendor is putting the deposit at risk.

3.   PURCHASE OR OPTION?

3.1   If there is a question mark over whether a deposit is excessive or if a deposit is to be paid to the vendor's solicitors as agents for the vendor, the vendor might be best advised not to exchange contracts for the sale but to grant an option to the purchaser instead with the purchaser paying what would have been the deposit as an option price.

3.2   For example, if there is any uncertainty as to whether a potential deposit might be too high and therefore, irrecoverable, if the vendor grants the purchaser an option, taking as an option price the amount that would otherwise have been taken as a deposit, then I cannot see how there could be an attack on the level of the 'deposit'. The money will belong to the vendor. It will comprise the price that the purchaser will have paid for the benefit of the option. Any question that the money represents a deposit which needs to be forfeited by the vendor will have been dealt with. Needless to say, the purchaser will have major concerns here, primarily that he would have actually parted with possession of the option price. It is not often going to be an effective way for a vendor to protect his position.

3.3   From the purchaser's point of view there are also concerns over the protection of a deposit. It is normally a worry for a purchaser parting with a 10% deposit (which might be a substantial sum of money) to ensure that if for any reason he is entitled to the deposit back in circumstances where the vendor has not performed his contractual obligations, the deposit is capable of being returned. If the deposit is paid to a vendor either by being held by his solicitor as agents for the vendor or by way of an option price then the purchaser has no control. If the deposit is held by the vendor's solicitor as stakeholder then the purchaser can be sure that nothing untoward will happen to the money.

4.   BASIS UPON WHICH THE DEPOSIT IS HELD

4.1   The most common form of deposit is one held by the vendor's solicitors as stakeholder. This requires the vendor's solicitors to hold the deposit in their client account and effectively protect it for the purchaser. If a deposit is held 'as agents' then the vendor's solicitors are entitled to send the deposit to the vendor who may do with it as he wishes. If there is then a dispute which requires the purchaser to seek recovery of the deposit it may be very difficult for him to obtain it back. In practice it may have been passed to the vendor who may have disappeared with it or spent it. The vendors may even have become insolvent.

4.2   There are many situations where vendors seek to hold deposits as agent and clearly the advice to purchasers in those circumstances is that there can be no guarantee that there will ever be a return of that deposit. Purchasers should therefore avoid paying deposits as agents wherever possible. It will also be necessary for the parties to agree what happens to the interest on deposits between exchange and completion. Often the sums involved may be substantial and the question of who keeps the interest should be negotiated at the outset.

4.3   Option prices in lieu of a deposit may be acceptable to some purchasers but obviously only in cases where they would otherwise have paid a deposit to the vendor's solicitors as agents for the vendor.

4.4   If an option price is taken in lieu of a deposit it is important for the purchaser to protect his position as best he can by a restriction or notice on the vendor's title.

C.   GETTING RENT FROM SUBTENANTS WHERE THERE IS DEFAULT BY THE IMMEDIATE TENANT

1.   THE LANDLORD'S DILEMMA

1.1   Picture the scenario. A landlord has granted a lease to a tenant and authorised the tenant to sublet. The tenant has sublet and the subtenant, complying with its obligations, pays the rent on time. The tenant, however, fails to pay the rent. In these circumstances a landlord may be extremely frustrated to find itself in the unenviable situation where its tenant is receiving rent which may in fact be greater than the rent due to be paid by the tenant to the landlord but that same tenant is in breach of his obligations to pay the rent to the landlord. All is not lost here and apart from the normal remedies which are open to the landlord in these circumstances and arising out of the landlord/tenant relationship, Section 6 of the Law of Distress Amendment Act 1908 may also assist the landlord.

1.2   The 1908 Act authorises the landlord to serve a notice upon the subtenant directing him to pay the subtenancy rent, not to the tenant who is the immediate landlord, but direct to the superior landlord. There seems to be no reason why this should not survive the insolvency of the immediate tenant although there is apparently no case law on the subject.

1.3   So by way of example, if a landlord grants a lease to a tenant at say a rental of £100,000 per annum and the tenant sublets the whole premises at a rent of say £150,000 per anum (i.e. receiving a £50,000 profit rent) it is open to the landlord to serve notice upon the subtenant requiring the subtenant to pay £50,000 to the intermediate landlord and the £100,000 (i.e. the same figure as payable by the tenant to its landlord) to the superior landlord.

   This procedure can often help a landlord in recovering moneys due to it very quickly. By paying in this way the subtenant is discharging his obligations in the sublease and sums paid pursuant to Section 6 are credited against sublease rent payments due.

2.   ONE MAJOR PROBLEM WITH THE 1908 ACT PROCEDURE

2.1   It is not unusual for each of the head lease and the sublease to require payment of rent on the usual quarter-days. Any default by the tenant will therefore not occur until after the quarter-day. In such a situation the landlord is not entitled to serve the Section 6 notice until after the quarter-day by which time the subtenant may well have already paid his rent to the tenant. If this were to happen then the superior landlord could still serve notice and this would require the subtenant to pay part of the rent due on the next quarter-day to the superior landlord. The superior landlord would, however, always be behind the game. You will appreciate that it is possible for this to happen on every rent payment date.

2.2   One way around this would be for a landlord to try to persuade a tenant to provide that the sublease rent payment days are later than the usual quarter-days. I have seen some situations where sublease rent payment days are some ten or fourteen days after the usual quarter-day for payment of the head lease rent and this gives the landlord a period in which to see whether rent is paid under the head lease and, if not, serve notice under Section 6 before the subtenant will have paid the intermediate landlord. If there is no such window and the sub-tenant simply pays his rent on the same day that the head land-lord is due to collect it from the immediate tenant it may well be that the landlord will be too late when he serves his Section 6 notice. He will have to wait for the next rent payment day to catch up.

2.3   This raises the important question of whether a landlord would be reasonable in imposing a condition in a licence to sublet that the rent payment days in the sublease are later than the usual quarter-days. I have seen licences imposing such a provision and I have to say that if there is no empowering provision in the lease I think such a condition is probably unreasonable; parti-cularly following the decision of ***Straudley v Mount Eden Land 1996 EGCS 153*** (also referred to in Chapter 3, paragraph 3.21) where the court did not give the landlord the right to add to the powers that it already had by imposing new conditions in licences.

2.4   A tenant will no doubt wish to object to such a condition since it may well be his intention to discharge his head lease rent out of the sublease income. Imposing a fourteen-day window will effectively prevent the tenant from doing that and I think land-lords may well be advised to expect a challenge by a tenant if a licence to underlet imposes such a condition where there is no provision in the lease enabling the landlord to require it. Given the 1988 Act's statutory duty to act reasonably, landlords need to be aware of this. This variation in rent payment dates is something that should be considered right at the very outset when leases are negotiated since that might be the opportune time to seek to impose a provision in the lease allowing a land-lord to impose such a condition in licence to underlet.

2.5   It seems to me that if the alienation clause in a lease permits subletting with landlord's consent and provides clearly that the sublease must require rent to be paid fourteen days after the rent payment days in the head lease then the landlord would be perfectly reasonable in requesting such a condition when being asked to consent to a particular subletting. Tenants might be adverse to agreeing such a provision when negotiating a head lease but equally at that time it might be difficult for them to resist this type of provision; after all they would be negotiating a head lease and no doubt purporting to have the wherewithal to pay the rent under the head lease without the need to sublet either the whole or part of the premises and on that basis it will be more difficult for the tenant to state that it needs the sublease rent in order to discharge the head lease obligations.

2.6 As always, VAT is a consideration. One may have a situation where the subtenant is obliged to pay rent together with VAT direct to the superior landlord. If the superior landlord has elected to waive the exemption, the rent payable under the head lease will be subject to VAT. However if the subtenant has had to pay direct, irrespective of the VAT position in the sublease the subtenant may have a difficulty in claiming back the tax. The supply in respect of which VAT on the head lease rent is payable relates to the rent which flows between the head landlord and the head tenant. Where a notice under Section 6 of the 1908 Act is served the payment is made by the subtenant. Whilst the subtenant will have to pay VAT with the rent it is difficult to see how it would receive a tax invoice which would enable it to obtain a credit for the VAT. The VAT is payable in relation to the rent due by the head tenant not the subtenant. The position is very similar to that where a third party discharges another's bill. If a surveyor renders a bill to his client but a third party pays that bill, the third party is not entitled to receive the VAT invoice since the supply of the service by the surveyor is between him and his client and therefore without the tax invoice the third party is unable to claim back the tax. A Section 6 notice is very similar. Clearly where one is on the receiving end of a Section 6 notice, specialist VAT advice should be taken.

D.   SET-OFF AGAINST RENT

I.   GENERAL

1.1 Where a landlord has an obligation to his tenant, for example in relation to repairs, then if the landlord breaches that obligation the tenant will have a right of action against him. However, since the tenant has continuing obligations to pay rent the most practical remedy and often the most expedient, is for the tenant to stop paying the rent and set off, against the liability to pay rent, the damages claim.

1.2   It is for precisely that reason that leases often provide a covenant by the tenant to pay its rent on each quarter-day, whether or not the rent is demanded 'without deduction or set-off'. Where those words are used a tenant cannot exercise the remedy of set-off. The ability to exercise that remedy is one which may apply but if the parties specifically state in the contract that it should not, there is no reason why the remedy cannot be excluded.

1.3   The 1990s have seen a run of cases in relation to set-off, beginning with two decisions in 1993. *Akehurst* v *Stena Sealink Limited* **February 1993** was an unreported decision where the covenant in the lease provided for payment of rent without any deduction. There was no specific reference to set-off but the High Court said that this requirement to pay without deduction included all kinds of deductions including a deduction by way of set-off.

1.4   *Famous Army Stores* v *Meehan* **1993 9 EG 111** was another case in the same year on the same point and in fact was an earlier case than *Akehurst*, although reported later. Again the judge felt that the words excluded a right of set-off.

1.5   The Court of Appeal considered the position in *Connaught Restaurants* v *Indoor Leisure Limited* **1993 46 EG 184**. This case reversed the position under *Akehurst* and *Famous Army Stores*. *Connaught* concerned a breach of a repairing obligation by the landlord which led to the tenant not paying his rent. The sole issue in the appeal was whether the lessee's right of set-off had been excluded by the words in the rent payment clause requiring rent to be paid 'without any deduction'. The Court of Appeal considered the two 1993 first instance decisions to which I have just referred and also a New Zealand case, *Grant* v *NZM Scene Limited* **1989 1 NZLR 8**, where reference to payment of rent, free and clear of deductions, was not sufficient to exclude set-off. The Court of Appeal followed the New Zealand case and not the two United Kingdom cases. It felt that clear words would be needed to exclude set-off and the word 'deduction' was not sufficient. Since *Connaught* it is absolutely crystal clear that if one wishes to exclude the right of set-off then one must say so expressly and an obligation to pay without deduction is not sufficient to give rise to this interpretation.

1.6 *Electricity Supply Nominees Limited* v *IAF Group Limited* **1993 37 EG 155** was an interesting case considering whether a reference to payment of rent 'without deduction or set-off whatsoever' offended Section 3 of the Unfair Contract Terms Act 1977.

1.7 If this section applied then the anti-set-off position would have been ineffective. The court had to consider whether the act applied. Paragraph 1(b) of Schedule 1 to the 1977 Act excepts from the provisions of Section 3 'any contract so far as it relates to the creation or transfer of an interest in land'. It was held by the court that the exception includes all matters integral to a lease and since it was common ground that parties may contract out of a right of set-off, the court concluded that Section 3 of the 1977 Act did not apply because of paragraph 1(b) of the Schedule.

1.8 So the position now is that a right to set-off can be excluded in contract and the exclusion would not fall foul of the Unfair Contract Terms Act. However, to exclude it one must choose one's words carefully.

1.9 If the parties are going to use the set-off remedy, they must check that the right of set-off has in fact arisen. This was graphically illustrated in the case of the *Trustees of the Sloane Stanley Estate* v *Barribal* **1994 2 EGLR 8**. Here, a tenant paid the landlord less than the rent which was reserved. There was no prohibition on the right of set-off and the deduction that had been made was the owner's drainage rate which had not been paid by the landlord. The landlord had served a notice to quit and this case was brought since it was necessary in deciding whether the notice was valid to ascertain whether the tenant had complied with its notice to pay rent arrears.

1.10 In November 1990 the landlord had served notice on the tenant pursuant to Case D, Schedule 3, Agricultural Holdings Act 1986 requiring the tenant to pay £10,750 (half a year's rent). This was the amount at that time in arrears. A two-month period was given for compliance (as is the legislative requirement) and three days before the expiry of that period the tenant paid the rent minus a figure of just over £900. This was the owner's drainage rate. One week after the expiry of the two-month period the tenant paid that drainage rate to the authority. Was the landlord's notice valid? If it was, the tenant could not resist it. The tenant had argued that his obligations had been complied with, since he was entitled under the Land Drainage Act to deduct the owner's drainage rate from rent.

1.11   The matter went before an arbitrator who rejected the tenant's contention and the Court of Appeal restored this ruling after a High Court appeal had been successful. It was clear that under the Land Drainage Act an occupier is entitled to deduct any amount paid 'on account of an owner's drainage rate'. The right to deduct can be excluded but there was no such exclusion in this agreement. The Court of Appeal made it clear that the right to deduct arises only once the tenant has actually paid the rate, in this case the tenant had not done this until after he had deducted the sum from the rent and indeed this was after the two-month statutory period.

1.12   The case is a very clear illustration that if one is advising a tenant to exercise a right of set-off, one must ensure that the right actually exists at the time.

1.13   One final point on set-off is the inter-relationship with distress. *Eller v Grovecrest Investments Limited* **1994 2 EGLR 45** concerned a situation where the tenant was continually complaining about nuisance and a breach of covenant by his landlord. The tenant decided to put some pressure on the landlord by not paying the rent. The landlord responded by sending in the bailiffs and the tenant sought an injunction to prevent the landlord proceeding with distraint on the basis that the landlord could not exercise this remedy where there was an equitable right of set-off against rent in respect of a damages claim. Previous authorities had always made it clear that distress was a remedy to which set-off did not apply, but the Court of Appeal felt the authorities were based on procedural routes which were no longer appropriate.

1.14 The judge felt that he could ignore the authorities and it is now clear law that a landlord cannot distrain where the tenant has a proper right of set-off.

1.15 This must surely be correct, since any alternative decision would allow the landlord to obtain more by distraining than it could by an action in the courts. This is surely contrary to policy and the Court of Appeal felt that set-off applied to distraint in the same way as it would to an action.

1.16 Accordingly, set-off can be a useful and speedy remedy allowing the tenant to simply take what it believes it is due from moneys that it would otherwise have to pay to a landlord; it neatly avoids the necessity to sue and then enforce a judgment debt following a victory in the courts. However, and perhaps because it is such a useful remedy, most commercial leases exclude the right of set-off. If it is intended to exclude that right then the cases now make it clear that one must say so and in clear language.

E.   EXCLUSIVITY AGREEMENTS

1.   THE CONCEPT

1.1 Exclusivity agreements (or as they are sometimes called, lock-out agreements) are used where the parties to a deal agree that for a period after the deal has been agreed in principle, but before contractually committed, the vendor will not deal elsewhere. The purchaser is given an exclusive period within which to acquire and therefore has some insurance against the possibility of being gazumped.

1.2 The normal problem facing a purchaser who believes a deal has been agreed is that, until contracts have been exchanged, a vendor may change his mind, refuse to go ahead with the deal or simply try to re-negotiate. In land deals, until there is a written contract the transaction may be called off by either party.

1.3 One such agreement came under the scrutiny of the Court of Appeal in June 1993 in the case of *Pitt* v *PHH Asset Management*

Limited **1993 40 EG 149**. In this case there was an agreement between a vendor and purchaser that the vendor would not negotiate with other prospective purchasers for a short stipulated period. The Court of Appeal had to decide whether the lock-out agreement was enforceable and it felt that it was.

1.4　In *Pitt* the prospective purchaser wrote to the estate agent in the following terms:

> Your client has decided it is in his best interests to stay with my offer subject to contract. The vendor will not consider any further offers for the property on the basis that I will exchange contracts within a period of two weeks of receipt of that contract.

1.5　The vendor agreed to those terms and sent contracts to the prospective purchaser. After having done so they promptly sold at a higher price to the other offerer and contracts were exchanged before the two-week period ended. So much for promises. The Court of Appeal was only concerned to ascertain whether there was a binding contract independent of the continuing negotiations for the sale of the land. You will note that the letter uses the expression 'subject to contract' but goes on to make it clear that the vendor will not consider any further offers for a period. Since the relevant paragraph of the agent's letter was clearly agreed by the vendor and was not subject to contract, there was no reason why that agreement should not be binding and the Court of Appeal held it was. It was not considered to be subject to contract.

1.6　Accordingly it is now quite clear that agreements of this nature are enforceable. Any contract that is entered into underhand (and I deal with contracts under seal in a moment) is only legally enforceable if there is valuable consideration for the contract. Although the purchaser will be incurring legal costs, searches, survey fees, etc. it is normal to specify a specific nominal consideration. The consideration does not have to be adequate although it must be real and a consideration of only a few pounds will be sufficient.

1.7　However, if one wants to avoid any problems in deciding whether there is consideration, the exclusivity agreement may be entered into under seal and I would recommend that lock-out agreements are always executed under seal so that the question of consideration is avoided completely.

1.8   In *Pitt* the Court of Appeal felt that there was value to the vendor both in the removal of the purchaser's threat to make difficulties for the other offerer and also in promising to get on with the sale by limiting himself to a two-week period. This was sufficient consideration. None the less, I believe that the safest route is to execute exclusivity agreements under seal.

2.   THE CONTENTS

2.1   So, if one is agreeing to enter into a lock-out agreement what should the document say? Normally it will provide for the parties to use reasonable endeavours to do a deal within a certain fixed time-scale but it is not really possible to compel a vendor to exchange. At the time that the lock-out agreement is negotiated (i.e. right at the very outset of the transaction) the parties cannot commit to the deal. If they could, then they would not need the lock-out agreement; they might be able to move straight to exchange. On this analysis one would appreciate that it is not going to be possible to compel a reluctant vendor to exchange at the end of that exclusivity period. Detailed terms may not have been agreed.

2.2   However, I would recommend that provisions are inserted requiring the vendor to act reasonably, deal with all reasonable requests of the purchaser, answer his enquiries and the like so that as much as possible can be done to prevent the vendor from simply waiting out the period, refusing to exchange at the end of it and dealing elsewhere. Lock-out agreements should impose an obligation on the parties to act in good faith: after all, this is no more than what should be expected of them in any event.

2.3   The agreement will have to last for a fixed period of time. Where the agreement is to be entered into in relation to premises that require planning consent for the purchaser's intended use or redevelopment of them and where the purchaser intends to put in a planning application during the lock-out period, it is important that the period continues for so long as is necessary to enable the planning process to be complete. This can easily be provided for by extending any end date until after a planning decision notice is received. It is likely of course that the parties will have exchanged contracts before then, but clearly a purchaser would not want a lock-out period to come to an end if it had applied for planning and was awaiting a decision.

3. ENDING THE AGREEMENT

3.1   Where there is a reasonable amount to be done in putting the deal together during the exclusivity period, there are situations where the parties might fall out and the vendor would want to be able to free himself from the exclusivity obligations and the inherent inability to deal elsewhere during this period. After all, if the vendor knows that a deal is not going to be done because the parties have fallen out on a major principle, the vendor may well want to be able to start negotiations elsewhere. It is not unusual for an exclusivity agreement to seek to deal with matters of this nature but again the purchaser needs to be certain that the vendor cannot manufacture the dispute in order to simply get out of the agreement and sell to a third party.

4. BREACH OF THE AGREEMENT

4.1   What happens if the vendor breaches the exclusivity agreement? I am not aware of any situation where the court has decided on a level of damages. In *Pitt* the parties agreed themselves that abortive costs would be paid plus, I believe, a nominal sum for nuisance. Perhaps, therefore, if there was a clear case of breach of an exclusivity agreement the court might award exemplary damages but this is not at all clear and certainly there is a general reluctance of the court to award such damages. I do not think that injunctive relief is likely to be sought, or even if it is sought, I doubt it would be awarded very often. The nature of a lock-out agreement is to bind the parties to do no more than to talk to one another for a period and not to deal elsewhere during that period but since it is going to be almost impossible to require the seller to sell to the buyer an injunction is not going to help an enormous amount and I cannot imagine that the courts would be terribly keen to award an injunction.

5.   GENERAL

5.1   Lock-out agreements are useful if only to concentrate the mind of the vendor on the fact that he has 'done a deal' and should not treat this as irrelevant and carry on negotiating elsewhere. Bearing in mind the courts will enforce a lock-out agreement, it is important that the parties do not inadvertently enter into one and if it is not intended that any period of exclusivity is to be binding, the parties must make it clear that any such period that may have been mentioned is clearly subject to contract. The parties must make sure that they do not create a binding collateral contract if it is not their intention to enter into a legal commitment to lock-out others.

5.2   The basic effect of an exclusivity agreement is to prevent a vendor from dealing elsewhere; the agreement is not going to compel him to enter into contracts with the prospective purchaser who is party to the agreement.

5.3   If the purchaser wants to be in a position of being able to force the vendor to do a deal with it, then either the exclusivity agreement will have to specifically require the vendor to exchange at the end of that period and there will have to be a basis for resolving any dispute between the parties as to the terms of the contract documentation or alternatively, the purchaser will have to enter into a formal option to acquire the land and, again, if that option is entered into at the beginning of the transaction there will have to be a process for settling the contract documentation.

5.4   Exclusivity agreements are by and large there to protect the purchaser from being gazumped or finding that the vendor withdraws from a transaction after significant costs are incurred by the purchaser. Vendors who agree to give such a commitment not to deal elsewhere during a specific period might feel more comforted by taking a commitment from the purchaser not to try and do a deal with a different property within a defined area of the subject premises within the same period. A vendor who has effectively reserved for the purchaser an exclusive period within which to exchange contracts on a particular property and where he might take on commitments to deal with enquiries speedily and do its best to enter into a contract within the exclusivity period may well feel that it ought to be protected from the purchaser who relies on that but at the same time negotiates for a competing property.

5.5 The question of costs is often one that will help to focus the parties' attention. There is no reason why the exclusivity agreement cannot make one party liable for the other's costs if, prior to the end of the exclusivity period, contracts have not been exchanged due to some act or default of one of the parties.

F.   SIDE LETTERS AND COMFORT LETTERS

I.   SIDE LETTERS

I.I Quite often side letters can play an important part in negotiations between landlords and tenants. The parties may want to agree something between themselves but do not want the agreement elevated to a term of the lease. For example, there are certain concessions that might be offered to the first tenant but which a landlord would not want to repeat for assignees. Circumstances might exist, for example, whereby an original tenant whose quality of fit out is well known to the landlord is permitted to change its shop front or fascia or perhaps just carry out internal alterations without having to seek consent from the landlord but on a personal basis. The landlord is content in its belief that it knows that the quality of any replaced fit out will be first class and therefore does not need to involve itself in approving plans, specifications, etc. Obviously the landlord does not know the identity of likely assignees and therefore cannot give a commitment beyond the first tenant. The landlord might want to document such a concession by a personal side letter in order to ensure that it is outside the scope of the lease itself and not available to successors.

1.2 We will look briefly at the legal effect of these side letters but one point needs to be borne in mind at all times (only for agreements for lease – not leases): the trap of Section 2, Law of Property (Miscellaneous Provisions) Act 1989. This Section states that an agreement for the grant of a lease must contain all the terms in it or by reference to it and therefore if a side letter relates to an important aspect of the transaction and it is not referred to in the agreement there may be a danger that the whole agreement will be void. This will not be the case if the side letter is merely an independent or collateral contract and it is important to note that side letters do not cause problems under Section 2 where they relate to a completed lease – just agreements for lease. This was decided in the 1992 case of *Tootal Clothing Limited* v *The Guinea Properties Management Limited* **1992 64 P&CR 452**.

1.3 Personally I have always abhorred the use of side letters to document a concession given for the benefit of original tenants. If an original tenant is given a personal concession in relation to alterations, user or anything else for that matter, then there is absolutely no reason why that cannot be inserted in the lease itself but being made clear that it only applies to the original tenant. The concession might have to last a long period of time. If it is contained in the lease and expressed to be a personal concession to the original tenant there is less chance of it getting forgotten, mislaid, etc. Putting the concession in the lease will not of itself elevate it to a term of which assignees will have the benefit. Any such concession will of course be seen by prospective assignees carrying out their due diligence, and they may therefore seek a similar concession but so what? If there are good reasons to resist such a request the landlord will no doubt do so. If the landlord wants to extend the concession then it will be able to do so. It cannot be compelled to. Until October 1994 there was a further good reason for putting concessions in leases, namely that if the concession was incorporated in a side letter rather than in the lease there was always the danger that the landlord's successors in title would not be bound by any concession given in the side letter. Indeed this was often the very reason why landlords wanted to include concessions in this way.

1.4 This problem has now disappeared as a result of the Court of Appeal decision of *System Floors Limited* v *Ruralpride Limited and Another* **1995 07 EG 125**. Here the side letter included terms whereby the landlord stated that the rights granted were personal to the original tenant and would cease to have effect upon determination, surrender or expiration of the lease. Later the same year the landlord sold its reversion to Ruralpride and the High Court judge had held the side letter imposed personal obligations which were not binding on Ruralpride. The original tenant appealed and won. The Court of Appeal held that the landlord's covenants ran with the reversion and since the obligations contained in the side letter were entered into by the landlord 'with reference to the subject matter of the lease', they went with the reversionary estate. The fact that the benefit of the covenant was personal was irrelevant. The burden of the covenant clearly touched and concerned the land and ran with the estate.

1.5 Accordingly, if successors in title are going to be fixed with liability then there is virtually no reason why the concession should not be simply inserted in the lease. *Lotteryking Limited and Rollerball Limited* v *Amec Properties Limited* **1995 28 EG 100** perhaps adds even more credence to this, stating that even if the successor in title had no notice of the side agreement it would be bound by it.

1.6 My clear message is for you to ensure that personal concessions be included in leases. This avoids an awful lot of problems. It would be possible to ensure that the personal concession does not bind the landlord's successors. Clear and unambiguous language would be needed here but quite frankly I cannot see any situation where a tenant would want to go along with this. If a tenant is receiving a concession which is important to it, then the tenant must be able to ensure that it can have the benefit of that concession. If the landlord is able to relieve itself of all responsibility to grant the concession merely by disposing of the reversion (which will of course not require the tenant's consent) this does not seem to me to be very good practice for tenants. If the concession is intended to be worth the paper it is written on, it must bind landlords. *Ruralpride* makes it clear that this is likely to be the case even if it is in a side letter and therefore it is going to be difficult for landlords to grant a concession with one hand and promptly dispose of its freehold and take away the concession with the other hand.

2.   COMFORT LETTERS

2.1   I think it is worth making it clear that a side letter is not the same as a comfort letter. The latter is not intended to have binding legal effect but is where one party gives some form of comfort to the other. One sees this type of letter utilized in all sorts of documents where one party states that it wants to protect its legal position by retaining certain rights but is happy to confirm by way of comfort only that perhaps it will not act in accordance with its legal rights. I must emphasize that whilst one does see this type of thing quite regularly in all sorts of legal documentation it is no more than a comfort and does not alter the legal position of the parties.

G.   REPAIRS

1.   TYPE OF REPAIR COVENANT

1.1   Most modern commercial leases contain a repair obligation. Either the landlord carries out repairs and charges them back to the tenant or the tenant takes on a direct repairing obligation. Certainly in self-contained properties it is normal for the tenant to take on board an obligation to keep premises in good and substantial repair although you will see that earlier in this chapter where I have talked about service charges, I canvassed the possibility of an indirect repair obligation even in self-contained premises. The terms of any deal between a landlord and its tenant will of course decide the extent of the repairing obligation and this may well vary according to the length of the term of the lease, the condition of the building, the purposes of the letting, etc. For example, in a short-term lease where perhaps the landlord is letting premises prior to an intended re-development, it would not be normal for the landlord to seek to impose strict repairing obligations upon a tenant, nor would a tenant, properly advised, accept any such, since they may find that the cost of repairs is disproportionately high in comparison to the length of time the tenant is going to occupy and have the benefit of the premises.

1.2 Obviously the exact form of the repair obligation needs to be very carefully thought through.

1.3 In new buildings, for example, tenants must be very careful that they do not have any obligation to carry out repairs as a result of some inherent defect that might arise following construction. Tenants may wish to completely exclude any such liability or, alternatively, provide for the landlord to seek to recover from contractors or professionals who have given warranties in relation to the building and only if the landlords fail to make a recovery, perhaps due to the insolvency of the professional or the contractor, should the tenant have any kind of liability.

1.4 In all leases where the landlord insures, there should be an exclusion of any damage caused by any insured risks; the insured risks definition should of course be comprehensive so that there is no question of the tenant having an obligation to repair if the premises are destroyed or damaged by a risk which the landlord should perhaps have insured against but did not. Frequently one sees the exception to a repair clause geared to damage caused by fire whereas the landlord might in fact have an obligation to insure many other risks. There is absolutely no reason whatsoever why a landlord should be able to impose a repair obligation upon the tenant in these circumstances. All the landlord should seek to do is to ensure that it does not have a shortfall between the amount that can be recovered under the insurance policy and the tenant's obligation under a direct repairing obligation.

1.5 Leases can either impose a full repairing liability or perhaps some form of limited liability. If there is to be a limitation on the repair obligation then this can be dealt with by annexing a schedule of condition. The parties should satisfy themselves as to the condition of the premises at the date the lease is granted and annex the schedule to the lease. The schedule might include many photographs. This record of the condition of the premises would then be the benchmark for future repairs. The schedule of condition is effectively a statement of the condition of the property at the date of the grant of the lease and the repair obligation will no doubt state that the tenant is not responsible to put the premises in any better state of repair and condition than that evidenced by the schedule of condition.

1.6   Whilst this part of this chapter is not intended to be a detailed analysis of repair covenants (and there are many books that deal with this huge topic including the major text books *Woodfall on Landlord and Tenant* and *Hill and Redman's Law of Landlord and Tenant* – see Recommended reading) tenants should always bear in mind that there is little difference between an obligation to keep in repair and put in repair where the lease also contains an obligation to yield up premises in repair. It was made clear in the 19th century in the case of ***Proudfoot* v *Hart* 1890 25 QBD 42** that there is no substantive difference between the expression 'keep in repair' and 'put in repair' and one must bear in mind that as soon as a repair obligation is taken up there may be obligations to actually put the premises in repair. However, as we shall shortly see, where a tenant has a positive obligation to carry out repairs within a reasonable period of taking up the lease, it will be foregoing its Leasehold Property (Repairs) Act 1938 rights since Section 3 of the 1938 Act says that the Act will not apply in those circumstances.

1.7   When considering obligations to repair some thought must also be given to decoration covenants. Most leases provide obligations to decorate externally every three years or so and internally every five years or so and frequently the landlords seek control over colour schemes, supervision of the works of decoration and the like. This is very often a problem for tenants of commercial premises, particularly multiple retailers who may have maintenance programmes that do not coincide with the dates set out in leases. It is my experience that most landlords will not object to personal concessions allowing decoration outside those specific times so long as the basic state of repair and decoration of the premises is maintained. In any event, there may be very good practical reasons why the landlord should agree to such a concession simply on the pragmatic basis that the landlord will not necessarily be able to recover any damages if the tenant has failed to comply strictly with a decoration covenant. There may be no diminution in the value of the reversion.

2. BREACH

2.1 So what happens if the premises are the subject of a full repair obligation and the tenant is in breach of that obligation?

2.2 First of all the landlord will almost certainly have the right to forfeit the lease. In recent times this has not been a terribly attractive remedy since landlords have hardly wanted the ability to forfeit and take back premises that might be very difficult to re-let. It may have been difficult enough to let them in the first place! Having said that, in a bull market the ability to forfeit is quite a threat to be able to hang over a tenant and it must not be forgotten. Prior to forfeiture for a repair breach the landlord will have to serve notice under the Law of Property Act 1925, Section 146. This notice must be served in all cases where the landlord is seeking to forfeit except where forfeiture is for non-payment of rent. As you may know there are protection provisions for tenants in the Leasehold Property (Repairs) Act 1938 and, in addition, a right to apply for relief from forfeiture.

2.3 Since forfeiture has not been the most practical remedy in recent times, when it has been difficult to let premises, I do not wish to spend a great deal of time talking about it in this book which of course is devoted to more topical matters. If you want to know any more about forfeiture then you should look at the more detailed books on repair particularly *Woodfall on Landlord and Tenant*. If you are advising a tenant who has been threatened with forfeiture by his landlord then do remember to advise your clients to check that the appropriate notices have been served and even if they have been you may well want to advise the tenant to make an application for relief from forfeiture. I should like to move on to the other remedies that are available to a landlord where it does not wish to forfeit.

2.4 The main remedy here is the right to seek damages. The tenant will have taken on the obligation to keep the premises in good and substantial repair. This is a contractual obligation. If the tenant breaches his contract then in the same way as any other party breaching a contract may be liable for damages, the tenant may face an application for damages for breach of his obligations to repair.

2.5   Before moving on to the level of damages that might be awarded one must consider the Leasehold Property (Repairs) Act 1938. Where a lease is originally granted for a term of at least seven years and three or more years remain unexpired at the date that the landlord serves a notice of dilapidations or a Section 146 notice or proceedings are started, then before the landlord can enforce a right to damages (or indeed forfeiture, as we have already seen) then the landlord must send notice to the tenant of the tenant's right to serve a counter-notice claiming the benefit of the protection afforded by the 1938 Act. This landlord's notice must be in a form which complies with Section 146 and the tenant's time for response is twenty-eight days. Once the tenant claims that protection the landlord may not enforce a right to damages before obtaining the leave of the court. Leave will only be granted if the landlord establishes one of five grounds which are:

2.5.1   The remedy is required to protect other occupiers where the tenant in breach is out of occupation; or

2.5.2   The remedy is required to comply with statutory obligations; or

2.5.3   The remedy is required to prevent a substantial diminution in the value of the landlord's reversion (as to that a little more shortly) or there has already been substantial diminution; or

2.5.4   The expense of carrying out repairs now is relatively small compared to the costs that would be incurred if the repairs are postponed; or

2.5.5   There are some other special circumstances rendering it just and equitable for the repairs to be carried out.

Assuming that there is a dispute between the parties as to whether one of those five grounds exists, effectively two court hearings would be needed. A full trial will be required to decide whether one of the grounds has been proved as well as the proceedings to establish the level of damages.

Section 3, Law of Property (Repairs) Act 1938 says that the Act does not apply to an obligation to put in repair upon the tenant taking possession or within a reasonable time thereafter.

3.   SHORT-TERM LEASES

3.1   So, if there is a lease granted for at least seven years where at least three years remain, a landlord cannot enforce a claim for damages for breach of an obligation to keep in repair without going through the 1938 Act procedure. This does confer a level of protection for tenants and before a tenant agrees to take a short-term lease it must consider the fact that it is giving up this protection. For example a tenant taking a five-year lease with a repair obligation would not have the benefit of the 1938 Act even in the first two years since, although there would be more than three years remaining, the lease would not have originally been granted for a term of seven years or more. The position is different, of course, if the same tenant were to take a ten-year lease with a tenant's break at year five, and this in itself may well be an incentive for tenants to take a longer lease with a break. The tenant will have achieved pretty much the same objective: namely a commitment that can be brought to an end at year five and will have the benefit of the 1938 Act.

3.2   Perhaps, however, the most important thing for a tenant to consider when taking a short-term lease irrespective of whether that commitment is originally short or just potentially so (by virtue of the existence of a tenant's break after a relatively short period of time) is the level and extent of its repairing obligations. Tenants should ensure that they do not commit to such a lease only to find that after a relatively short period of occupation substantial repairs need to be carried out and that they have to fund these.

Tenants should be wary of this both where the repair obligations are direct or indirect by virtue of service charge provisions.

4. LEVEL OF DAMAGES

4.1 Assuming one has a repair obligation and either the 1938 Act does not apply, or its procedures have been complied with, what damages would a tenant be liable for? Section 18(1), Landlord and Tenant Act 1927 says that where a landlord seeks damages to compensate it for premises being in disrepair, those damages are limited to the loss in value of the landlord's reversionary interest. There may be fairly substantial items in disrepair which have little or no effect on the landlords reversionary interest and it may be very difficult indeed for the landlord to show loss. For example, if there are premises in disrepair and then a new tenant takes over the premises without demanding some form of concession to reflect the fact that it must carry out the repairs, it is difficult to see where there is diminution in the value of the reversion. One will need to carefully contrast premises that are in disrepair with premises that are in need of improvement. In 1987 the case of *Mayfair and Another v Barclays Bank PLC* **1987 26 EGLR** concerned a situation where the new tenant did demand a reduction in rent but this was to induce it to carry out improvements. The effect of this was that the investment value of the landlord's reversion produced a figure above that for the property repaired but unimproved and therefore again the landlord had suffered no diminution in value of the reversionary interest.

4.2 Section 18 also makes it clear that damages would not be recoverable at the end of the lease if the landlord intends to demolish and the tenant's surveyors will need to try and ascertain whether there are redevelopment or refurbishment proposals well before discussions take place in relation to any damages.

4.3 What happens where the property has a negative value and needs to be refurbished? *Shortlands Investments Limited v Cargill PLC* **1995 8 EG 163** concerned a situation where a property was in disrepair but the property itself had a negative value. Did the disrepair contribute towards a diminution in the value of the reversion? The court held that it did and awarded damages by reference to the value that the property had in its unrepaired stated compared to that which it ought to have had if the tenant had complied with its repairing obligations. The fact that one was dealing with negative figures was irrelevant.

4.4 So where there is a direct repairing obligation the tenant will have an obligation to pay for repairs but may find that Section 18 comes to its rescue. As I mentioned in Part A of this chapter (Service Charges) this is one good reason why landlords might want to re-think whether their tenants should be responsible for repairs indirectly through a service charge. Section 18 does not deal with indirect repair obligations in this way and therefore if a landlord has to repair and the tenant is obligated to pay towards the repairs by virtue of the service charge there is no statutory ceiling on the amount that is claimable. So long as the service charge cost is directly attributable and referable to the repair (and not improvements to the premises) the tenant should be responsible to pay it. None the less, landlords are still somewhat reticent to impose indirect repair obligations through a service charge in a self-contained building.

5. SELF-HELP REMEDIES

5.1 Accordingly, commercial tenants are protected not only by the 1938 Act but also by the provisions of Section 18. These statutory protections do not apply, however, to clauses that state that a tenant must keep premises in repair and where they fail to do so the landlord has the right to enter the premises, carry out the repairs and charge the tenant for the cost of so doing, recovering those charges as debt from the tenant as if they were rent arrears. Provisions of this nature are commonplace in commercial leases and I fear have not been given the respect they deserve by both tenants' solicitors and their surveyors. This procedure clearly avoids the 1938 Act because the claim is for a debt and not damages and for the same reason Section 18 does not apply.

5.2 Perhaps the reason that clauses of this nature have not been given the respect they deserve emanates from the fact that until November 1995 there were conflicting court decisions as to the effect of such clauses and whether they obviate the necessity to serve the 1938 Act notice.

5.3 It is now clear from *Jervis* v *Harris* **1995 EGCS 177** that land-lords can use this procedure to avoid the constraints of the 1938 Act and Section 18.

5.4 It is now crystal clear that if the clause is appropriately worded a landlord may carry out repairs which the tenant has failed to do and recover the cost without having to comply with the 1938 Act. The dangers of abuse are self-evident and tenants must be sure that the ability to exercise this self-help remedy does not enable the landlord to make the tenant's life a misery by con-stantly requiring minor repairs to be carried out on pain, if not of death, of an obligation to pay the landlord its cost for carry-ing out the repairs if the tenant fails to remedy the breach.

5.5 A tenant can amend provisions of this nature by inserting the protections that would otherwise apply to the repairs in ques-tion by effectively imposing contractually the protection of the 1938 Act. It can also be made absolutely clear that clauses of this nature only apply to major repairs or where the tenant has failed to comply with obligations which are substantial and material.

5.6 Landlords must make sure that they do not utilize this proce-dure in order to force a tenant to carry out what are effectively improvements. If they do works which constitute improve-ments as opposed to repairs and seek to charge them back under such a clause, a tenant may well be able to resist the obligation to pay and of course in those circumstances the landlord will have expended the money and not have the remedy of recovery.

5.7 I do not think, therefore, that the *Jervis* v *Harris* type clause is necessarily the panacea to all the landlords ills but it does help concentrate the tenant's mind considerably.

Equally, tenants must make sure that landlords do not use it to bully them to carry out repairs that may not be absolutely necessary. One word of caution for landlords planning to use this remedy in new leases under the 1995 Act: once they have gone in and carried out the repairs and rendered a bill to their tenant, depending on the wording of the clause it is quite pos-sible that they would have caused a liquidated sum to be due from their tenant. In this event, if the tenant failed to pay up and the landlord wished to recover the money from a former tenant, then the landlord would have to serve its demand under Section 17, 1995 Act within six months. This would not be the case if the moneys in question were simply damages sought for breach of a repair obligation, since in this case the moneys would not constitute a fixed sum.

5.8   Perhaps the biggest irony of this type of clause lies in the fact that it enables a landlord to do work itself and charge back to the tenant, thus ensuring firstly that the repairs are carried out and secondly that the landlord obtains a full recovery. This produces exactly the same effect as the indirect repair obligations through a service charge and perhaps gives more credence to the suggestion that even in self-contained buildings one should try and deal with repairs in this way rather than in the traditional manner. Certainly landlords who might otherwise wish to utilize the *Jervis* procedure may well be far more comfortable with all repairs being dealt with through an indirect liability through a service charge.

6.   EFFECT OF A REPAIR CLAUSE

6.1   Before leaving the question of repairs, just a short word on the 1994 case of ***British Telecommunications PLC v Sun Life Assurance Society PLC* 1995 EGCS 139**. Here the Court of Appeal was asked to consider whether or not a landlord's obligation to repair the external walls and main structure of a building was, or included, an obligation to keep the property in repair *at all times*, so that the landlord would be in breach of covenant just as soon as the property ceased to be in a state of good repair. The relevant facts of *Sun Life* were as follows.

6.2   In 1986 part of the exterior brickwork of a building where BT were the tenant became out of repair. Sun Life did not put in hand works to carry out the necessary remedial work until February 1988. The tenant alleged that the landlord was in breach of covenant as soon as the brickwork became out of repair. If this was accepted, the tenant would have been entitled to such damages as it may have been able to prove, without having to concern itself as to whether or not the landlord proceeded to carry out the repairs with sufficient promptness.

6.3   The landlord's case was that it was not in breach of covenant since its duty to repair only required it to carry out repairs within a reasonable time after the defect became apparent.

6.4   The relevant landlord's repairing clause was contained in the head lease. The clause included the following obligations:

> from time to time and at all times during the said term to uphold maintain cleanse and keep in complete good and substantial repair and condition the demised premises and car parking accommodation for the time being erected or built thereon ... including all party and other walls boundary walls and fences and drains belonging to the demised premises ...

6.5   The question that the court had to answer was whether the landlord was under an obligation to keep the premises in repair at all times, so that the obligation would be broken as soon as the premises became out of repair? Alteratively, as contended by the landlord, was the obligation to repair only applicable when the disrepair became evident?

6.6   In the High Court the tenant's contention was accepted. This contention was that the words 'to keep in repair' were specifically included in the repair covenant not only to make it clear which party should carry out the repairs but also to make it clear where the liability should lie if the premises should for any reason fall into disrepair. The obligation to keep in repair imposed an obligation to 'have them in repair at all times during the term and if they are at any time out of repair [the person giving the covenant] is guilty of a breach of covenant'. The Court of Appeal dismissed the appeal and it is therefore clear law (whether a landlord or a tenant is responsible for repair) that where there is an obligation to keep a building in repair the liability imposed in the covenant is absolute. If the building is not kept in repair at all times the covenanting party will be in breach of covenant and liable for damages to the party who has the benefit of the covenant.

6.7   Very careful thought must therefore be given to inclusion of the word 'keep'. If there is an obligation to keep in repair there must be an early warning system so that the covenantor, be he landlord or tenant, can make sure that he is appraised of the repair position at all times. This is particularly important, for example, if the obligation to keep in repair affects, say, an ability to break or renew. If there is an option to renew, provided the tenant has complied with his repair obligations, this will not be of much help if the tenant has not so complied because at the relevant time he has not 'kept' the premises in repair. All the more reason to make certain that options to break, renew and the like are not geared to compliance with clauses containing liabilities to repair. (See Chapter 4 for more on this subject.)

It may be that there would be an exception to this rule if the defect is outside the covenantor's control, but the principle remains the same: if one agrees to keep premises in repair then they must be in repair at all times.

7.   CONCLUSION

7.1   The question of repairs is one that needs to be considered in great detail. Quite apart from the general principle of who is to be responsible for repair, the terms of the repair clause need to be looked at in the context of the length of the term that the tenant is taking and the type and condition of the premises that are being let to the tenant. It is all very well for the landlord to seek a clear lease with the full tenant's repair obligation but this may be intrinsically unfair on the tenant in certain cases.

H.   VAT

I.   GENERAL

1.1   No book on property is really complete without some reference to VAT. VAT is a very complicated tax which, quite frankly, should be considered at all times in relation to any property transaction. For that reason it deserves a mention in this book; equally it is far too complex a subject to receive comprehensive treatment in this book, and in any event I am no tax expert. For more details on VAT please look at one of the specific textbooks on the subject (see Recommended reading) or take specialist advice. The property journals also frequently carry articles devoted to property VAT.

1.2   We have already seen in Chapter 6 that the right to charge VAT needs to be expressed in leases where an election to waive the VAT exemption has been made prior to the grant of a lease.

1.3   The reference in Chapter 6, of course, was to renewal leases but the position is exactly the same for any lease granted. Any lease is prima facie exempt unless the landlord chooses to waive the exemption.

2.   THE 1996 BUDGET AMENDMENTS

2.1   Until the 1996 Budget the decision to waive the exemption and opt to tax a building was entirely within the discretion of the landlord. If he wanted to do so he could charge VAT. If he did not then he had the choice to treat the lease as an exempt supply and not charge VAT. The 1996 Budget changed all that for commercial property transactions entered into from Budget Day (26 November 1996). Whilst this is particularly relevant for leases the position is identical with a sale of an old building (one more than three years old) where, again, unless there is an election to waive the exemption the sale is treated as an exempt supply. Sales of new buildings are standard rated. (See paragraphs 3 and 4 below.)

2.2   The proposal in the 1996 Budget was to disapply options to tax from Royal Assent of the Finance Bill if the person to whom the supply is made can recover less than 80% of the VAT that would have been chargeable on the supply. It is expected that the Finance Bill will receive Royal Assent in the Spring of 1997. The proposals outlined in the Budget are contained in Clause 37 of the Finance Bill.

2.3   The Budget was unclear as to how the 80% test was to be measured although it is likely to be based on the actual use to which the tenant puts the relevant property. In looking at the 80% test it is necessary to see whether the tenant's use of the particular premises in each VAT prescribed accounting period exceeds the percentage. This is likely to give rise to great uncertainty.

2.4 The Government did not intend these changes to affect leases executed before Budget Day or sales completed before Budget Day, however, subject to that there was to be minimal relief save that it was suggested that leases entered into on or before 30 May 1997 pursuant to a pre-Budget Day agreement for lease would not be caught.

2.5 All in all, these changes have created uproar in the property industry and there has been a great deal of lobbying particularly by the British Property Federation. The changes were introduced to catch various leasing structures which had been thought up by VAT exempt occupiers in an effort to spread the VAT cost and reduce the cashflow implications of irrecoverable VAT. However, when the new rules were introduced they were not restricted in their application to transactions between connected parties.

2.6 Do not forget that if a landlord cannot charge VAT to a tenant he is not able to recover input tax incurred in respect of the property and this may lead to a position where the landlord has irrecoverable VAT on service charge costs, professional's fees, etc. Where there are multi-let buildings the situation could well arise where, in relation to leases granted before the Budget Day, VAT is charged on the rents but not on leases granted to some of the tenants after Budget Day.

2.7 As I have said, the property industry has reacted violently to these proposed changes and the very fact that they will catch many transactions which were clearly outside the mischief of the proposed legislation. If the proposals were to become law without significant amendment, it would not be safe any longer to assume that one can always elect to waive the VAT exemption and clearly a close liaison between landlords and their VAT advisers needs to be maintained.

2.8 Many other issues need to be resolved. The new rules will apply to leases granted on or after 26 November 1996 (subject to transitional relief) and therefore landlords would be adversely affected in a manner over which they have no control where a new lease is granted after Budget Day 1996 under the 1954 Act as a renewal to a lease which was in force before that day.

Similarly, landlords may have a problem if there was a contractual right to renew a pre-Budget Day lease. The grant of overriding leases under the 1995 Act could also create problems; any such lease granted after the 1996 Budget is likely to be granted in respect of a lease entered into before that day, and again this could expose the landlord to a VAT problem.

2.9   We have already seen practitioners' drafting provisions in leases in an effort to control the tenant's use of premises so as to ensure that the tenant does not use those premises for any purpose which will reduce the ability of the landlord to recover input tax credits. Such provisions normally include an indemnity for extra VAT that the landlord has to pay, or cannot recover. Such clauses must be used with caution, particularly at this time when the legislation has not been settled. There may be adverse rent review consequences and, in addition, receipts by a landlord under a VAT indemnity may themselves create additional tax burdens for landlords.

2.10   This is all very new and, as I have said, the provisions are not yet in force. I believe Customs are trying to introduce a further test so that the new rules will only apply where an exempt, or partially exempt, occupier has funded capital costs of acquisition or development. This was a suggestion of the British Property Federation. If it is possible to introduce a test of this nature then a great deal will have been achieved and the new rules will not catch many ordinary commercial transactions. If this cannot be done – and I believe Customs are concerned that it will not be possible to do so in a way that will prevent abuse – then there are suggestions to introduce other measures intended to alleviate the effect of the new rules including:

2.10.1   Extending the transitional period to three years so that leases granted before 26 November 1999 pursuant to pre-Budget Day agreements for lease would not be caught;

2.10.2   Excluding retail lettings (but not lettings to banks and building societies) and pubs from the rules. Small workshops and markets would also be excluded. It is not proposed to exclude office accommodation, and if this does happen, landlords may need to cater for this in user clauses so that they do not find themselves in a position where a shop use could change to an office use and thus leave them with a VAT problem if the tenant who occupied the premises under an office use did not satisfy the 80% test; and

2.10.3 Providing an obligation on tenants to tell landlords of any change in their use of the land.

2.11 As I have said, these VAT changes were designed to close a specific loophole and it is a shame that the Budget proposals were so wide; they are and are perceived to be the proverbial sledge-hammer to crack a nut. They clearly will soon be on the statute book in some form or other and, before leases are granted, landlords should satisfy themselves that they do not have a potential VAT problem as a result of the tenant's proposed use.

2.12 For the rest of this part of this chapter I am assuming that the landlord can waive the exemption entirely within his discretion and of course the position in relation to the waiver of the exemption and the choice of whether or not to opt to tax is one which applies equally for leases and sales of old properties.

3. GENERAL PRINCIPLES

3.1 If there is a contract for the sale of an old property which is an exempt supply, then prima-facie VAT is not charged on the sale price. If the vendor elects to charge VAT, and subject to paragraph 2, above, the election is entirely within his own discretion, the purchaser must pay VAT. If, however, the vendor's election precedes the date of the contract and the contract is silent as to VAT and does not give the vendor the option to charge, then again the sale price would be deemed inclusive of VAT and the purchaser need not pay the tax as a result of Section 89 of the VAT Act 1994.

3.2 If, however, the contract is silent as to VAT and then the vendor elects, the purchaser will have to pay VAT. Again Section 89(2) of the VAT Act comes to the vendor's rescue. The vendor's election will have had the effect of changing the tax status surrounding the supply and under Sections 89(1) and (2), VAT Act where there is a change in the tax charged on a supply, including a change attributable to the making of an election under paragraph (2) of Schedule 10 to the VAT Act, the purchaser will have to pay the VAT.

3.3 Accordingly, vendors and purchasers must carefully check the VAT position before entering into sale contracts.

4. TRANSFERS OF A GOING CONCERN

4.1 The next concern in relation to VAT relates to what is called a transfer of going concern (TOGC). If a property is an investment property and let us say the whole of that property is let to one tenant and VAT is charged on the rents, then when that property is sold to a purchaser who elects to waive the exemption and serves notice on HM Customs and Excise, there would be very little point in the purchaser paying VAT on the purchase price and simply recovering it from Customs. The purchaser will suffer a cashflow disadvantage and Customs would suffer additional administrative work.

4.2 Accordingly, in those circumstances where the purchaser is purchasing a going concern and investment properties fall within this category, the purchaser need not pay VAT. If the vendor has not elected and if the purchaser does not elect, there will be no VAT charged on the sale price. If the vendor and the purchaser are both registered for VAT, even without an election it is possible for the transaction to be treated as a TOGC in certain cases. Once the vendor has elected, if the purchaser elects and serves notice on customs, then the property can be treated as TOGC. This would not be the case if the purchaser has not elected and in those circumstances VAT would be charged on the price.

4.3 Difficult questions arise where property is part let and the safe advice is for a ruling to be obtained from Customs. If this cannot be obtained before contracts are exchanged, the vendor should reserve the right in the contract to recover VAT on the basis that if Customs rule that the transaction is not a TOGC, there will have been no VAT paid.

4.4   Again, in order to protect vendors from a purchaser who might not be able to come up with the money afterwards, the vendor might, wish to insist on recovering the VAT at the outset and placing it in a special, designated account pending a ruling.

4.5   It is important to remember that all these situations apply only when dealing with old buildings, i.e. buildings more than three years old. Where there is a building less than three years old, VAT must be charged on the purchase price. There is no discretion.

4.6   The question of TOGC relief is an increasingly complex one and is made more worrying by the fact that if VAT is paid wrongly, it may not be recoverable as input tax. Accordingly, if a property sale should have been treated as a TOGC and is not, then if the vendor mistakenly pays what it thought was VAT, it is possible, although perhaps unlikely in practice, that Customs could refuse a VAT reclaim by that purchaser.

5.   SURRENDERS

5.1   Surrenders of leases equally caused much *angst* until the much publicised **Lubbock Fine** case in 1995. It is now clear that a surrender of a lease is exempt from VAT where a landlord pays his tenant for the tenant to surrender up the unexpired portion of the lease. This will not apply, however, if there has been an option to tax and in this case the surrender will be standard rated.

6.   CAPITAL INDUCEMENTS

6.1   VAT is also important in relation to capital contributions that are sometimes made by landlords to their tenants or prospective tenants. Where a tenant receives a capital contribution, perhaps for fitting out, then it must charge VAT on that contribution and if it does not do so it may lose out considerably. If, for example, a landlord provides a potential tenant with a fitting out contribution of, say, £100,000 then if the document does not say that the sum is exclusive of VAT, VAT is deemed to have been included. If there was a £100,000 contribution then, at current VAT rates, the tenant would be deemed to have received £85,106.40 towards fitting out and the balance of £14,893.60 would be VAT for which the tenant would have to account to Customs. For this reason tenants should insist on VAT being paid in addition to any fitting out contribution. There is an interesting case of *ES Poyser and Sons Limited* v *Capital and Counties PLC* decided in the Nottingham County court in January 1991 where such a provision was held by the County court judge to equate to an obligation by the landlord to contribute the sum (in that case £55,000) net after VAT. I am not sure that it was correctly decided and the safest route is to add VAT to any capital contribution.

6.2 Similarly where there is a substantial rent-free period being given by the landlord to the tenant there may be VAT consequences that need to be thought through and once again specialist VAT advice should be taken in such circumstances.

7. VAT AND RENT REVIEWS

7.1 One should always have an eye on the inter-relationship between VAT and rent reviews. If a lease gives the right to charge VAT, then whether or not an election to waive the VAT exemption has been made, the potential for a VAT charge does, of course, exist. Bearing in mind that not all tenants can recover the VAT that they have to pay, it would be possible on a review of such a lease for the tenant (even one who does have the ability to recover VAT) to argue that any notional lease to a new tenant might be to a tenant who does not have such ability. In those circumstances, the notional tenant may well be seeking a rent reduction to reflect the fact that it does not have the right to recover VAT.

7.2 For example, if one is dealing with a letting in the financial sector, the tenant might well argue that other financial tenants, banks, institutions and the like do not have the ability to recover all their VAT as input tax. In these circumstances, if the landlord were to elect to waive the exemption, then it may well find that the market for the premises excludes some tenants who would not have the right to recover all their VAT. They would either not want to take the premises or perhaps would only do so at a discount to reflect the fact that in real terms the rental cost is greater because they are not able to recover all the VAT that is payable on the rent. This is something that can and often is considered in the drafting of rent review clauses by an assumption that any potential tenant has a full VAT recovery. A false assumption of this nature seems to be intrinsically unfair on a tenant and I would urge tenants and their advisers not to agree any such without carefully thinking through the consequences.

7.3   Much will depend on the negotiating position of the parties as to whether a false assumption should be inserted and if inserted whether it can be resisted but it is something to watch out for.

7.4   In the situation postulated in the diagram below, where the landlord elects to waive the exemption it is likely that all the tenants in the office premises, except for Ian Shurrance Associates, the insurance company, will have a full recovery position. For those tenants that can recover, the position as to whether VAT is charged will be neutral. Ian Shurrance might take a different view and might well argue for a rent reduction. It may also be possible for the other tenants to argue for a rent reduction on the basis that there is the possibility of an assignment by them to a tenant that does not have a full recovery status. It is situations such as this where the question of a false assumption will need to be given considerable thought.

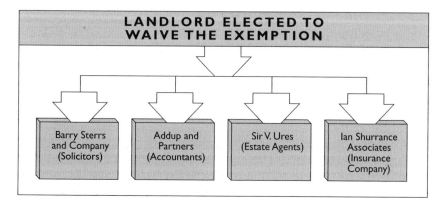

LANDLORD ELECTED TO WAIVE THE EXEMPTION

| Barry Sterrs and Company (Solicitors) | Addup and Partners (Accountants) | Sir V. Ures (Estate Agents) | Ian Shurrance Associates (Insurance Company) |

7.5   Now that the law is to be changed so that elections cannot be made where a tenant fails the 80% test, it is possible for a landlord to be prejudiced on review. Landlords waive the VAT exemption so that they can charge VAT in order to ensure that they obtain full VAT recovery. This is quite important where they are concerned with a property which they have developed or where they are paying sums with large VAT elements attached to them.

7.6   Where a landlord lets property in the expectation of being able to waive the exemption and charge VAT so that the landlord is able to recover the VAT that it is paying out in relation to that property, if the landlord subsequently finds that the tenant fails the 80% test and therefore Customs disallow the option to tax, that in itself might affect the landlord's VAT recovery position. There is just the possibility that this could affect a rent review under the lease. If the above scenario is a possibility then the landlord might be able to allege that it is always a possibility and therefore seek to obtain a higher rent on review to compensate it for the prospects of a tenant coming along who will not be able to meet the 80% criteria and thus cause the landlord a VAT problem.

7.7   Bearing in mind VAT elections must be in respect of the whole building, I am not sure how one will deal with a situation where one of the tenants in a building does not have the right to recover at least 80% of its VAT and this is something that will have to be looked at in detail when the draft legislation is available.

7.8   It is difficult to advise how to deal with this since at today's date the legislative framework behind the Budget Day announcement has not been drafted.

8.   CONCLUSION

8.1   Perhaps I should make a short apology for this whistle-stop tour through VAT at the end of this book. As I say, it is an extremely complex subject and one which should be borne in mind on all property transactions so that the appropriate VAT advice can be obtained. It is, however, a complicated tax and by mentioning it in this book I am merely trying to draw attention to its existence and the need to be thinking about it. For that reason this is not a detailed analysis of VAT and as mentioned earlier, other books already fulfil that function.

Absolute user clause	A lease which prohibits any change of use.
AGA	An authorised guarantee agreement under the Landlord and Tenant (Covenants) Act 1995.
Agent for the vendor	Basis upon which a deposit can be held enabling the solicitors holding the deposit to account to the vendor. (To be distinguished from the stakeholder.)
Alienation	Assignment or underletting of a lease.
Assumptions	Matters to be taken into account in valuing premises on review.
Authorised guarantor	The person giving an AGA.
Break clause	The right (for either landlord or tenant) to determine a lease early.
Comfort letter	A letter written by one party to a transaction indicating in a non-legally-binding manner the way in which it might implement its legal rights or refrain from doing so.
Condition precedent	A condition that must be carried out as a prerequisite to any clause taking effect.
Contractual guarantee	A guarantee given contractually and which is not an AGA.
Contractual guarantor	The person giving a contractual guarantee.
Discretionary criteria	Criteria for objecting to assignment under the Landlord and Tenant (Covenants) Act 1995 which are not factual criteria and where the landlord must still act reasonably or where the matter must be referred to a third party for determination.
Disregards	Matters not taken into account in valuing premises on review.
Excluded assignments	Assignments which do not give rise to release of tenant liability under the Landlord and Tenant (Covenants) Act 1995.
Factual criteria	Criteria for refusing consent to assignment which are capable of objective analysis.

Former tenant	The person who remains liable under privity of contract or an AGA. This may be a former tenant or a former guarantor.
Headline rent	The rent that would be payable for premises ignoring any concessions or incentives given to the prospective lessee.
Keep open clause	An obligation to continuously trade from premises.
Lock-out agreement or exclusivity agreement	An arrangement whereby the parties agree with each other to deal exclusively in relation to a property for a specific period.
New tenancy	A lease which is a new tenancy under the Landlord and Tenant (Covenants) Act 1995.
Notional lease	The notional terms of the lease utilized for the purposes of valuing premises on a rent review.
Old tenancy	A lease which is not a new tenancy under the Landlord and Tenant (Covenants) Act 1995.
Original tenant liability	The liability of an original tenant irrespective of subsequent assignments. This only applies in relation to old leases or where a tenant retains liability under an AGA.
Overriding lease	A lease granted under the Landlord and Tenant (Covenants) Act 1995 to a former tenant who pays in full arrears demanded of him.
Personal covenants	Covenants that are designed to apply only to the person who gives the covenant; the covenant is not expressed or designed to apply to successors in title.
Privity of contract	The doctrine whereby original tenants remain liable throughout the duration of the term.
Privity of estate	The doctrine whereby tenants other than original tenants remain liable only whilst they hold an estate in the property.
Qualified absolute user clause	A user clause in a lease which prohibits change of use without landlord's consent but which does not expressly provide that the landlord cannot act unreasonably.
Qualified user clause	A user clause in a lease which prohibits change of use without landlord's consent but where it is stated expressly that the landlord cannot act unreasonably.
Ratchet review clause	A traditional upward-only review where rent cannot go below that which is payable immediately before the review date.

Schedule of condition

A schedule attached to a lease setting out the current condition of the premises. Utilized in situations where a landlord has agreed that a tenant will have liabilities to repair limited to the state and condition of the premises at the date the lease is granted.

Severance clause

A clause severing from a document that part of the document that is illegal or which would make the document invalid.

Stakeholder

Basis upon which a deposit is to be held requiring the vendor's solicitors to retain the deposit in a stakeholder account. (To be distinguished from agent for the vendor.)

Threshold review clause

A rent review where rent can go up or down but not below the rent originally agreed between the parties.

Time of the essence clause

A clause where there are time-scales set out which are fundamental to the contract.

Upward-only reviews

A rent review whereby the rent can never go below the rent previously payable.

Use classes

One of the classes of use in the Town and Country Planning (Use Class) Order 1987.

RECOMMENDED READING

TEXTBOOKS

Barnes, M, (ed.), *Hill and Redman's Law of Landlord and Tenant*, Butterworth, 1996.

Bernstein, R and Reynolds, K, *Rent Review Handbook*, Sweet and Maxwell, 1996.

Crooks, R, *Tolley's VAT on Construction, Land and Property*, Tolley, 1996.

Fox-Andrews, J, *Business Tenancies*, Estates Gazette, 1995.

Lewison, K, (ed.), *Woodfall on Landlord and Tenant*, Sweet and Maxwell, 1996.

Riley, A and Rogers, P, *Privity of Contract: A Practitioner's Guide to the Landlord and Tenant (Covenants) Act 1995*, College of Law, Guildford, 1995.

Sainer, T, *Landlord and Tenant Fact Book*, Gee Publishing, 1992.

PERIODICALS

Estates Gazette. This is a weekly publication which no surveyor should be without. Apart from keeping up to date with property issues, there are regular articles on a variety of legal topics as well as law reports and a 'Mainly for Students' feature.

Property Week. Again a weekly publication with regular legal features.

Property Law Bulletin

ARTICLES IN THE *ESTATES GAZETTE*

British Property Federation, McKenna and Company and Estates Gazette, *Privity on Parade*, p154, 12 October 1996.

Cullen, S and Pollerton, R, *Must a surety guarantee an AGA?*, p118, 11 May 1996.

Fogel, S and Moross, T, *Extracts from The Blundell Memorial Lecture: Landlord and Tenant Reform*, p64, 10 August and p77, 17 August 1996.

Guant, J (QC) and Main, R, *Extracts from The Blundell Memorial Lecture: Virtual reality – defining the world of rent reviews*, p88, 20 August and p107, 27 August 1994.

Miller, K and Bibring, M, *Business Tenants' Compensation*, p39, 28 July 1990.

NON-STATUTORY GUIDELINES

RICS, *Commercial Property Leases in England and Wales Code of Practice*, RICS Books, 1995.

RICS, PMA, ISVA, BPF *et al.*, *Service Charges in Commercial Properties – A Guide to Good Practice*, 1995.

STATUTES

Landland and Tenant (Covenants) Act 1995 (1995 Act)

Landlord and Tenant Act 1954, Part II (1954 Act)

Landlord and Tenant Act 1927 (1927 Act)

Landlord and Tenant Act 1988 (1988 Act)

LIVERPOOL
JOHN MOORES UNIVERSITY
AVRIL ROBARTS LRC
TEL. 0151 231 4022

INDEX

LAW CASES

LIVERPOOL
JOHN MOORES UNIVERSITY
AVRIL ROBARTS LRC
TITHEBARN STREET
LIVERPOOL L2 2ER
TEL. 0151 231 4022